T0377303

# Globalization, Planning and Local Economic Development

This textbook is concerned with economic development at the local, community or regional scale. Its aim is to provide students with a comprehensive introduction to contemporary thinking about locally based economic development, how growth can be planned and how that development can be realized.

This book:

- Provides students with a thorough understanding of current debates around local and regional development and how that body of work can assist them in helping communities grow;
- Equips students with a 'toolkit' of strategies that enable them to both plan for development and deliver that development through their professional lives;
- Offers a roadmap for economic development that helps students make sense of place-based development by providing a 'meta narrative' of how regions grow and how those processes can be enhanced. This integrating perspective will be organized around the concept of competitiveness and how that concept can be understood and operationalized in various ways;
- Aims to improve the performance of economic development agencies by providing current and future staff with a better set of strategies that are more appropriate to their needs;
- Socializes students into the world of economic development planning, providing them with an entry point into a rewarding career;
- Introduces students to a range of techniques essential to success in economic development planning.

In addition to a wealth of case studies and pedagogical features, the book is also complemented by online resources. In offering a full toolkit of economic development knowledge, techniques and strategies, this text will thoroughly prepare students for a career in urban planning, transport planning, human geography, applied economic analysis, geographic information systems, and/or work as an economic development practitioner.

**Andrew Beer** is Dean, Research and Innovation at the University of South Australia Business School. He previously worked at the University of Adelaide and the Flinders University of South Australia, and holds a Bachelor of Arts from the University of Adelaide and a PhD from the Australian National University.

**Terry L. Clower** is the North Virginia Chair and Professor of Public Policy at George Mason University's Schar School of Policy and Government. He is also Director of GMU's Center for Regional Analysis, the most widely recognized university-based regional economic research unit in the National Capital Region. Previously he was the Director of the Center for Economic Development and Research at the University of North Texas.

'Place matters! This red thread through this textbook written by two recognized scholars calls for active care and smart governance for cities and regions. This fine opus offers practical and pedagogical guidelines for professionals and students in urban and regional planning. Both the local and the global arena of competitiveness and of endogenous and external forces are systematically and comprehensively mapped out. This book is a great source of new insights in place-based policy strategies.'

**Peter Nijkamp**, *Universiteit Jheronimus Academy of Data Science (JADS), The Netherlands*

'This book is highly recommended in understanding what is happening locally and globally in planning and economic development. It will be a hugely helpful source of information and insight for those going into – or already working in – careers in economic development, urban planning, transport planning, spatial data analysis and applied economic analysis, and indeed the wider world of public policy. Clear, well written, great coverage and with many interesting examples – a must-read.'

**David Bailey**, *Aston Business School, Aston University, UK*

# Globalization, Planning and Local Economic Development

Andrew Beer and Terry L. Clower

Routledge
Taylor & Francis Group

LONDON AND NEW YORK

First published 2020
by Routledge
2 Park Square, Milton Park, Abingdon, Oxon OX14 4RN

and by Routledge
52 Vanderbilt Avenue, New York, NY 10017

*Routledge is an imprint of the Taylor & Francis Group, an informa business*

*British Library Cataloguing-in-Publication Data*
A catalogue record for this book is available from the British Library

*Library of Congress Cataloging-in-Publication Data*
Names: Beer, Andrew, author. | Clower, Terry L., author.
Title: Globalization, planning and local economic development /
    Andrew Beer and Terry L. Clower.
Description: 1 Edition. | New York : Routledge, 2020. |
    Includes bibliographical references and index.
Identifiers: LCCN 2019014908| ISBN 9781138810303 (hardback) |
    ISBN 9781138810310 (pbk.) | ISBN 9781315749624 (ebook)
Subjects: LCSH: Regional economics. | Economic development. |
    Regional planning.
Classification: LCC HT388 .B434 2020 | DDC 330.9—dc23
LC record available at https://lccn.loc.gov/2019014908

ISBN: 978-1-138-81030-3 (hbk)
ISBN: 978-1-138-81031-0 (pbk)
ISBN: 978-1-315-74962-4 (ebk)

Typeset in Times New Roman
by Apex CoVantage, LLC

Visit the companion website: www.gpaled.com

# *Contents*

# Figures

# Tables

# *Boxes*

# *Preface*

This book is a product of our long history working with practitioners, teaching undergraduate and postgraduate students, and engaging in discussions with colleagues in our home nations and elsewhere about how individuals, and groups of individuals, can make a difference to the prosperity of cities, communities and regions. We have both performed multiple roles in the field of economic development and this experience pushed us to realize that there is a need for a text that helps us understand this fast-moving discipline and profession. We saw that there was a need for a comprehensive source that helps readers understand what is happening locally and globally in the field of planning and economic development, and how they can best work to position their community for the future.

Undergraduate and graduate students are a particular focus for this book. We see this text equipping them for a future in economic development, urban planning, transport planning, spatial data analysis and modelling, and applied economic analysis. It will also be of value to those who go on to work in government sectors, as a sound understanding of what drives prosperity and well-being should be a cornerstone of all public service. Having both taught for many years, and on three continents, we see that there is a clear need for students to have access to a text that introduces them to why local economic development is important and why economic development practitioners and planners are some of the most important members of the community. It is these individuals who can help drive job and wages growth, helping many who would otherwise have very limited economic opportunity. Second, students need to be introduced to contemporary thinking on why cities, regions, places and communities grow. We would all accept that our world has gone through a major economic transformation, as first information and communication technologies (ICT), and secondly biotechnologies have reshaped the ways in which we work, socialize and relate to others. In the future, artificial intelligence (AI) may exert an even greater impact. These new technologies have also driven fast-paced changes in the ways economies grow or decline. Students need to understand what these growth dynamics are so that they can help create and implement the strategies that will help their cities and localities grow in the future. Third, this book aims to socialize students into the world of economic development: helping them to understand the field and make positive contributions as they take up the challenge of working in this dynamic area. And we recognize, of course, that many individuals enter the field later in their working career. For this group, this book serves as a primer that adds to their insights from prior life experience, as well as putting more economic development 'tools' in their professional toolkit. Fourth, we believe that any book of this type needs to help students understand the basic techniques and approaches that form the core of professional life as an economic development practitioner or planner. Students need a firm understanding and competence in these basic skills in order to find their first employment opportunity. Analytical, practical and governance techniques are therefore an important focus for the book.

Finally, we would add that we consider local development to be a fundamentally important determinant of the prosperity and quality of life of regions, cities and towns. We hope that this text helps communities create a brighter future and encourages students to go into the profession.

# *Acknowledgments*

Thanks go to the many people, organizations and institutions that helped make the writing of this book possible. Andrew Beer was able to spend a substantial period of time on this monograph thanks to study leave when he worked at the University of Adelaide. Thanks have to go to Julie Clower and Christine Steele who put up with the two of us launching into detailed discussions about the book at apparently random points in time in all the oddest places.

Conversations with economic development practitioners, town planners, consultants, academics and government officials were crucial to the evolution of this book. Thanks go to Professor Phil McCann for his ideas on what the book could – and should – look like, and as always his insights were both profound and welcome. We acknowledge the hospitality and support of our colleagues Dennis Clayton at the City of Weatherford, Kristine Peters at KPPM Project Management and the Hallett Community and Sports Association, Anne Moroney at the Barossa Regional Development Australia Committee, Greg Ratsch from the City of Salisbury, Peter Tregilgas from the Mid North Coast Regional Development Australia Committee and many others working in the profession.

Special thanks go to our colleagues at the University of Adelaide, the University of North Texas, George Mason University and the University of South Australia, including Lisa Gage and Louise O'Loughlin. They helped with the creation of figures and tables, while other colleagues provided helpful commentary on the manuscript. Thank you to Sandy Horne who played such an important role in the finalization of the manuscript. As always, we are both grateful to her for her professionalism, attention to detail and inquiring mind. Many thanks go to Professor Marie Wilson for allowing Andrew Beer the time to complete this work.

# *Abbreviations*

| | |
|---|---|
| ABS | Australian Bureau of Statistics |
| AI | Artificial intelligence |
| BID | Business improvement district |
| CEDS | Comprehensive economic development strategy |
| CGE | Computable general equilibrium |
| EDA | Economic development administration |
| EU | European Union |
| FDI | Foreign direct investment |
| GDP | Gross domestic product |
| GSP | Gross state product |
| ICT | Information and communication technologies |
| MEP | Manufacturing extension program |
| NAFTA | North American Free Trade Agreement |
| NRP | New rural paradigm |
| OECD | Organisation for Economic Co-operation and Development |
| R&D | Research and development |
| SBDC | Small Business Development Center |
| SREDC | San Diego Regional Economic Development Corporation |
| TIF | Tax increment financing |
| UCSD | University of California San Diego |

# 1 Introduction

This chapter:

▶ Addresses why cities, regions and communities need to take active measures to plan for their future economy;

▶ Reviews the arguments that both support and oppose efforts to develop locally or regionally;

▶ Argues there is now a substantial body of evidence on what is effective, and what is not effective, in local economic development;

▶ Notes the range of strategies potentially available to encourage growth locally and that the globalization of the economy has generated new opportunities for many communities, and that this should provide a further spur for action.

WE ALL LIVE, work and enjoy ourselves in a city, a town, a village or a region. Increasingly these places are confronted by social, technological, demographic and political developments that have transformed their economic base and raised questions about the ongoing prosperity of many. In many cities and communities the established economic order has been challenged by a suite of changes, including the shift amongst economically advanced nations from a reliance upon manufacturing employment to jobs based on services; the rise of China as an economic and technological superpower; the global economic crisis in 2007–2008 and the resulting legacy of sluggish growth in many regions and communities; the liberalization of trade between nations; growing questions of environmental sustainability at the regional and global scales; and the aging of the workforce.

Governments have struggled to find strategies to ensure the prosperity of all parts of the nation in the face of change that is beyond their control. Increasingly there has been a fracturing of economic well-being and growth at the national scale, with some places adjusting to the new economic opportunities more rapidly than others. This has meant that as individuals, our quality of life and economic prospects are now more influenced than in the past by the prosperity and physical resources offered by the places in which we live. Indeed, Richard Florida (2008) has argued that the rise of the creative economy means that where you live is now one of the most important decisions in your life: shaping your job opportunities, lifetime earnings and the quality of your environment. Localities with strong economies, good infrastructure and burgeoning industries are more likely to offer their residents high levels of amenity, rising incomes and secure employment. By contrast, cities, communities and towns suffering from the decline of important employment sectors are less likely to attract investment, they find it more difficult to develop and sustain appropriate infrastructure and they are more likely to lose population and influence when compared with more prosperous regions.

Places – cities, regions, towns and other, smaller, settlements – therefore matter (OECD 2009). They are important to the individual, the household, the community and – as will be argued later – the nation as a whole. There are no truly wealthy nations comprised entirely of poor regions and towns and, as the OECD (2012a p 15) observes, 'very underdeveloped regions can often impose high costs on national budgets.' This book sets out to shed light on three things: first, it examines why governments, communities, elected officials and professional staff in town planning, city management and national, state and local governments need to pay close attention to the economies of their regions, towns and cities. Second, *Globalization, Planning and Local Development* sets out to provide the concepts and knowledge needed to successfully navigate current thinking around growth and how and why these economic drivers are shaping the prospects of regions and cities. Third, and perhaps most importantly, in this book we document the strategies and actions available to communities and regions as they plan for a better future.

## ■ 1.1  Planning for economic development

Communities across the globe are confronted by a fundamental question: why should we plan for economic development when national governments already give the issue a great deal of attention, and we know that globalization means many of the decisions affecting growth are taken outside the region, and commonly in other countries? Surely, given the fundamental dynamics of the economy, comparable development would take place locally if no action was taken?

These are critical challenges and it is important to acknowledge that some communities and local governments do not prioritize economic growth and instead emphasize other issues, such as meeting social needs, ensuring the protection of the environment or building a sense of community. While each of these other aspects of social and economic well-being is important, and deserving of local action, engaging with questions of economic development at the city, region or community level is crucial for four major reasons:

- First, economic development empowers a community to shape its future. It provides greater choice with respect to pathways for future development, it can enable the emergence of a better-educated and more skilled population and it can provide the resources needed to reduce adverse impacts on the environment, while continuing to enjoy greater prosperity.
- Second, the processes of economic globalization have made localities more, not less, important. Decision makers based in New York, London, Berlin

or Shanghai will have little knowledge of the conditions and opportunities in America's Midwest, central Europe or rural New Zealand in respect of potentially hosting a new factory, or attracting additional investment in an existing plant. Those making such critical choices are unlikely to have detailed insight into individual cities or regions. Part of the challenge of economic development in the 21st century, therefore, is for communities to raise their profile globally in order to attract investments, secure new markets and become a known destination for tourism and other activities. Academics have referred to this as the process of 'glocalization': a simultaneous refocusing on both global networks and individual localities, with both crucial to the prospects for growth.

- Third, community-based economic development has become more important as the economy has changed – especially in developed nations. This has meant the conditions needed to foster growth have become more complex. Countries such as the United States, Canada, the United Kingdom, Australia, France and Germany now rely upon services – such as tourism, retailing, business services, education, Research and Development, et cetera – to generate the major share of employment and household income. Both manufacturing and agriculture remain important parts of the economy, but they too have transformed, relying heavily on more technologically sophisticated and knowledge-intensive production systems than previously. Development at the local level now depends on the provision of a sophisticated array of infrastructure – transport, telecommunications, et cetera – as well as access to an appropriately skilled workforce, specialist suppliers and high-quality resources. The sheer complexity of our contemporary economy demands coordination at the city or regional scale in order to ensure that appropriate investments are made in the first instance, and then used to their full potential.
- Fourth, the failure to plan and take steps to secure growth can result in missed opportunities and sluggish performance for the local economy. In addition, cities, regions and communities that do not develop economically are likely to be confronted by adverse outcomes – including their potential demise. Economic globalization has reduced the willingness and capacity of national governments to support regions or cities in decline, and communities can quickly discover they have been left behind economically. This results in a raft of problems including entrenched long-term unemployment, a declining tax base, a shrinking workforce, poor access to infrastructure, a loss of skilled workers and young people, and limited visibility amongst key private sector and government decision makers.

There is not a universal consensus on the importance of local action to secure development. At the global scale, some have argued that a focus on national development alone is not only sufficient, but also the most productive strategy for ensuring prosperity (World Bank 2009). Those who advocate for this position would discourage central governments and local communities alike from investing in local growth, arguing that market processes alone will guarantee development and ensure resources are used wisely. It is their view that community or government action promoting the growth of particular places does so at the cost of aggregate national growth. That is, the time, effort and money put into achieving growth at the city or community scale could be more usefully employed elsewhere. In addition, it is argued that such strategies have a poor track record of success. Economic activity, the World Bank (2009) contends, is inevitably 'lumpy' and governments should therefore focus on the 'spatially blind provision of essential public services and balanced regulation of land, labor and product markets.' (Gill 2010 p 3) Academic researchers have also been critical of local and regional development efforts, with Freebairn (2003) arguing that regional policies reduce competitiveness by discouraging industry from establishing in the most productive locations.

Locally based economic development efforts have been criticized for encouraging communities, cities or governments to invest in infrastructure for which there is either uncertain or limited demand (Daley and Lancy 2011). Others have noted that locally based economic development efforts often exhibit perverse effects, including facilitating 'rent seeking' behavior as firms seek locations that offer the most favorable subsidies (Malecki 1999) and become 'footloose' – moving as one set of incentives expires and others become available elsewhere. There is clear evidence of such game playing in the US, the UK, Australia and other nations (Beer et al. 2003). At a more fundamental level, Glaeser (2012) has argued that the major metropolitan regions now dominate economic growth, both at a national and a global scale, and in consequence there should be a focus on facilitating their role as engines of growth rather than distributing employment and productive capacity more broadly.

A second group of researchers and institutions has responded to this argument by assembling a substantial body of evidence that suggests that locally and regionally based growth is essential for national well-being. The OECD examined the growth of regions across the developed world over a ten-year period (OECD 2010, 2012a and b) and concluded that spatially blind policies – of the type advocated by the World Bank – are a necessary, but not sufficient, condition for growth, and that such policies are likely to have unintended negative consequences (Garcilazo et al. 2010). The research (2010) observed that across the nations within the OECD, regions with lower rates of growth accounted for 44 percent of aggregate growth between 1995 and 2005 and that fewer than half the metropolitan regions in the OECD had growth rates higher than their national average. In part, these arguments presented by the OECD (2009) set out to reverse conventional interpretations of regional growth processes and outcomes. In their view, the persistence of growth and income disparities between more developed and less developed regions did not reflect a failure of regional policy *per se*, but instead highlighted the potential for future growth in less developed regions. From this perspective, if failure was evident, it was in the type of regional policies and programs implemented by governments. Growth, the OECD (2009) argued, results not from the simple application of increased investment in infrastructure or research and development (R&D), but instead 'the key appears to be how assets are used, how different actors interact and how synergies are exploited.' (OECD 2009 p 3) In short, one of the world's leading authorities on economic development proposed that growth is achieved through positive interactions between factors such as infrastructure provision, educational attainments, innovation and the promotion of an entrepreneurial culture. Critically, such synergies are best planned for at the local, city or community scale.

The body of work produced by the OECD (2009, 2010) can be interpreted in a number of ways, but it has two clear implications for this book and its audience. First, generating growth locally is important for economic prosperity and well-being, not only in the immediate region, but also nationally. If a nation is to grow in the 21st century, in large measure it will need to do so from the community level up. This was a point appreciated by Lord Heseltine in his development of a strategy for economic growth in the UK. He argued that encouraging growth at the local level is central to securing a prosperous future and that this is best achieved by devolving power, responsibility and resources to the regions so that they can shape their own future (Heseltine 2012). Second, truly integrated local development is only possible at the local level, and while central governments and nationwide programs can assist with the process through grants, networks and information sharing, cities, regions and communities are fundamental to success.

##  1.2 New models of thinking about local economic development

Over recent decades our understanding of how economies grow has expanded greatly. There is now more published work and more robust evidence on the drivers of economic growth than at any time in the past. This new knowledge should inform the growth strategies of cities, regions and communities globally.

Twenty to thirty years ago the economic foundations of most developed nations were still undergoing a process of transition as they left behind their reliance on manufacturing industries and moved to post-industrial economies. The way we thought about economic development and its determinants was often constrained by a lingering focus on manufacturing as the most significant part of the productive economy, and models of economic development that were restricted by poor data and limited theorization. We have now moved on considerably in our understanding of the processes driving economic development and how to achieve it locally. We better understand how the creation and dispersion of knowledge shapes the prospects for growth, what types of technology are likely to have positive spillovers into other industries and the importance of transport infrastructure in encouraging growth.

Green Leigh and Blakely (2013) identified five phases of economic development in the USA, which they summarized as:

- **Phase 1. Industrial recruitment** commencing in the 1930s and continuing into the 21st century.
- **Phase 2. Business retention and incubation** was added to the portfolio of activities for some economic development agencies from the 1960s. From the 1960s economic development evolved to embrace the expansion of business-related activities to include the expansion of established businesses and incubate new firms.
- **Phase 3. Fostering entrepreneurship and working to achieve social equity** emerged as key strategies in the late 1970s and early 1990s. Considerable emphasis was placed on the development of new and emerging

technologies as a pathway to a more prosperous future for the city or region, including those who would otherwise struggle to find employment. The building of industry clusters by facilitating access to venture capital, training of the workforce, and marketing internationally typified this phase.

- **Phase 4. Environmentally sustainable economic development** emerged as an important goal in the 1990s as the USA and other nations became more aware of environmental issues and attempted to incorporate sustainability in every aspect of economic and community life.
- **Phase 5. Market approaches** to meet local demand and address social goals came to the forefront in this fifth, most recent, phase. Some areas of focus have included the revitalization of degraded inner-city areas, and building public–private partnerships with minority firms (Green Leigh and Blakely 2013 p 62). This perspective sought to address the fact that many inner urban areas have not reached their economic and social potential and represented largely untapped markets with respect to consumer expenditure, residential development and services. Strategies were implemented to encourage investment in these places and create a more vibrant market economy at the local level.

Other nations passed through different trajectories. Taking the United Kingdom as an example, local economic development has – until recently – largely been overshadowed by a focus on regions, with policies informed by three distinct paradigms (Hildreth and Bailey 2013). Regional development policies introduced in the first part of the 20th century persisted in one form or another until the mid-1970s, and drew upon Keynesian economics to provide intellectual support for public sector expenditure on industry. The regional policies that persisted in the UK from the 1930s to the 1970s had – at best – a mixed history, with governments providing substantial investment packages to firms in the hope of turning around the processes of de-industrialization. Many of these actions failed, with the House of Commons Expenditure Committee concluding: 'Much has been spent and much may well have been wasted. Regional policy has been empiricism run mad, a game of hit and miss, played with more enthusiasm than success.' (McCallum 1979; House of Commons 1973 cited in Garretsen et al. 2013)

Regional development policies were abandoned by the Conservative Governments of the late 1970s which enacted a more market-oriented philosophy that drew upon neoclassical economics (Haughton et al. 2003; Hildreth and Bailey 2013). Both urban regeneration and inner-city development emerged as major policy initiatives during this period, with high profile developments including the London Docklands. As Haughton et al. (2003) noted, there was a strong emphasis on property-based redevelopment, with major projects supported in London, as well as in regional centers such as Leeds and Sheffield.

The election of the Blair Labour Government in 1997 ushered in what Hildreth and Bailey (2013) dubbed 'the new regional policy.' Regional Development Agencies (RDAs) were introduced into the UK, partly to gain access to European Union funding, but more importantly as a strategy for better integrating local conditions into the development of each region. Seven RDAs covered all of England and had substantial budgets, well in excess of £1 billion annually. Wales, Scotland and Northern Ireland were each covered separately as part of the emerging, devolved governance of the UK. The RDAs were active in business promotion and support, infrastructure provision, workforce training, community building, property development and innovation support. In 2010 the new Cameron Coalition Government abolished the RDAs and created a new policy framework to support Local Enterprise Partnerships (LEPs), which were to be led by business but involved both local governments and the community. When compared with their predecessors, the LEPs have less funding and a more restrictive mandate for involvement in local economies. They are also more locally focused with 38 separate LEPs in England alone and a complex relationship with a more recent UK Government initiative – Combined Authorities.

Contemporary thinking about how and why regional economies grow has evolved and informed some of these developments in the practice of local or regional development. Within economics, the rise of new growth theory and endogenous models of regional growth (Stimson et al. 2009) has highlighted the importance of the factors found within a region – the quality of the labor force, propensity for innovation, the history of entrepreneurial activity, et cetera – in explaining differential rates of growth. These new perspectives have challenged researchers, policymakers and practitioners alike to consider how best to generate growth from the resources within a region. One of the pivotal questions, therefore, is: if the keys to a region's growth are already embedded in that place, what actions, strategies and processes are needed to unlock growth? Geographers and other social scientists have explored comparable ideas with a considerable volume of work in the early part of the 21st century focused on 'new regionalism' and the impact of institutions on economic development (see, for example, Rainnie and Grobbelaar 2005; Amin 1999). The intellectual development of the field has also been affected by Krugman's 'new economic geography' which shows that economic integration will result in greater specialization within individual regions (Krugman 1991, 2011). Krugman's work has been interpreted variously to either support the need for place-based intervention or deny the effectiveness of such actions, but it has unquestionably emphasized the tendency of economic processes to concentrate economic activity in a small number of regions – a process planners refer to as cumulative causation.

Developments in our broader understanding of the drivers of growth locally or regionally have been matched, and often outstripped, by the addition of theories at the meso level on why regions or places grow. This has included work on the impact of industry clusters on growth (Porter 1990), a focus on the role of innovation and the knowledge economy in driving development (Cooke and De Propris 2011) and a debate on the significance of related economic activities in helping businesses and industries grow (McCann and Ortega-Argiles 2013). Researchers and policymakers have examined the relative impact of the development of a specialized versus a diversified local economy on growth prospects, as well as how to develop a resilient economy, one able to withstand environmental, economic and social shocks (Pike et al. 2010). Recently, governments, including the agencies of the European Union, have begun to explore 'smart specialization' strategies as a way of putting into practice recent thinking on how best to take advantage of the opportunities for growth.

Policy and academic debates have helped create a high level of dynamism within the field of local economic development. New ideas have flooded into the field and there is a need to be aware of the origins and limitations of these concepts as communities seek to apply them to their own circumstances. It is important to acknowledge that linear or uni-dimensional approaches to local economic development are rare, if not completely absent. Green Leigh and Blakely's (2013) five stages to economic development discussed above suggest that over time one approach has supplanted its predecessor, such that successive strategies have been rolled out over the decades, with clear points of delineation as new ideas have been adopted. The reality, however, is far different: instead, local development tends to find expression as a melting pot of ideas and programs with, for example, the simultaneous implementation of firm recruitment and urban regeneration polices, often overlaid with a sustainable development agenda. The practice of economic development at the local level sees communities employ any and all of the strategies potentially available to them, and the greater their stock of knowledge about these mechanisms, the better their prospects for success.

## ■ 1.3 Generating more prosperous communities

*Globalization, Planning and Local Economic Development* maps out the strategies and actions available to communities and cities in order to achieve a better future economically, socially and environmentally. A great deal has been written on economic growth at the local level and how policies can, and should, be reset to promote local prosperity. A lot less has been written on *how* to achieve growth at the local level. In part this gap is perfectly understandable, the circumstances – opportunities, risks and history – of each region or urban area are unique, and there is no 'one size fits all' strategy to be applied universally. Moreover, there are often competing solutions offered up by consultants, local political entities, central government directives and academic research. The task of selecting the most appropriate development solutions is difficult, especially when confronted by a raft of apparently contradictory ideas and theories on how best to promote growth (Perry 2010). Which path should a community choose, a high technology route or one that seeks to reduce the cost of production in more conventional industries? Are the two necessarily opposing trajectories? And, is it possible to combine the two to maximize outcomes? Such questions simply emphasize the magnitude of the decisions confronting individual communities, community leaders and professionals as they examine their development possibilities. These questions are often faced under circumstances that can make those given the task of finding an answer feel information rich, but knowledge poor. The magnitude of this effort is often made greater by the need to find solutions in the face of crisis, when there may be little time to engage in an orderly search for answers.

It is important to consider economic development as both a process and an outcome. This perspective has two distinct dimensions. First, while locality-based development needs to focus on particular goals or outcomes, the challenge to remain competitive within the global economy remains, even after all targets have been met. Economic development efforts need to be sustained in order to adapt to changing conditions and in order to tap into emerging opportunities. Second, successful economic development needs to combine a goal orientation with a commitment to achieving the most appropriate processes to facilitate development. In large measure, establishing a good institutional framework – one that engages with stakeholders, includes mechanisms to ensure a clear vision for the future and identifies the strategies to achieve those goals – ensures that the opportunities for growth are maximized.

While not every city or community with strong processes will achieve their economic objectives – and not all places that grow will have a strong economic development framework – on average, well-prepared economic development strategies will result in better outcomes. In a series of highly influential reports, the OECD (2009, 2010, 2012a and b) commented on the importance of institutional arrangements – the local organizations and systems put in place to facilitate development – in explaining why growth happens in some localities but not others. There is clear evidence that encouraging growth is a multifaceted task that isn't simply a responsibility of town planners or economic development practitioners. Instead, success is dependent upon the capacity to span the boundaries that exist between government agencies, as well those that sit between government and private sector organizations. It is important to acknowledge also that measures designed to foster growth also add to the resilience of the economy.

Questions of geographic or spatial scale are fundamental to understanding, and influencing, the processes that drive growth. Often the terms local economic development and regional economic development are used interchangeably and we have followed this practice in a number of places in *Globalization, Planning and Local Economic Development*. In part this reflects variation in practice at the global scale: activities that would be presented as local economic development in the US would be discussed as regional development in New Zealand or the UK, and in many parts of the European Union. More fundamentally, some factors are important at only one scale, while others exert a substantial impact at more than one geographic level (Figure 1.1): access to utility networks – electricity, gas, water, telecommunications, transport – are critical for individual sites, but also significant at the regional scale, where it may be a question of the availability of high-speed broadband connections, or the adequacy of major transport routes. Other factors span all the way from individual property to state- or region-wide significance, and may be highly influential at each level. It is important to acknowledge some issues can only be addressed effectively at a particular geographic scale, and that attempts to do otherwise are fruitless.

Success in local or regional economic development is achieved by addressing local needs and opportunities. Successful city or community economic development is unlikely to emerge by following strategies prominent in the popular or industry press, but poorly matched to local conditions. Moreover, economic development strategies shouldn't be shaped to fit the guidelines of an external funding body – such as a central government agency.

Learning from others is one of the ways communities can empower themselves and their economic development efforts. In the past there was a tendency to view economic development as a set of processes unique to a nation and its institutional, social and economic structure. There is now, however, a growing recognition that the strategies and learnings of cities, towns and communities in

**FIGURE 1.1**   Economic factors by spatial scale

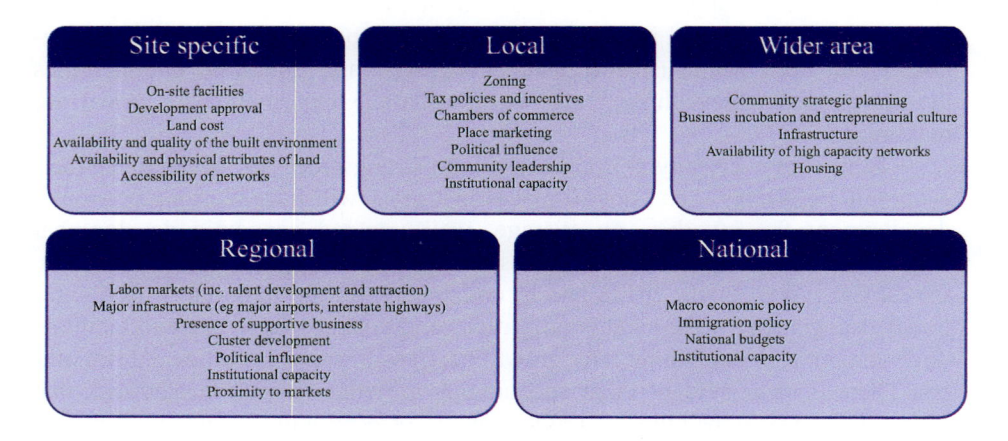

other parts of the world are directly applicable in attempting to address local conditions. For example, the challenges confronting declining towns in rural Canada, Australia or the US have strong similarities, but there are also parallels with many European and South American localities. Similarly, a US oil and gas town such as Midland in West Texas is likely to be confronted by the same difficulties with respect to providing worker housing, shaping a long-term future for the region and adjusting to cycles of boom and bust as Chinchilla in Queensland, Australia, or the parts of Scotland tied to North Sea oil and gas. The growth of global industries and production systems in areas as diverse as technology development, manufacturing and resource extraction has meant there is now greater benefit than ever before in a city, community or region emulating the success of a comparable local economy on the other side of the globe. Increasingly there is convergence in how places – cities, regions, towns – seek to grow. Many of the strategies and approaches deployed locally have the capacity to span international boundaries, providing useful insights to practitioners in apparently very different contexts. This is partly an outcome of deliberate programs of knowledge transfer and learning, but at a more fundamental level, it is a product of the evolution of the global economy.

In considering how places develop locally we have to acknowledge that globalization has meant all locations are affected by a broadly uniform set of processes and growth dynamics. Where once we might have considered issues of development in China, India or Malaysia as different from those evident in the US, Finland or Canada, we must now accept the equalizing dynamic of global capital flows and production systems. The divide between what was traditionally considered the developed and developing world is not nearly as sharp as it was in the 1980s or 1990s. We need to accept that an advanced industry – information and communication technology – now represents the single largest employment sector in China, with low added-value industries such as textile, clothing and footwear, moving to lower wage nations in South and South East Asia. The pace of China's transformation has been remarkable, but it is indicative of the rapidity of global economic change more generally. It is important to acknowledge that differences remain between and within nations with respect to the level of resources devoted to locally based development – with the European Union, for example, committing €74 billion to territorial cohesion over a four-year period – but the philosophies and approaches to action traverse national borders.

Cities, regions and communities that examine the success of other places around the globe are more likely to identify appropriate growth strategies when compared with those that take a narrower view. There is a second and equally important source of information available to localities seeking growth: the review of the evidence based on what has worked in other communities, why it has worked and how it has achieved success. There is now more published material on the outcomes of programs intended to promote local or regional growth than at any time in the past and *Globalization, Planning and Local Economic Development* seeks to introduce the reader to this set of resources.

Over the last decades we have come to know a great deal more about the detail of economic development strategies. We now have a far better idea of what will be effective in stimulating development in individual cities and communities, why it is likely to have an impact and how it can be best implemented. Examples include:

- The research literature indicates that the most effective city and community-based economic development strategies in the United States are:
  - The provision of business support and advice to individual enterprises;
  - The preparation of land and the development of sites for incoming or expanding firms;
  - The provision of grants or loans that enable businesses to establish or grow; the establishment of networks and the formation of partnerships;
  - Measures to secure inward investment and promote the region (Clower 2003).
- Innovation is recognized as an important driver of economic performance and it is possible to draw a number of firm conclusions on how best to boost innovation:
  - Firms operating internationally are 40 to 70 percent more likely to innovate than domestically oriented firms;
  - Small firms will be more innovative and profitable if family members work in the business (Adjei et al. 2016);
  - Businesses are more likely to be both innovative and profitable if they are located close to their suppliers and customers (Oerlemans and Meeus 2005);
  - Innovation tends to be concentrated in both small and large firms. Mid-sized firms tend to be less innovative and therefore a less productive target for local development assistance (McCann and Ortega-Argiles 2013 p 193).
- In responding to an adverse event such as the closure of a major employer, cities, regions and communities need to respond by:
  - Providing a number of different forms of assistance;

- o    Obtaining as much information as possible about likely further developments; delineating clear responsibilities in developing recovery actions;
- o    Implementing flexible programs for recovery (Cook et al. 2013).
- Support provided to small businesses (up to 50 employees) is likely to be more effective than assistance to larger firms (Mouque 2012 p 11).

This still-expanding stock of knowledge represents an enormous resource for cities and communities seeking to improve their economic futures. This evidence base provides a solid foundation for the development of more effective – and locally appropriate – economic development strategies and actions.

## ■ 1.4 Conclusion

This chapter has introduced some of the key ideas that inform the development of the remainder of this book: the need for city, local or community-based approaches to economic growth; the impact of the global economy and the need for places to guarantee their place within it; and the emerging capacity to develop better economic development strategies by examining international experience, while also drawing upon a growing evidence base on what is effective and why. In this chapter we have argued that the case for promoting economic development at the city or community scale is clear-cut. Regions and towns that engage with a local development agenda are likely to prosper, while those that do not plan for, and invest in, local or community development implicitly accept a lower level of prosperity and a more limited role in determining the community's future. There is, of course, no guarantee that cities and communities striving to improve their economic performance will grow: some places will be adversely affected by processes beyond their control, while others develop without apparent effort or in spite of measures to control growth. There is clear evidence, however, that efforts to encourage growth locally or regionally have positive results, help create a more resilient economy, assist in the process of economic transformation and contribute to social cohesion and rising skill levels within the workforce.

## *Key messages*

- Advances in our understanding of the drivers of local or regional growth have informed the development of new economic development policies and practices;
- Strong national institutions – such as financial and legal systems – are a precondition for growth but do not assure growth;
- In the 21st century, nations need to grow from the bottom up, which means that community or local development is a priority;
- Local economic development needs to be considered as both an outcome and a process;

- The new economic geography shows that in the absence of other action, economic processes tend to concentrate development in relatively few locations;
- Communities use a range of strategies to achieve growth and the list of potential strategies has grown over time.

## Discussion questions

- Reflecting on the material covered in this chapter, think about the place or places in which you have lived and consider what the important industries are and where growth opportunities might lie for this community.
- What do you know about the economic development strategies and programs that are being pursued, and where might you find out more?
- As a group, list the economic development agencies active in your community and the activities they have in place in order to achieve a more prosperous future.

## References

Adjei, E.K., Eriksson, R.H. and Lindgren, U. 2016 Social proximity and firm performance: the importance of family member ties in workplaces, *Regional Studies, Regional Science*, 3:1, pp 303–319. DOI: 10.1080/21681376.2016. 1189354.

Amin, A. 1999 An institutionalist perspective on regional development, *International Journal of Urban and Regional Research*, 23, pp 365–378.

Beer, A., Haughton, G. and Maude, A. 2003 *Developing Locally: Lessons in Economic Development from Four Nations,* Policy Press, Bristol.

Clower, T. 2003 Local and Regional Economic Development Agencies in the United States of America. In Beer, A., Haughton, G. and Maude, A. *Developing Locally, Lessons from Economic Development Agencies in Four Nations*, Policy Press, Bristol.

Cook, J., Pringle, S. and Bailey, D. 2013 *Economic Shocks Research: A Report to the Department for Business, Innovation and Skills*, SQW Ltd and Coventry University Business School, London.

Cooke, P. and De Propris, L. 2011 A policy agenda for EU Smart Growth: the role of creative and cultural clusters, *Policy Studies*, 32:4, pp 365–375.

Daley, J. and Lancy, A. 2011 *Investing in Regions: Making a Difference*, Grattan Institute, Melbourne.

Florida, R. 2008 *Who's Your City?* Basic Books, New York.

Freebairn, J. 2003 Economic policy for rural and regional Australia, *The Australian Journal of Agricultural and Resource Economics*, 47, pp 389–414.

Garcilazo, J., Oliveira Martins, J. and Tompson, W. 2010 Why policies need to be place based in order to be people centred, *Vox*, November.

Garretsen, H., McCann, P., Martin, R. and Tyler, P. 2013 The future of regional policy, *Cambridge Journal of Regions, Economy and Society*, 6, pp 179–186.

Gill, I. 2010 Regional development policies: place-based or people-centred, *Vox*, October.

Glaeser, E. 2012 *Triumph of the City*, Penguin, New York.

Green Leigh, N. and Blakely, E. 2013 *Planning Local Economic Development: Theory and Practice.* 5th edition. Sage Publications, New York.

Haughton, G., Beer, A. and Maude, A. 2003 Understanding international divergence and convergence in local and regional economic development. In Beer, A., Haughton, G. and Maude, A. (eds) *Developing Locally*, Policy Press, Bristol, pp 15–37.

Heseltine, M. 2012 *No Stone Unturned in Pursuit of Growth*, House of Lords, London.

Hildreth, P. and Bailey, D. 2013 The economics behind the move to 'localism' in England, *Cambridge Journal of Regions, Economy and Society*, 6, pp 233–249.

Krugman, P. 1991 *Geography and Trade*, MIT Press, Cambridge, MA.

Krugman, P. 2011 The new economic geography: now middle aged, *Regional Studies*, 45:1, pp 1–7.

Malecki, E. 1999 Soft variables in regional science, *Review of Regional Studies*, 30:1, pp 61–69.

McCann, P. and Ortega-Argiles, R. 2013 Smart specialization, regional growth and applications to European Union cohesion policy, *Regional Studies*. DOI: 10.1080/00343404.2013.799769.

Mouque, D. 2012 *What Are Counterfactual Evaluations Teaching Us About Enterprises and Innovation Support?* Regional Focus, 2/12, Directorate General for Regional and Urban Policy Brussels.

OECD 2009 *How Regions Grow: Trends and Analysis*, OECD, Paris.

OECD 2010 *Regions Matter*, OECD, Paris.

OECD 2012a *Promoting Growth in All Regions*, OECD, Paris.

OECD 2012b *Growth in All Regions*, OECD, Paris.

Oerlemans, L. and Meeus, M. 2005 Do organizational and spatial proximity impact on firm performance? *Regional Studies*, 39:1, pp 89–104. DOI: 10.1080/0034340052000320896.

Perry, M. 2010 *Controversies in Local Economic Development*, Routledge, London.

Pike, A., Dawley, S. and Tomaney, J. 2010 Resilience, adaptation and adaptability, *Cambridge Journal of Regions, Economy and Society*, 3, pp 59–70.

Porter, M. 1990 *The Competitive Advantage of Nations*, The Free Press, New York.

Rainnie, A. and Grobbelaar, M. 2005 *New Regionalism in Australia*, Ashgate, Aldershot.

Stimson, R., Stough, R. and Salazar, M. 2009 *Leadership and Institutions in Regional Endogenous Development*, Edward Elgar, Cheltenham.

World Bank 2009 *World Development Report 2009 – Reshaping Economic Geography*, Washington, DC, World Bank.

# 2

# The challenge of local economic development

This chapter:

▶ Considers four case study communities confronted by economic change;

▶ Provides concrete examples of the issues and challenges that are discussed in later chapters;

▶ Examines the processes of change and how they have affected each community;

▶ Focuses upon:
  ▶ The nature of the challenges;
  ▶ The processes for identifying potential solutions;
  ▶ The steps taken to reposition the local economy;
  ▶ How success has been measured or evaluated;
  ▶ What is needed to sustain solutions in order to build or rebuild economies.

ALL ECONOMIES GO through change – whether it is at the national, regional, local or community scale. Change is brought about by the emergence of new technologies, the rise of new business models – think about the success of Airbnb, Uber, Amazon, et cetera – environmental change, investment in new or enhanced infrastructure, population growth or decline, shifts in the preferences of consumers, or the relatively straightforward decision of one or more businesses to relocate.

Change is a good thing: it often results in income growth, the opening up of new opportunities, and a chance to work for a better future. But it needs to be actively managed. Often it calls for the formulation of new plans and the establishment of innovative development instruments better suited to shifting conditions, and this in turn may result in the formation of new alliances between businesses or the creation of new government entities in order to deliver a better future. This chapter examines four communities affected by change and how they have, or have not, adequately responded to the issues that have emerged before them. Additional examples are provided in the Web-based supplementary material (www.gpaled. com). Importantly, all case studies were selected because they provide lessons that are transferrable to other places and other times. They illustrate both the nature of the problems many places are forced to deal with, and the ways in which authorities and businesses have found solutions.

# ■ 2.1  San Diego

San Diego is the eighth largest city in the United States with a population of 1.4 million. It is the county seat of San Diego County and is the economic center of the San Diego–Chula Vista–Carlsbad metropolitan area, the 17th-largest metro area in the US with a population of 3.3 million in 2017. It is located on the coast in southern California, adjacent to Tijuana, Mexico. The combined San Diego–Tijuana population is about 4.4 million. The border crossing at San Ysidro, which connects the two cities, is often referred to as the busiest in the world. According to the US Department of Transportation, there were 32.2 million ground transportation or pedestrian crossings into the US at San Ysidro in 2017.

In addition to its famous cross-border tourism connections, San Diego and Tijuana have multiple industrial channels through *maquiladora* (twin-plant) operations. Maquiladoras are characterized by manufacturing/assembly facilities located in Mexico with administrative, design and component development operations housed in adjacent US cities. According to the City of San Diego,[1] there are more than 570 maquiladora plants operating in Tijuana with direct connections to US companies.

## 2.1.1 The challenge facing San Diego

San Diego's development through the 20th century was tied to the expansion of the military, with the US Navy establishing a presence in 1907. The Coast Guard and the US Marine Corps also have bases in and around the city. The US Navy remains important as the city has the only major submarine and shipbuilding yards on the US West Coast and is the home port of the world's largest naval fleet. San Diego's economy experienced a substantial downturn in the 1990s as the Cold War came to an end and as it refocused on new industries.

## 2.1.2 Identifying solutions for San Diego

San Diego in the early 1990s was fortunate in that the seeds for its regrowth were already firmly planted. The University of California at San Diego (UCSD) has long been a global leader for basic research in the health sciences and, as San Diego's military-driven economy waned, the city rode the wave of the biotechnology revolution. By 2004 the prestigious Milken Institute ranked San Diego as the top metropolitan area in the US for biosciences (DeVol et al. 2004).

The World Bank attributed San Diego's success to academics, local business and political interests coming together to create a productive environment (Wu 2005). UCSD and its CONNECT program was identified as being central to this growth, with the Scripps Institute and the Salk Institute also important. Other researchers have argued that San Diego's growth as a bioscience center is a function of university research *and* related spin-off companies and other firms working in the life sciences (Walcott 2002).

The community also benefited from the North American Free Trade agreement. It boosted the value of maquiladora operations, allowing manufacturers in San Diego to take advantage of lower production and assembly costs in Mexico while accessing highly skilled designers, engineers and professional services in the US. Effectively, the components that are shipped into Mexico for assembly and then returned as finished products into the US move with little or no tariffs, and thus boost competitiveness and economic development on both sides of the border.

### 2.1.3 Repositioning San Diego's economy

The regeneration of San Diego's economy was not simply a matter of good luck. Public and private sector agencies worked hard to capitalize on their intellectual assets and the promise that it offered for jobs and economic growth in advanced technologies and high value-added services.

The San Diego Regional Economic Development Corporation (SREDC) has played its part in attracting and retaining companies in the San Diego region and has done so by working one on one with these businesses to assist their relocation and expansion. The SREDC is a private, not-for-profit corporation, funded by a broad coalition of public companies, trade associations, universities and local governments. The SREDC offers a range of services, including:

- Site selection assistance;
- Incentive and business tax information;
- Information on key contacts in business and local government;
- Demographic, wage and other data;
- Assistance in navigating local government requirements;
- Access to workforce training and recruitment.

UCSD has been active in encouraging innovation and new firm formation within the region. The SREDC has worked closely with the UCSD's CONNECT program in nurturing high technology entrepreneurship and facilitating interaction with the university. Other agencies active in encouraging the growth of high technology companies in the region include:

- BIOCOM San Diego – a regional association for biotechnology, medical device and bio-agriculture companies;
- Centers for Applied Competitive Technologies – one of 12 state-funded advanced technology centers designed to help manufacturers modernize their manufacturing and production technologies;
- CONNECT – which links entrepreneurs with inventors in technology and life sciences in San Diego County;
- MIT Enterprise Forum, San Diego – conducts events and workshops to address business challenges facing San Diego entrepreneurs;
- Bio, Tech and Beyond – a life sciences-focused business incubator offering low-cost lab space, shared equipment and collaborative work spaces.

Government investment in designated real estate – i.e. laboratories – has also been critical. Biotechnology companies need access to specialist laboratories that are very different from conventional commercial office space. This is especially true for companies that require wet-lab facilities that are often not available outside of university or major research centers. Providing appropriate facilities for technology development has assisted business startups and the growth of small enterprises into larger businesses. In turn, this has increased the region's ability to attract federal life sciences research funding. BIOCOM reports that in fiscal year 2016, San Diego County organizations attracted almost $833 million in National Institutes of Health grants (BIOCOM 2017).

## 2.1.4 Measuring success in San Diego's economy

In 2006 a consultant working for a city eager to reproduce San Diego's success concluded that

> San Diego is in a league of its own. . . . San Diego has economic development momentum because it has reached a critical mass in one of the most dynamic industries in the new economy – biosciences. Further, Greater San Diego is working hard to build critical mass in other sectors as well, and given its track record it is likely to succeed.
>
> (KMK Consulting 2006)

San Diego's success in promoting the life sciences industry cluster is demonstrated by ongoing gains in bio-pharmaceuticals manufacturing, medical devices and diagnostic equipment manufacturing. By 2016, the concentration of these industries was double the US average (BIOCOM 2017). Overall, San Diego enjoys broad economic gains with county level employment growing by more than 313,000 jobs (+18%) from 2010 through the 2018 third quarter.[2]

## 2.1.5 Sustaining the rebuilding of San Diego's economy

San Diego faces opportunities and challenges. The resurgence in federal defense spending since the early 2000s has solidified military bases and supported key traditional sectors of the San Diego economy, namely aerospace and space-related industries. The commercialization of space travel and exploration is also creating economic opportunities. However, San Diego also faces challenges, natural and man-made. Based on cost of living data from the Council for Community and Economic Research, it has the 13th highest cost of living among US metro areas. Housing costs are more than 2.2 times the national average. Even with relatively high salaries for skilled workers, it is increasingly challenging for under-40 workers to live well in the community, which creates concerns about out-migration of skilled labor. While San Diego has, according to many, the most pleasant weather conditions in the continental US, the increase of severe weather events threatens homes in the region, particularly from mudslides. Like many of the nation's top metro areas, the key issue moving into the third decade of the 21st century will be the region's ability to continue to attract and retain the high-skilled labor that drives its success in life sciences and other advanced industries.

The re-negotiation of the North American Free Trade Agreement[3] and a growing appetite in the US and elsewhere for trade restrictions more generally could threaten the success of maquiladoras. In addition, much of San Diego's recent success, especially in developing a thriving life sciences industry cluster, is based on the quality and quantity of key academic and research institutions. However, California's state budget is under increasing stress, and this includes the substantial costs of rebuilding large areas of the state after environmental disasters. Regional universities and research institutions in San Diego will need to look for funding away from state government, and perhaps even federal research spending, given current federal administration priorities. Finally, San Diego will need to address fundamental urban design issues that integrate Smart Growth principles and address housing affordability in order to maintain their competitive advantages.

## ■ 2.2 Washington, DC

In this case we examine the Washington, DC metropolitan area which includes counties in northern Virginia and southern Maryland and the District of Columbia. As the National Capital Region, the DC metro area enjoys many benefits, including being the site for more than 360,000 federal workers with average salaries in the range of $100,000. But even this contribution to the economy is the result of a major shift in government-as-employer in the region. Under President Bill Clinton, the federal government underwent a major privatization program that saw great reductions in the federal government civilian labor force in exchange for a rapid increase in federal procurement spending.

Between 1992 and 2000, federal procurement spending in the National Capital Region almost doubled from $15.6 billion to $29.3 billion. The War on Terror and related conflicts in the early 2000s pushed regional federal spending even higher. By the 2008 presidential election, government contractors in the DC region were getting almost $69 billion per year in federal procurement spending. This figure rose again through American Recovery Act spending in the aftermath of the financial crisis and Great Recession, rising to $82.4 billion in fiscal year 2010. The federal government has been a driver and backstop to the regional economy. The opportunities provided by federal government employment, government contractors, and political positions attracted talented workers from across the country and around the world. It is generally considered that the Washington, DC region has the most educated workforce in the country, surpassing even the west coast technology centers in San Francisco and Silicon Valley.

In the early days of the internet, the DC region, and particularly what became known as the Dulles Corridor, saw the growth of Internet-based companies that became household names such as AOL (America Online). Also, with the presence of the Pentagon and the Defense Advanced Research Projects Agency (DARPA), telecommunications infrastructure development focused on the region, and especially northern Virginia, with massive fiber-optic cable channels delivering the fastest broadband speeds available. Today, some estimates say that 70 percent of the world's Internet traffic passes through servers located in the DC region, which gives the area a strategic advantage in communications-dependent technology sectors.

Due in large part to its federal spending-driven success, the DC region has not developed widely accepted regional organizations providing economic development activities across local jurisdictions, much less across state and district boundaries. When it comes to economic development cooperation across Maryland, Virginia and the District of Columbia, the Potomac River is deep and wide.

## 2.2.1 The challenge facing Washington, DC

In 2010, the Center for Regional Analysis at George Mason University estimated that the federal government directly or indirectly created about 40 percent of all regional economic activity. As long as federal spending kept growing, the region prospered. But DC had become a company town, and just like a coal mining town in West Virginia, a logging community in British Columbia or a mill town in 1960s western Pennsylvania, the regional economy was overexposed to one sector and had become fragile. After the Republican Party gained majorities in the House of Representatives and Senate in the mid-term elections of 2006, fiscal conservatism became the mantra, with much credit going to Tea Party activism and the House Freedom Caucus in calling for restraint in federal spending. The result was the Budget Control Act (BCA) of 2011, which effectively said that if congressional budget writers could not agree on a budget with reduced spending, automatic spending cuts, called sequestration, would be triggered.

In 2013, congressional Republicans and Democrats could not reach a budget agreement, resulting in a series of sequestration spending cuts and a federal hiring freeze (federal employees retiring or resigning their jobs could not be replaced except in specific circumstances) that lowered the total federal workforce. Between fiscal years 2010 and 2013, federal procurement spending in the DC metro region was reduced by more than $13 billion per year. The regional economy entered a short but painful recession. With further rounds of automatic cuts included in the BCA, and political gridlock between congress and the White House, the outlook among businesses in early 2014 was bleak. Regional leaders began to publicly discuss the need to diversify the regional economy away from federal government dominance, but the lack of a regional economic development leadership group has meant that economic diversification strategies have been locally based, with little coordination across jurisdictions. This is not to say that there have not been attempts by business and cross-jurisdiction groups to step into the void of regional economic development leadership, but success has been limited. A relatively new concern has emerged among regional leaders as members of the Trump administration have begun examining opportunities to move large segments of federal agencies away from the National Capital Region. While it is unclear if this relocation of thousands of federal jobs will be implemented, it has the attention of the economic development community.

## 2.2.2 Repositioning the DC economy

Several business groups and individual leaders have made attempts at creating a vision of a DC metro area economy that can grow and thrive with a relatively smaller federal presence. One notable effort sponsored by a group of property developers identified the sectors of the regional economy that could grow independent of federal spending.[4] These target industries include:

- Advanced healthcare services;
- Information and communications technology;
- Science and security technology (including cybersecurity);
- Advocacy;
- Business and financial services;
- Media and information; and,
- Business and leisure travel.

Some of these targets are based on long-standing competitive advantages enjoyed by the region. It is no surprise that the National Capital Region is home to a large cohort of organizations and firms that advocate and lobby Congress. As private sector firms increasingly need near-military grade security to protect organization and customer records and data, they see the DC region as a source of the latest security technology, as well as a ready source of workers (separated military) who can pass security clearances and have an aptitude and attitude for data security.

Other proposed sectors of opportunity extend the impact of government programs. For example, with the National Institutes of Health and John Hopkins medical research complex, suburban Maryland captures more federally supported bio-health and medical research dollars than any other region of the nation. This has led to the development of a significant cluster of pharmaceutical and other health discovery businesses. In an extension of this strength, a major hospital group in northern Virginia is making major investments in personalized medicine, which can be described as turning the bench science supported by NIH grants into clinical practice. Wider efforts are underway to challenge Boston and San Diego as centers of medical innovation entrepreneurship. An important lesson from this case is that most change in the structure of a region's economy begins incrementally. Effectively, the strategy for future success in the DC region depends in large part on businesses (contractors) continuing to provide services to federal agencies, but expanding their customer base into the private sector.

## 2.2.3 Measuring success

The efforts to diversify the economic base of the National Capital Region has had mixed success to date, though these efforts are only a few years old. A key lesson, and source of frustration, for many communities trying to change their economic trajectory is that changing the structure of an economy is a long-term effort. As with steering a super tanker, the vessel will turn, but not quickly. Several of the targeted sectors have shown growth, but over the past few years the overall US economy has moved into a period of solid, if not spectacular, growth. While the DC region has seen growth in bio-health and advocacy, other regions of the nation have grown faster in these industries. The one sector that is showing increasing local competitive advantage is cybersecurity. However, the biggest threat to these efforts may come from the federal government.

In spring of 2018, with Republicans in control of the White House and both houses of Congress, the provisions of the Budget Control Act were nullified and a new budget with very large increases in federal government spending, largely in military and security outlays, was enacted. The immediate pressure of economic diversification may be temporarily relieved, but most business and elected leaders in the region realize that long-term success requires continuing effort – and this is where the absence of a regional economic development agency with the influence to shape local economic development planning has been felt.

The efforts to reshape the regional economy in DC took a major leap forward when it was announced that Amazon chose northern Virginia (across the Potomac River from DC) as one of two sites to host their second headquarters (Amazon HQ2). (The second site is on New York's Long Island.) As details are released on the most public, and frenzied, economic development site location process since the Boeing Company relocated its headquarters to Chicago, we will create a detailed case study that will be available on the textbook website.

### 2.2.4 Sustaining economic diversification efforts in the DC region

If Amazon grows as expected over the next 10–15 years, HQ2 will add about 25,000 new direct employees to the DC region, plus other related jobs that may bring the total jobs effect to more than 75,000. However, while highly important, HQ2 will not be the dominant industry in the DC region. There are already more than 750,000 jobs in professional and business services in the region, most of which are tied to federal spending. The recent boost in federal spending could be considered a temporary economic stimulus since it has been driven by increasing federal deficit spending – meaning that the US is expanding the amount of money the federal government must borrow to match its spending – and is not sustainable in the long run.

Coordinating a shift in economic development strategies that can be effectively implemented across dozens of local jurisdictions located in three states[5] calls for, and perhaps requires, a multi-jurisdictional entity that can influence local strategies and actions while still allowing local economic development plans to reflect the particular wants and needs of their residents. Moreover, economic diversification as described above is but one challenge facing the DC region. As with many major cities, the cost of living in and around DC is high, especially the cost of housing, and transport corridors are congested. Some have suggested the arrival of Amazon HQ2 will exacerbate local accommodation problems and increase commuting times. Moreover, with regional unemployment rates of 4 percent, or below, the 'Amazon effect' may include the region losing businesses as some employers get pushed out of the local labor market.

Given that challenges such as transportation and housing availability are regional in nature, a coordinating entity may need to start by taking on these issues, gaining credibility among businesses, elected leaders and the public, and then take on the challenge of changing 'business as usual' in a government-driven regional economy. The danger is complacency – Amazon addresses the DC region's problems of a relative decline in federally supported economic activity and as a set of communities it may choose to focus on something else. However, experience shows any community that finds itself heavily reliant on government spending, whether it is military bases or the presence of large state or local government institutions, is vulnerable to austerity-driven reductions and may find their economic security compromised. The path to change will most likely be along well-established business patterns, applied to new markets – but even achieving incremental change may require partnerships and new structural collaborations that are more efficiently provided through a regional lens. Getting an Amazon bump is a great economic development achievement, but the DC region must be careful not to shift too many eggs to only one other economic basket.

#  2.3 Chattanooga

Chattanooga, Tennessee is a community that achieved success, suffered from the negative spillovers of that success, and has seen tremendous recovery through local – endogenous – efforts. The resources that underwrote much of the relatively recent development efforts can be traced to the last decade of the 19th century when two Chattanooga businessmen purchased the formula for an elixir from an Atlanta pharmacist. This elixir became Coca-Cola and through aggressive investment and shrewd product licensing, created the family fortunes of the Lyndhurst and Benwood foundations. But hold that thought for a few minutes.

Chattanooga is strategically located in south-eastern Tennessee along the Tennessee River. The city became an early industrial hub in the southern US, at one time being one of the largest cities in the US and known as the Pittsburgh of the South, or the Dynamo of Dixie (Eichenthal and Windeknecht 2008). With river and rail transportation services, key industries included manufacturing, metalworks, iron foundries, as well as more traditional southern US industries including textiles and furniture making. The Great Depression of the 1930s hit the region hard, but growth began again as a result of new hydroelectric plants built by the Tennessee Valley Authority, which gave manufacturing a competitive advantage on power availability and costs. Moreover, the expansion of Fort Oglethorpe in the buildup to World War II brought in thousands of residents, and resulting service sector business opportunities. Other key local industries of this era included patent medicines and insurance services.

## 2.3.1 Chattanooga's challenge

Chattanooga's success came at a steep environmental cost, comparable again to Pittsburgh and other early 20th century manufacturing areas, but the growing level of pollution was a relatively minor concern to the business leaders and workers who were riding the wave of post-war industrial success. But like much of the industrial Midwest, as post-war industrial capacity recovered in Europe and Asia during 1950s and 1960s, Chattanooga found itself suffering from a drop in industrial activity and employment. Germany quickly regained industrial strength with a reputation of high quality, sophisticated manufacturing, while Asia, particularly Japan, under the guidance of Edward Demming and others, were increasingly attracting manufacturing activities with a relatively low-wage, highly productive workforce.

With heavy industry concentrated in the city center, the population declined slightly between 1950 and 1960, but annexation masked the steep rate of population decline in the city core. Population density for the City of Chattanooga in 1930 was about 7,500 residents per square mile. By year 2000, density had dropped to 1,100 residents per square mile (Eichenthal and Windeknecht 2008). The loss of manufacturing jobs happened relatively quickly and the negative spillovers of industrial pollution hindered any shifting of the regional economy to nonindustrial sectors. In 1969, Chattanooga was known widely as the most polluted city in America. The loss of jobs in Chattanooga's urban core was exacerbated by growing racial imbalances in what was later called "white flight" from urban neighborhoods to suburban enclaves. Research over the past 40 years has led us to think of this phenomenon in economic as well as racial terms – white flight became middle income flight as minority groups gained enough economic success to join the exodus to the suburbs. The concentration of poverty increased in the city with an attendant loss in purchasing power, which resulted in abandoned commercial properties and a city that lost tax revenues, including property taxes, sales taxes and income from business licenses. City leaders knew they needed to attract new investment, but that investment was not likely to happen without cleaning up leftover environmental challenges, and recreating a sense of place for the urban core. However, unlike the federal government, cities rely on balanced budgets, and the city simply did not have the resources to implement a major urban renewal plan.

## 2.3.2 Remaking Chattanooga

While Chattanooga suffered from the loss of key industries, environmental degradation, and population out-migration from the urban core, it still possessed key locational advantages: a temperate climate, nearby forest preserves, transportation networks and proximity to major markets (Atlanta, Nashville, Charlotte), and a downtown riverfront (Lambe and de Zeeuw 2016). With a population in the city of more than 175,000 and a metro area population of more than 500,000, Chattanooga is large enough to sustain a sizable services industry. The city enjoyed business-friendly labor laws (right-to-work), relatively low taxes, and an aggressive state incentive program, but still needed to recreate a sense of place. This is where we return to the Coca-Cola fortunes.

Local leaders realized that for Chattanooga to grow and thrive economically, there would need to be a massive program of reinvestment into the city center, supported by public *and* private funding. The investments started with planning in the 1980s for a riverfront park across the river from downtown and an urban design studio that focused redevelopment efforts downtown, including an aquarium, cultural institutions and amenities. By 2005, funding for revitalization planning and projects had risen to $120 million through private donations and public–private civic partnerships (Lambe and de Zeeuw 2016; Katz 2015). The region received a manufacturing boost in 2008 when Volkswagen announced it had selected Chattanooga as the site for the world's first LEED Platinum auto assembly plant with a $1 billion investment and projected employment of 2,000. By 2018, the VW plant, which builds the Passat, Atlas and other vehicles, had expanded employment to more than 3,000 and total investment of $2.3 billion (VW 2018). However, the vision for Chattanooga was not to return to its manufacturing roots, but to create a downtown-based innovation district with a highly developed innovation ecosystem of research institutions, talent and collaboration (Katz 2015). This included building and supporting neighborhood organizations and funding education reform initiatives. Through these efforts, Chattanooga gained a network of volunteers and community leaders who could effectively employ social capital to support redevelopment efforts.

In 2015, local private investment raised $415 million for placemaking in downtown Chattanooga with hundreds of hotel rooms and thousands of apartments to create live–work–play spaces. With a restored riverfront, increasing retail outlets and a revived sense of place, Chattanooga has become one of the most successful urban recovery stories in the US. It repeatedly appears on lists of the 'best places to live.' According to Lambe and de Zeeuw (2016), the key elements to Chattanooga's revitalization have been:

1.  Civically oriented public–private partnerships characterized by funder patience;
2.  Local philanthropy (funding institutions with long-term connections to the community);
3.  Engaged public leaders;
4.  Forward-looking, not looking for 'good old days,' and not opposed by leaders of the past;
5.  Aggressively marketing their story.

### 2.3.3 Measuring success in Chattanooga

It has taken time for the recovery of the City of Chattanooga to take hold, but progress is being made. Between August of 2013 and August of 2018, jobs in the city increased from 69,800 to 82,520, according to the Tennessee Department of Labor and Workforce Development, an increase of 18 percent. The metropolitan area, where the VW plant is located, has grown faster, but this is a good result after decades of decline. The marketing campaign promoting Chattanooga as a 'gig city' with innovation and entrepreneurship at its heart has, perhaps, been more successful than the actual economic performance, but this is a city on the move. More importantly, it is now moving in the right direction.

### 2.3.4 Spreading the success

Even with its success, the story of Chattanooga has its detractors. Cohen (2015) notes that the revitalization occurring in the city center has led to gentrification and displacement of the city's working class and poor. While thousands of new apartments have been added to the housing inventory, most are renting at price points well beyond the reach of households below median incomes. Some of the newly or redeveloped properties include affordable units, but not enough to meet demand. This problem is not unique to Chattanooga. A relative decline in affordable housing usually means economic growth, though not necessarily economic development, is occurring. There is still more to be done in revitalizing Chattanooga's urban core, especially across the river. Moreover, the technology-centric approach to industrial redevelopment that has sparked a resurgence in Chattanooga's economy has placed an economic barrier on residents, especially urban residents, who do not have in-demand skills (Lambe and de Zeeuw 2016). Innovations in the delivery of primary and secondary education will need to be implemented for the city's continued success.

## ■ 2.4 Concordia, Kansas

Concordia, Kansas is the county seat for Cloud County located in the north-eastern part of the state. The regional economy is dominated by agricultural production led by grains, primarily wheat, and livestock (cattle). There are a number of smaller communities near Concordia that traditionally served as hubs of farming activity with small retailers and farm-related services dominating the town economies, as well as hosting local kindergarten to year 12 education. As the county seat, Concordia also has government employment and financial services, and is a regional retail hub with larger stores, including some national chains, and durable goods retailing (appliances, automobiles, farm equipment). Nonetheless, Concordia has always been a small town, with a peak population of 7,221 at the 1970 Census.

### 2.4.1 Concordia's challenge

The challenge for Concordia is the same as most agriculture-dominated regions in the US, Australia, Canada and other industrialized nations. While agricultural production is increasing, technology-driven productivity is reducing the need for farm labor. Tractors and combines are larger and more efficient and cellular-based technologies mean that farmers and ranchers can effectively move herds from one pasture to another with remotely controlled gates. More importantly there has been an intergenerational shift away from family farming. Family farms, which dominated the landscape in Concordia and other regions, have given way to industrial/corporate agriculture either because younger generations of farming families are leaving the sector, and the region, or the finances of 21st century agriculture cannot support family farm operations. The result is depopulation of farming communities.

Concordia has continued its decline in population with the 2017 Census esti-mate for the city totaling 5,099. The population is aging with more than 20 percent of the population 65 years or older. While more than 91 percent of all residents have at least a high school diploma, only 22 percent possess a bachelor's degree or higher. Median household income, based on American Community Survey data for 2012–2016, is a very modest $36,984, reflecting farm income and the rela-tively large percentage of pensioners. The population characteristics make it hard to attract the type of retail and hospitality businesses/amenities associated with talent attraction in the 21st century.

While the State of Kansas has had success in key industries such as farm equipment and aircraft manufacturing, it has leveraged its agricultural sector exper-tise into a leadership position in biosciences by funding research, development and commercialization of new discoveries in agrisciences. Kansas is also located in the heart of the nation's 'wind corridor,' ranked second for wind potential and thus an ideal location for the rapidly expanding renewable energy sector. However, Concordia's small size and relatively remote location has been an impediment to attracting these state-focused clusters.

### 2.4.2 A strategy for Concordia

For many years, Concordia and north-eastern Kansas have attracted hunters in fall and winter for the region's plentiful stock of game birds including pheasant, dove, turkey and quail, as well as white-tailed deer. The state's wildlife agencies have managed game stock through season length and bag limits. Hunters travel from near and far, bringing new income through hospitality sector spending, hunt-ing supplies, outfitter and guide services, and access payments (leases) to local land owners. In June 2014, Roger Brooks International consultancy conducted an assessment of city's core competencies and recommended an economic develop-ment strategy focused on developing the tourism business.

### 2.4.3 Is this the answer for Concordia?

Case studies are often presented as providing an answer to a particular economic conundrum. In this case our intent is to demonstrate that sometimes your best strategy is to use whatever comparative advantage you possess to maintain the current economy. The first step for most distressed communities is to stop declin-ing! Is focusing on seasonal tourism a pathway to long-term success for Concor-dia? Probably not. The data suggest that even with success in attracting hunters, the city continues to shrink. Concordia is a story of many farming communities. Residents have strong family and historical linkages to their home, but simply do not have the scale of assets or resources to fundamentally shift their economy into new industries. In the European Union, such communities may receive sub-stantial funding for community initiatives that may jump-start new industries. In the US federalist system, those few programs sponsored by the US Department of Agriculture or the Economic Development Administration are much too small and spread too thin to help all of the Concordias in Kansas, Nebraska, Iowa and other states. We can cheer Concordia on from the sidelines, but it seems clear that they will need an external (exogenous) stimulus to successfully reshape the local economy.

## ■ 2.5 Conclusion

The cases presented in this chapter were selected to offer examples of economic development challenges and solutions, but are hardly exhaustive of the types of problems, opportunities and responses available to local economic development planners and practitioners. In the following chapters we cover the theory and practice of economic development. Chapter 3 introduces the theories and processes that shape our understanding of why regions prosper or decline. Students can consider how the local dominance of a narrow range of industries or institutions creates dependencies that shape the industrial structure of a region, like Washington, DC. Each of the presented cases also shows how internal (Chapter 6) and external (Chapter 5) forces act on a regional economy, but importantly also inform strategic decisions for future growth. Chattanooga's transformation illustrates both endogenous (local philanthropy) and exogenous (VW investments) strategies, as well as the employment of place branding (Chapter 7) and land use planning (Chapter 10) to reimagine the community. San Diego clearly engaged in successful economic development planning (Chapter 9) when they chose biotechnology as a pathway to growth, and all the cases show the influence of economic development practitioners (Chapter 11) in implementing economic development plans and strategies. But, economic development is a process, not an event. The need to continuously monitor empirically (Chapter 8) economic performance and to adapt to regional and global trends and technological change means that each of the cases presented have future challenges to address (Chapter 12).

As a reminder, we will continue to expand the catalog of case studies for this textbook on the website www.gpaled.com.

## *Key messages*

- Critical institutions can be a foundation for economic change;
- The presence of committed regional philanthropy, as private sources of funding and leadership, is a key contribution to endogenous redevelopment;
- The ability to diversify a regional economy is inextricably tied to economic sustainability;
- Rural communities increasingly face the challenge of insufficient resources to spur economic change and development;
- Assets and opportunities are necessary, but not sufficient conditions for economic development. Effective planning and leadership must be deployed to realize economic development success in an increasingly globalized economy.

## Discussion questions

- This chapter examined four very different case studies. Which cases are most similar to places you have experienced?
- For each case, what are the four key lessons which you think are applicable to other communities in the US or globally?
- What is the most unique feature of each case that is unlikely to be reproduced in other places?

## Notes

1  https://www.sandiego.gov/economic-development/sandiego/trade/mexico/maquiladoras.
2  Data from Economic Modelist Specialists, Inc. It includes covered and estimated non-covered employment.
3  In the fall of 2018, Canada, Mexico and the US agreed to terms on a trade agreement to replace NAFTA. The United States–Mexico–Canada Agreement (USMCA) will be reviewed and approved by the respective national legislatures over the next few years. The biggest proposed changes affect automotive assembly (maquiladora) domestic component content, select agricultural products and intellectual property.
4  *The Roadmap for the Washington Region's Future Economy* was prepared in late 2015 by Dr Stephen Fuller at the Center for Regional Analysis, George Mason University through a grant by the 2030 Group, an organization made up mostly of DC-area property developers.
5  The District of Columbia is not a state, but in terms of economic development and taxing authority, it has much of the authority and capabilities of states.

## References

BIOCOM 2017 The 2017 BIOCOM Databook. Available at https://laedc.org/wp-content/uploads/2017/05/biocom-2017-economic-impact-report-databook.pdf.

Cohen, R. 2015 Chattanooga: a model of urban revitalization, or inequality and gentrification, *Non-Profit Quarterly*, October 9.

DeVol, R., Wong, P., Junghoon, K., Bedroussian, A. and Knepp, R. 2004 America's biotech and life science clusters: San Diego's position and economic contributions. Milken Institute, June 1. Available at https://assets1c.milkeninstitute.org/assets/Publication/ResearchReport/PDF/biotech_clusters.pdf.

Eichenthal, D. and Windeknecht, T. 2008 *A Restoring Prosperity Case Study: Chattanooga, Tennessee*, Metropolitan Program at Brookings, DC: Brookings Institution.

Katz, B. 2015 An innovation district grows in Chattanooga, *The Avenue*, Brookings Institution, September 29.

KMK Consulting 2006 *Tucson Economic Blueprint, Strategic Analysis Report*, Tucson Regional Economic Opportunities, Tucson.

Lambe, W. and de Zeeuw, M. 2016 *The Small Cities Study Tour: Chattanooga's Comeback*. Available at https://www.frbatlanta.org/community-development/publications/partners-update/2016/01/160203-small-cities-tour-chattanoogas-comeback.aspx.

VW 2018 10 years ago "it's Chattanooga" announced by Volkswagen, Volkswagen press release, July 16. Available at www.media.vw.com.

Walcott, S.M. 2002 Analyzing an innovative environment: San Diego as a bioscience beachhead, *Economic Development Quarterly*, 16, pp 99–114.

Wu, W. 2005 *Dynamic Cities and Creative Clusters*, World Bank Policy Research Working Paper 3509.

# 3 Why places grow

This chapter:

- ▶ Introduces economic models that have sought to explain how regions grow;

- ▶ Notes the evolution of these models over time;

- ▶ Identifies some of the key variables critical to development;

- ▶ Reviews the substantial body of work produced by the OECD on the determinants of regional growth, including analysis of how impacts vary by location;

- ▶ Finds that the measures needed to promote growth vary by location, current growth rates and pathways, and industrial structure;

- ▶ Considers competitiveness and how it relates to the growth of cities, regions and communities;

- ▶ Concludes that while competitiveness at the city or regional scale is sometimes a contested concept, it is an identifiable phenomenon;

- ▶ Determines that even though places can be 'locked in' to particular development pathways, places have the capacity to improve their competitiveness through local action.

PLANNERS, COMMUNITIES, ECONOMIC development professionals and government officials alike need to understand the processes that generate growth locally if they are to ensure a more prosperous future. One of the important themes in this book is that communities, cities and regions have the capacity to shape their economic future, and that intelligent planning, relationship building and business support can help achieve that end. To realize these goals and develop effective actions, cities and communities need to understand the contemporary drivers of growth. They benefit from appreciating the economic processes that are important for the economy overall, but more importantly, they need to have clear insights into which drivers of growth are likely to affect their community or city.

The globalized economy affects small rural communities, ex-urban cities, and major metropolitan centers in varying ways, which in turn generates differentiated opportunities for development and the need for highly targeted economic development strategies and actions. There is a wide range of strategies or actions to promote economic growth, but local or regional economic development often falls short of expectations because inappropriate measures are chosen, or there is inadequate commitment to implementation. And, as will be discussed later, a sustained drive to achieve growth often differentiates economically successful cities and communities from those that lag behind.

This chapter begins by providing an overview of current writing on the drivers of growth at the city, regional or community level. The chapter examines research into the determinants of development at the city, regional and city scale – and what that research means for those planning local action. The chapter then examines the comprehensive body of work produced by the OECD on regional growth and its causes. The OECD's contributions to our understanding of the drivers of local or community-scale growth are the focus of this section because they represent the most substantial body of evidence currently available. In addition, the OECD has been able to distinguish how places are affected by economic processes depending on whether they are large or small regions, urban or rural, and fast-growing or lagging territories. The final section of this chapter considers the issue of competitiveness and how it is understood regionally and locally. It argues that while the concept of competitiveness presents a number of challenges, it remains an important issue, and one which can be enhanced through the actions of governments, community groups, business associations and professionals.

## ■ 3.1  Understanding the drivers of growth

Why places grow is a complex question and one which has occupied the minds of regional scientists, geographers, economists, planners and policymakers for more than 60 years. In many ways understanding why regions grow was the intellectual challenge that stimulated the establishment of the discipline of regional science in the 1950s and has remained central to all forms of regional research and policy since then. It is a difficult question, and one made more challenging because growth processes change over time with the transformation of the global economy affecting all cities, communities and regions. Growth processes vary by location, with both the natural features of a location, such as access to natural resources, and human-created qualities – including access to markets, population size, et cetera – affecting the prospects for development. Even broadly comparable places will be substantially different: London's growth dynamics may be very different from those evident in San Francisco, Berlin or Detroit, and a world apart from those evident in rural Kansas or Devon.

Much of the analysis of why places grow has focused on regions, rather than cities, suburbs or communities, simply because more and better data is available at the regional scale, and because attempts to undertake more fine-grained analyses are likely to become overly complex. However, a number of lessons or insights can be taken from regional growth models, especially with respect to understanding which factors are important, why they are important, and how they can be influenced.

### 3.1.1 Modeling growth

The early explanations of regional growth were relatively straightforward and offered very broad explanations that, it could be argued, provided little to inform or assist economic development planning. However, such models are important because they tell a story of how our thinking has evolved, and provide insights into which factors need to be addressed if cities and communities are to grow. Neoclassical economics drew upon early work from the 1940s that argued that growth – as measured by the production function $(Y)$ – was an outcome of increasing investment in capital stock $(K)$ such as factories, machinery or infrastructure, as an outcome of growth in the workforce $(L)$, or as a consequence of growth in both (Stimson et al. 2009 p 4). This relationship was then represented as:

$$Y = f (K, L)$$

Later research by Solow (1956) and others challenged this model, noting that only 15 percent of growth in the US in the early 20th century could be explained by increases in capital and labor (Stimson et al. 2009). They argued that technological change $(T)$ was the missing factor in understanding growth and that development was better understood as a product of:

$$Y = f (K, L, T)$$

However, while this modification is intuitively attractive, it raises considerable difficulties because technological change is both unpredictable and 'lumpy'. It is difficult to measure, it is difficult – if not impossible – to predict technological advances and it is hard to assess which technological changes will have an impact on overall productivity. And, as Stimson et al. (2009) noted, there are substantial differences in the economic performance of regions with otherwise comparable technological bases.

Export based theories of the development of regions highlight both foreign direct investment and the sale of goods and services to consumers outside the region as an important impetus for growth and as a driver of specialization within regions. Rostow (1960) emphasized the role of a leading sector or industry in driving growth at the regional scale, but also noted that as trade grows the region will develop competitive advantages relative to other places because of the emergence of economies of scale and scope.

Export base theory has strong links to economic base theory, which informs the activities of many local economic development practitioners and planners across the US and in other nations (Green Leigh and Blakely 2013). Economic base theory underlines the need to generate income and jobs by focusing on markets outside the region. Employment and wealth generated in exporting industries, it is believed, will then create new opportunities for non-exporting firms and result in growth for the community as a whole. In practical terms this results in a focus on attracting – and retaining – firms that are geared towards export markets, providing infrastructure that assists their relocation or expansion and developing a job-ready, and an appropriately skilled, workforce.

New growth theory is analytically distinct from conventional neoclassical models in that it separates out endogenous (internal) and exogenous (external) factors and recognizes internal factors as the fundamental drivers of growth (Stimson et al. 2009). New growth theory views development as a continuous process driven by 'the endogenous capability of a region to learn and innovate.' (Stimson et al. 2009 p 8) One form of endogenous growth model assumes that development is driven by the stock of human capital in a region, which in turn affects the region's capacity to innovate and close the gap with more developed regions (OECD 2009). A second approach sees growth being propelled by the accumulation of human capital over time, with development driven by this ongoing acquisition of intellectual and technical capacity.

New growth theory suggests that as development, or the absence of development, is an outcome of processes internal to the region, places can develop their own trajectories that may be positive, flat or negative. The factors that drive change internally include the level of education in the region, its institutional capacity, the strength of local entrepreneurship, et cetera, such that the production function can now be represented as:

$$Y = f(K, L, T, R, H)$$

where R represents research and development and H stands for human capital. Critically, new growth theory posits that endogenous growth processes drive increasing returns to scale, with the possibility that relatively small increases in some factors generate substantial uplift in regional output.

Economic models on the new economic geography set out to understand why consumers and firms tended to agglomerate in cities and regions and remain fixed in these localities. Building on Myrdal's (1957) work on cumulative causation, Krugman (1991) showed that the processes of circular causation gave rise to differentiated core and peripheral regions, with the differences between the two increasing over time. What is clear from this body of work is that there are fundamental, and perhaps unavoidable, risks for less developed places and that without purposeful action their disadvantages are likely to increase over time.

Neoclassical and later models of regional economic growth have helped us to understand why places grow but may have oversimplified matters, which in turn has made delivering growth more difficult. As Rodríguez-Pose (2013) observed, these models led to a standardized response to encouraging growth that consisted of making greater investment in infrastructure, enhancing education and training, as well as the promotion of innovation. These actions were expected to improve the well-being of well-performing and less developed regions alike. The models also encouraged top-down development, which was largely undifferentiated in its approach from nation to nation and from city to city. The models, however, were inadequate in key areas, both with respect to the policy prescriptions that emerged – with a growing critique of regional policy *per se* (World Bank 2009) – and increasing acknowledgment among researchers that the existing models simply did not explain the observed patters of growth. New approaches were therefore needed.

## ■ 3.2 The analysis of current growth patterns

A great deal has been written on the drivers of growth at the regional and local scale (Stimson et al. 2009) with much of this analysis undertaken by regional scientists interested in determining the nature and importance of a particular component of the regional economy, such as innovation, human capital, et cetera. Computable General Equilibrium (CGE) models are now widely used by researchers, policymakers and cities alike to provide fresh insights into how and why cities and regions grow.

Much of this work into the determinants of economic development regionally has enjoyed a high profile. Examples include Saxenian's (1994) work highlighting the importance of business culture in determining Silicon Valley's success relative to Route 54 outside Boston, and Richard Florida's (2003) writings on the emergence of a creative class and how human capital now shapes the growth prospects of regions and cities (Glaeser 2011). The challenge, of course, is that not all explanations are equally true in all locations and that often the conclusions – and policy advice – offered by individual analyses are shaped by other factors, such as the depth and spatial scale of the data used, the starting assumptions of the researcher, the availability of key information and the robustness of the models used. Students and economic development practitioners alike are therefore confronted by an apparent plethora of policy prescriptions, without clear guidance on the most appropriate way forward with respect to which strategies to adopt, how to implement them and how to measure their impact (Beer 2009). Greater clarity is needed.

Recent work by the OECD provides useful guidance on how places grow, and the sorts of strategies and mechanisms communities and governments can employ to secure their economic future. The OECD's work is important because it has several innate advantages that are often absent from other work. First, the OECD has been able to commit substantial time and resources to understanding regional growth dynamics, with their analysis and policy prescriptions becoming more sophisticated over time. Second, the OECD has been able to collect data from, and draw upon the experience of, virtually all developed economies. Their conclusions therefore can be generalized across city, state and national boundaries with some confidence. Third, the OECD has been able to construct its own data sets to inform its analyses and thereby generate more robust conclusions. As the OECD acknowledges, some of the data could be improved, and some of the measures are open to question – for example, the use of the value of freeways as a proxy for infrastructure generally – but it stands as a comprehensive source of information. Finally, the OECD is not wedded to a particular paradigm of development and is therefore able to think outside some theoretical boundaries. In its work the OECD retains a clear focus on economic growth and how it can be achieved. Other considerations, such as questions around quality of life and other dimensions of well-being, are not examined in this body of work, although they are present in other OECD publications.

## 3.2.1 The importance of context

Nationwide processes are critical to the growth prospects of cities, communities and regions and should shape the economic development strategies employed locally. The OECD (2009) found that elevated regional growth rates tend to be associated with high national growth rates, and that the direction of causation – whether regional performance affects national growth or vice versa – operates in both directions. In addition, regions with a high GDP rarely recorded negative growth rates (OECD 2009 p 31), possibly because they effectively function as growth machines, with high rates of labor demand, supply and innovation. In slow-growing or declining regions other processes appeared to be at work, with local factors such as falling labor force productivity, rising unemployment rates, falls in the percentage of population seeking work and adverse demography all contributing to decline.

Importantly, the OECD (2009) concluded that different sets of processes affected high-growth and low-growth regions. Places where the economy was expanding relatively rapidly benefited from population growth and increasing labor productivity – often as a consequence of investment in new technologies. By contrast, regions that lagged behind were characterized by falling population, declines in the percentage of the workforce economically active and falling productivity. This latter group was more likely to be predominantly rural rather than urban. The OECD (2009) observed that growth was likely to be significantly impeded when the labor force contracts, which could result from demographic change – such as the aging of the population – or from rising unemployment rates. The OECD (2009) also concluded that the most adverse outcomes arise when unemployment rates increase at the same time that the workforce is contracting – that is, individuals are leaving the world of paid work because of retirement, the belief that work cannot be found, or for other reasons.

Rural and urban regions remain substantially different with respect to their growth dynamics and opportunities. Many regions and communities across developed and developing nations remain firmly rooted in agriculture and its related industries. Such places often confront significant challenges because incomes tend to be smaller, growth rates lower and many of the key indices of health and well-being are not as favorable when compared with the major cities. One of the critical hurdles is that rural regions are simultaneously affected by the processes evident in all parts of the economy, but are also subject to additional, distinctive, economic forces. In 2006 the OECD developed a set of principles for rural regions which it labeled the New Rural Paradigm (NRP), which set out to establish a framework for how to enact best practices in rural development. This paradigm attempts to balance the unique features of rural regions with broader-scale economic processes. The NRP was based on four guiding concepts (OECD 2009 p 83):

1. A recognition that sectoral policies have limited capacity to achieve rural development goals;
2. A greater focus on investing in local competitiveness;
3. Emphasis on sustainable development and resource management;
4. Acknowledgement that rural regions constitute most of the territory of nations.

These principles lead to strategies for development that include:

- Diversification of rural economies;
- Upgrading transport and infrastructure links;
- Adopting better technologies to achieve and maintain a competitive edge in global markets;
- Provision of small-scale training to improve human capital and productivity;

- Restructuring agricultural industries;
- Finding new, and more efficient ways to provide public services.

These strategies in turn have implications for the practice of economic development at the city or community scale, as there is a clear orientation towards linking to global markets, engaging in appropriate innovation, managing resources effectively and in a way that opens up the possibility for diversifying the economy, and improving the skills of the workforce in order to anticipate change.

## 3.2.2  Regional growth dynamics

In their modeling of growth dynamics, the OECD (2010) focused on three key factors which they considered critical to understanding economic growth at the regional scale: public capital stock or infrastructure, human capital and innovation. While acknowledging that some drivers of growth cannot be included in econometric analysis because they change only gradually or data are not available, the OECD (2010) considered these three factors as the central pillars of local growth, a view informed by the economic growth models reviewed above.

The OECD (2010) argued that:

- **Infrastructure** is a 'foundation' of development, enabling private sector investment as governments provide the transport systems, telecommunications networks and other services that individual companies cannot afford;
- **Human capital** – the quality of the workforce – is acknowledged as the second pillar of growth, with some types of education in some types of region generating high returns with respect to regional growth (OECD 2010 p 43);
- **Innovation** is the third major determinant of locally based growth, with education attainment, research and development (R&D) investment and the presence of knowledge-intensive industries contributing to economic growth.

Importantly, the OECD (2010) recognized that many of these influences on growth are relatively slow acting – that is, they have long lead times – with investment in infrastructure and education taking at least three years to exert a measurable influence on growth, and innovation investments even longer. The relatively lengthy lead times between investment in communities' capacity and outcomes should not surprise either practitioners or students: economic development is better thought of as a marathon than a sprint. In some places communities or governments have sought to encourage greater levels of technological innovation in various ways, and while these aren't always successful, there is sufficient progress to suggest pathways forward. The knowledge economy will be a focus of a later discussion.

Other research by the OECD (2009) provided a more detailed breakdown of the factors contributing to growth locally. The research highlighted the role of:

- **Human capital** – including workforce size and skills;
- **Innovation** – research and development;

- **Distance from markets** – accessibility to markets provides an added advantage for places, while proximity is important in the innovation process;
- **Infrastructure** – as a necessary precondition for growth;
- **Spatial effects** – including spillovers from neighboring regions and the benefits arising from the agglomeration of activities.

The OECD (2012a and b) argued that in order to achieve growth locally or regionally, policies that improve the qualifications and expertise of low-skilled workers are critical. Put at its simplest, 'regions with insufficient human capital will not grow.' (OECD 2009 p 69) Importantly, the percentage of low-skilled workers in the region or community is seen to be more important than the percentage of tertiary (post-secondary education) qualified workers, with low-skilled workers serving as a drag on local economic performance. This suggests that in seeking to increase the rate of growth of a slow-growth locality, measures to encourage basic skills acquisition are likely to make a larger contribution than those focused on high technology and higher education. Simulation modeling undertaken by the OECD (2012b) showed that even a modest improvement in the skill sets of the workforce significantly boosted growth rates in less developed places. On the other hand, the development of an innovation economy and access to a highly skilled workforce were important for fast-growing regions and communities. The importance of innovation, however, should not be overstated, with OECD (2012a) modeling showing that increased expenditure on R&D had only one-third the impact of education and training expenditures of comparable magnitude. The OECD (2009) observed that research and development tends to have highly localized impacts, and while there are some indirect spillovers into neighboring communities, there are few direct impacts.

Distance from markets and spatial effects have been recognized by the OECD (2009, 2012a and b) as important, if not central, to the process of local growth. That is, they exert a relatively weak influence when compared with the quality of the workforce or the level of innovation. However, places with good access to markets have a competitive edge when compared with more remote communities. Being close to markets helps in developing knowledge industries, as it assists with face-to-face communication and the exchange of ideas. Being close to a fast-growing region also assists the development of a community or city, as there is a strong correlation between the performance of neighboring regions. In some instances, a community may be confronted by growth – whether they wish it or not – as development spills over from a larger center. In these cases, the key question may not be whether growth will occur, but instead, what quality of development will take place.

The OECD (2012a) argued that contrary to expectations, policies that target infrastructure are not usually the most effective strategies for promoting growth in places that are lagging behind the national economy. Infrastructure was acknowledged as an important driver of growth in fast-growing regions, but it was seen to be relatively unimportant in low-growth regions. The absence of infrastructure, the OECD (2012a and b) concluded, is not the binding constraint on development that has long been assumed. Instead of being seen as the preeminent tool for economic development, the OECD (2012b) proposed that infrastructure needs to be considered in conjunction with other policies in order to ensure that the full benefits of – often expensive – infrastructure investment are realized.

The OECD acknowledged that policy and governance are critical to achieving growth, recognizing its critical role in explaining both the success of fast-growing cities and regions and the impeded development of other places. The OECD (2012b) noted the importance of embracing a 'growth-oriented' ethos that consciously seeks to promote development. Policy frameworks that concentrated on securing external support for the city or the region were likely to result in the misallocation of resources, with government and community efforts directed towards securing further subsidies rather than taking advantage of local assets to achieve growth locally. Instead, policies need to be directed at building the internal – endogenous – drivers of growth; improving linkages between the important institutions within the region or community; and stimulating urban regeneration and the improvement of city fabric. Community and industry bodies were recognized as critical to encouraging economic progress. In part they are seen as mechanisms for developing and channeling local leadership, but they also serve an important role in debating growth strategies and exchanging information.

The OECD (2012b) drew together these insights through the examination of 23 case studies and concluded that the key factors for determining growth were 'soft' variables, rather than conventionally understood determinants of growth, such as infrastructure. Importantly, many of the determinants of growth in advanced regions were important also in less developed regions – but as impediments to economic activity rather than facilitators. Significantly, the policy environment and the institutional structure were critical in both sets of regions, but with opposing impacts: government processes drove development in fast-growing regions but slowed or stalled it entirely in slow-growth localities. Similarly, the business environment had a positive impact in high-growth regions, and a negative impact in lagging regions. There were some differences between the two sets of regions with respect to which factors could be considered a driver of growth, with demographic factors contributing to the slow growth of lagging regions, alongside the fragmentation of population and economic activity.

**TABLE 3.1**   Determinants of growth in leading and lagging regions

| Growth factors in leading regions | Impediments to growth in lagging regions |
| --- | --- |
| Policies | Institutions – including leadership |
| Connectivity of infrastructure | Policies |
| Institutions – including leadership | Density and cohesion, i.e. fragmentation |
| Human capital | Human capital |
| Innovation – including entrepreneurialism | Geography |
| Business environment | Connectivity of infrastructure |
| Geography | Business environment |
| Presence of natural assets | Demographic factors |
| Foreign direct investment | Innovation – including entrepreneurialism |

*Source:* OECD 2012b, pp 262 and 259.

### 3.2.3 Implications for policy and planning for local development

Recent work by the OECD has provided greater insights into what it considers to be effective strategies for economic development. Over the past decade the OECD (2009, 2010, 2012a) has argued that the growth of regions and places is driven by how effectively a number of the components of growth interact. Under this line of reasoning the whole is more than the sum of the parts, and this additional value is created through nuanced and effective local action that brings together the various components of growth into a coherent entity. While accepting that argument, it is important to retain a focus on each of these individual components, as those working locally need to ensure the presence and adequacy of all potential drivers of growth.

The OECD has articulated what it considers to be a 'new paradigm' in regional policies (OECD 2012b p 28) that emphasizes the importance of growth in every region of a nation's economy, the highly variable pattern of growth across regions, and that growth rates in any place principally depend on the assets already there: human capital, innovation and infrastructure. While the OECD (2012b) is justified in drawing out the distinction between its advocated policy framework and the subsidy-dependent approaches of the past, it is important to acknowledge that academic authors have advocated similar policy prescriptions for a considerable period, within the broad body of work known as 'new regionalism.' (see Rainnie and Grobbelaar 2005; Lovering 1999) The OECD's new paradigm of regional growth emphasizes

> a portfolio of integrated and coordinated investments aimed at mobilizing the endogenous resources and assets within regions. A key element in this new paradigm is a multidimensional approach which consists of integrating, coordinating and synchronizing these endogenous growth factors with pro-growth policies, adequate institutions and governance mechanisms so as to avoid potential un-intended consequences typically driven by actions taken in isolation.
>
> (OECD 2012a p 264)

Essentially, the OECD (2009) has advocated for comprehensive regional and local economic development strategy in order to promote growth. In part, this view is informed by a concern that too often one-off investments in a region's development – such as the construction of a freeway – have adverse impacts. Such measures are likely to result in the leakage of economic activity from the region as they are not linked to a broader suite of measures designed to retain and expand business in the region.

Perhaps one of the OECD's most basic insights on planning for growth has been a recognition that the strategies to be employed vary by location and the level of development already present in that community. The OECD (2012a) was able to distinguish between the strategies needed to sustain growth in fast-growing places, and those needed in places that are in decline or growing more slowly. Critically, from the perspective of the OECD (2012a) 'it is important to think in terms of *policy packages* rather than piecemeal measures.' (OECD 2012a p 24) Critically, success in the eyes of the OECD (2012a) was most commonly – but not exclusively – a consequence of better coordinated policies, improved regional capacities, infrastructure provision and the development of human capital. Success would appear to come in packages, and the OECD (2012a) noted that places that grew appeared to adhere to a common set of strategies, while places that lagged behind found many pathways to failure. Or as the OECD (2012a) notes, 'There are thus more "recipes" for failure than for success.'

Fundamentally the OECD argues that places can choose to be successful or not. The pathways to achieving economic growth are both known and realizable, and they involve a coordinated approach that addresses the impediments to growth on multiple fronts. Planners, economic development practitioners, business associations and others concerned with development locally have the ability to address both the 'soft' side of development planning and the 'harder,' infrastructure-related elements. The strategies for doing so are addressed later in this book.

## 3.3 Regional competitiveness

Over the last two decades the concept of regional or city 'competitiveness' has attracted a great deal of attention amongst national governments, regional authorities, cities and business groups. In large measure, this relatively recent interest in this concept is an outcome of the work of Michael Porter and his notion of 'regional competitive advantage' and the associated focus on industry business clusters (Budd and Hirmis 2010; Huggins 2010). Some authors have suggested that competitiveness has become a 'hegemonic discourse' – that is, a powerful and near universal discussion within public forums – because of the impact of globalization and the realization that new economic processes are at work (Bristow 2010).

Regional competitiveness has been variously defined. Storper (1997 p 20) envisioned *place competitiveness* as '[t]he ability of an economy to attract and maintain firms with stable or rising market shares in an activity while maintaining or increasing standards of living for those who participate in it.'

Bristow (2010 p 14) observed that regional competitiveness can be understood in two ways: firstly, narrow competition over market share and resources; and, secondly, as a determinant of a region's long-term economic future. Often the two ways of understanding regional competitiveness are confused and in the US this tendency is greater, given the use of incentives to attract businesses. Bristow (2005) has also suggested there is a risk of regional competitiveness as a concept being oversold: effectively overemphasizing the importance of regions or communities for firms.

For Porter (1990) regional competitiveness is something that is simultaneously both more complex and powerful than Storper's (1997) definition implies. Porter's (1990) formulation of regional competitiveness is about the creation of a set of conditions at the local scale that deliver long-term advantages to firms within that locality, thereby assisting them to maintain a viable position within global markets. From this perspective, the factors that contribute to regional competitiveness can include the clustering of firms in the same industry or in industries that are linked through their participation in a common supply chain, the use of related technologies or the need to access a common market. It can also include the development of a specialized workforce, the development of specific institutions and the provision of relevant infrastructure. Porter (1990) saw competitive advantage arising out of four interrelated drivers:

1. Factor conditions (the inputs into the production process, including labor);
2. Demand conditions;
3. Related and supporting industries;
4. Firm strategy, structure and rivalry.

The detail of Porter's ideas will be discussed later, but importantly he popularized the idea that regional competitiveness is important, that it is measurable, that it is a highly localized process (Kitson et al. 2010) and that it is amenable to change. Productivity lies at the heart of Porter's (1990) understanding of regional competitiveness, and productivity growth is seen as fundamental to produce a high and rising standard of living (Kitson et al. 2010).

Most economists and researchers agree that productivity growth is essential for raising living standards, but there is no consensus about how that translates into our understanding of economic growth at any spatial scale. Krugman (1994, 1996) has critiqued the concept of national competitiveness, and for him – and many other commentators – the critical factor is that it is firms and corporations that compete, not nations, cities or communities. Economic growth, employment and the creation of wealth comes from the actions of businesses and individuals, not from central governments or cities. Other authors have echoed these sentiments, with Boschma (2004) observing that economics recognizes that competition between firms is both real and a positive feature of market economies. The arrival of new firms and the demise of unsuccessful firms ensures that economic resources – staff, real estate, infrastructure, et cetera – are used efficiently and that costs of production are kept low. But places – nations, cities and regions – do not appear and disappear as businesses can: all cities and regions engage with the global marketplace with an already established history of development, and unsuccessful communities may suffer an economic downturn but remain part of the broader economic landscape.

It is important to acknowledge that the criticisms leveled at the concept of regional competitiveness constitute a building block for regional strategy because the failure to fully understand this core concept could – and almost certainly has – led to misguided economic development efforts. While acknowledging these perspectives, there is now a solid body of work that supports the theoretical foundations of regional competitiveness, as well as providing evidence that some places are more competitive – and productive – than others. At a conceptual level, a number of authors have shown that regions, cities and communities can and do compete for firms, labor and for access to markets through the provision of 'superior technological, social, infrastructural or institutional assets that are external to but which benefit individual firms. . . . These assets tend to give the region's firms, overall, a higher productivity than would otherwise be the case.' (Kitson et al. 2010 p 994)

These assets are sometimes referred to as 'regional externalities' or 'untraded interdependencies' – and can include the flow of tacit knowledge, networks of trust and local systems of collaboration. They are essentially the advantages a firm accrues simply from its location. These benefits often cannot be reproduced in another locality. Similar ideas have a very long history, with Marshall (1920) considering knowledge spillovers in his work on industrial districts at the start of the

20th century. Budd and Hirmis (2010) also noted the importance of the more tangible factors that affect the costs of doing business, including the cost of labor, rent and access to capital. They remind us that businesses constantly evaluate the costs of operation in one location relative to others.

At a more pragmatic level there is clear evidence that some regions are simply better places to do business than others. O'Farrell et al. (2006) examined the performance of comparable firms working in the business service sector in London and Scotland. They found that those based in London reported 23 percent greater productivity than those located in Scotland and, in addition, London-based businesses had a much greater export orientation. They concluded that one of the key differences between the two regions related to the nature of demand: in London, where the demand for business services was substantial, firms were able to specialize, working in niche markets where returns to effort were large. In Scotland, where demand was softer, firms were required to take on the role of a provider of generalist services, with much higher rates of competition among the providers of business services. Importantly, O'Farrell et al. (2006) also noted that the firms they studied in London had much more demanding customers, which in turn pushed them to find new markets, new products and new strategies which could then transform into new products for other customers.

All things considered, we must conclude that the competitiveness of places – cities, regions and communities – is a key concept that deserves both policy and practitioner attention. Places able to enhance their competitiveness are more likely to grow, and some of the necessary measures are discussed in the following section.

### 3.3.1 The components of a competitive economy

If cities, regions and communities can be differentiated according to their regional competitiveness, what are the factors that differentiate one location from another? Various ideas have been put forward by government agencies, nongovernment institutes and private sector companies, and there is a consensus that regional competitiveness is a multifaceted phenomenon with key components including – among other factors – the propensity for innovation, the quality of human capital, investment in infrastructure and entrepreneurial potential.

Figure 3.1 presents one interpretation of the determinants of regional competitiveness, highlighting the interrelated processes that create a more competitive environment.

There are strong commonalities between the findings of the OECD's analysis of the determinants of growth at the local or regional scale, endogenous growth models and the outcomes of work on regional competitiveness. Key factors include:

- Productive capital – including investment in plant and machinery;
- The importance of the quality and size of the labor force;
- The nature of the business environment, including attitudes to firm establishment and failure;
- The presence of institutions that encourage growth and assist firms;
- The local stock of infrastructure;
- The capacity to generate new intellectual capital – the knowledge economy.

**FIGURE 3.1**    The bases of regional competitive advantage

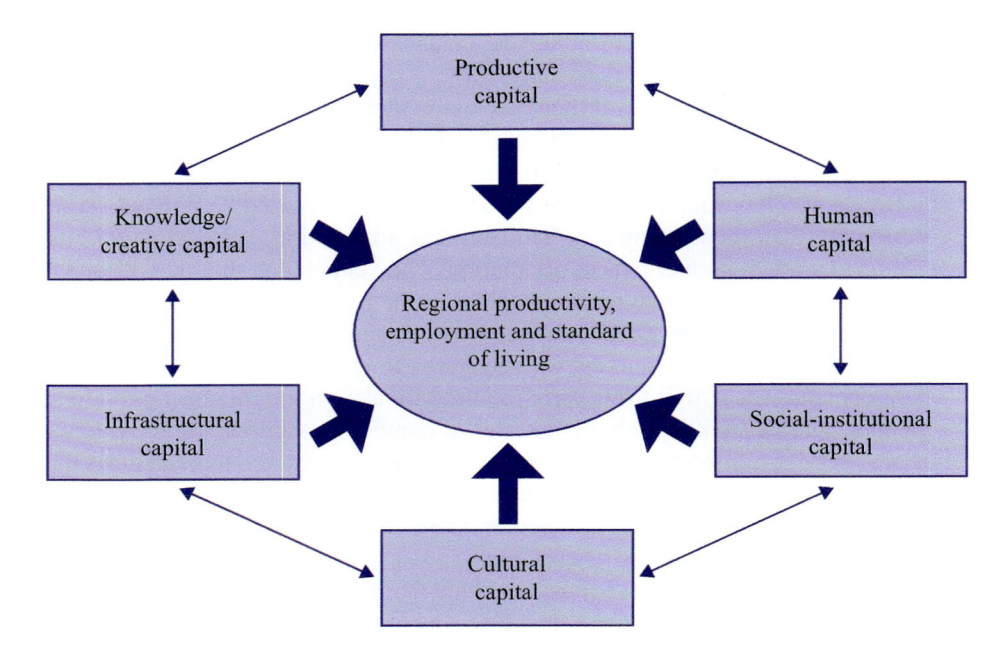

Each of these factors potentially contributes to the competitiveness of a region, though in varying degrees and in diverse ways.

Polese (2010) has suggested there are 'Four Golden Rules of Regional Growth' in the 21st century, which he summarized as:

- *Size matters*, because dynamic industries are naturally drawn to large cities or places within easy reach, with a diversified industrial base, an educated workforce and blessed with natural or architectural heritage;
- *Location matters* because industries are drawn to places best suited for commerce and interaction with markets;
- *Costs matter*, because in the absence of the two previous factors, places will grow in the presence of cost or resource availability advantages; but
- *Exceptions abound*, because unique events and accidents – technological change, history, politics – can cause growth or precipitate decline despite the presence of the three previous factors.

Polese's (2010) general rules capture both the complexity of growth processes and many of the readily apparent general trends. His first rule, however, suggests a degree of convergence with the theories of prominent economists such as Porter and Glaeser who argue that the further intensification of economic activity in the cities is inevitable. This point, however, remains open to debate, with Porter's (2010) analysis of the performance of America's regions finding that:

- There was little support for the notion that metropolitan regions will inevitably grow as neither large nor small regions were significantly better at increasing employment;

- Regions with higher wage growth were more active in the knowledge economy, as measured by patents lodged;
- Traded industries – those that produce goods or services for export from the region – accounted for only 32 percent of employment but were the most significant determinant of local wages. There was more muted evidence that they contributed to higher rates of employment.

In short, Porter (2010) concluded that urban structure – city or community size – was irrelevant to understanding the propensity to grow and be competitive on world markets, and on that basis he argued the building of industry clusters must be central to local or regional growth strategies, and that there is a need to upgrade all industry clusters rather than focus on leading edge technologies. From this perspective, measures are needed that ensure the effective functioning of businesses that export from the region.

## 3.3.2 Measuring, benchmarking and building competitiveness

Much of the discussion of regional competitiveness attempts to find the universal drivers of regional competitiveness, so that they can be both understood and reproduced in other locations. The World Economic Forum, for example, devised a Global Competitiveness Index at the national scale in which competitiveness is derived from eight variables that are measured qualitatively and quantitatively:

- Openness to change 1/6th;
- Government 1/6th;
- Infrastructure 1/9th;
- Finance 1/6th;
- Management 1/18th;
- Technology 1/9th;
- Labor 1/6th;
- Institutions 1/18th (Huggins 2010).

Huggins (2010) developed a comparable index of regional competitiveness for England that weighted its six indicators as 11 percent business density; 11 percent presence of knowledge-based industries; 11 percent economic participation of the labor force; 33 percent productivity; 17 percent earnings; and 17 percent unemployment. Both indicators give some sense of the relative importance of the various factors that contribute to competitiveness locally, regionally and nationally. Critically, such indicators explicitly suggest that in aggregate these factors accurately measure competitiveness, and improvements in the individual components will deliver benefits. There are, of course, many indicators around the world that claim to identify the most competitive cities or regions, with business publishers – such as the Huffington Post – or major financial institutions – including Citibank – often promoting individual indices. Often such measures are simply used as promotional material for individual cities (McCann 2013; Avraham 2004).

Attempts to measure or benchmark the competitiveness of cities, regions or communities are often flawed by subjective assessments, inadequate data and a flawed approach that attempts to apply a single set of measures to multiple locations, irrespective of context, development pathway, assets and location. Desrochers noted that attempts to identify universal explanations – as embedded in indicators – of regional competitiveness are likely to be 'defeated by particular circumstances; that the search for a single explanation for urban and regional growth is as understandable as it is futile; and that local development strategies must be tailored for local conditions.' (2010 p 1097)

We must therefore conclude that attempts to identify drivers of regional competitiveness that are applicable in all circumstances do not generate helpful outcomes at the local or community scale, and a more targeted approach is needed.

Storper (2014) considered development at the international scale, noting that the development outcomes and trajectories of nations often appear in clusters, with similar features and prospects in each grouping. From his perspective these 'development clubs' provide both a greater capacity to understand growth processes and better insights into how to bring about positive change. Similar approaches can be applied at the city, regional or community scale (Perry 2010), with localities first identifying a group of comparable communities and then developing a set of benchmarks to track progress. Huggins (2009) observed that benchmarking is commonly used in three ways:

1. Monitoring economic development and its progress;
2. Helping to gather information on 'best practices' in economic development for a community;
3. Promoting the image of the community, city or region.

The collection and analysis of data – benchmarking – can be an important tool for initiating development, setting policy directions, assessing progress and identifying challenges unique to your own community. The first two uses of benchmarking identified by Huggins (2009) are likely to have the most tangible benefits and can inform economic development planning in the short, medium and long term.

## ■ 3.4 Conclusion

This chapter has examined the current state of knowledge on why cities, regions and communities grow. It has shown that regional and city modeling has become more sophisticated over time, and that a great deal of this evolution has been driven by the differences between what the models thought were important, and what empirical investigations found to be significant. There are key messages to take from neoclassical and more recent models of regional economic growth, and this includes the need to focus on factors such as the size of the labor force, the level of investment in productive capital, the rate of technological development and uptake, the level of innovation or research and development in a region, and the quality of the labor force – including the current level of skills.

Many of the accepted orthodoxies of economic development have been called into question through this chapter. There is mounting evidence that hard infrastructure provision is not a key pathway to development and that less tangible factors, such as attitudes to business formation and the provision of a supportive environment for business are of greater significance. The chapter emphasizes the importance of considering the competitiveness of the city, region or community within which businesses sit. While it is possible to overemphasize the importance of location for individual firms, the highly mobile nature of global capital, the pace of technological innovation and shifts in consumer preferences underscore the contributions localities can make to the vibrancy of their economic environments.

## *Key messages*

- Economic development efforts need to be thought of as a 'package' of measures rather than single programs;
- Analysis confirms the importance of a number of factors as drivers of growth at the local, community and city scale. These include:
  - Innovation;
  - Infrastructure;
  - Human capital;
  - Location/geography;
  - Connectivity and distance to markets;
  - The quality of the business environment;
  - Institutional factors, such as the presence of appropriate agencies to engage in a development dialogue, and the quality of regional leadership;
  - The policy environment.
- The context of development is important, and context should shape how economic growth is approached locally;
  - Fast-growing regions require different assistance to sustain their growth when compared with the actions needed to trigger development in lagging cities or communities;
  - Cities and communities in fast-growing national economies are more likely to grow, but slow-growing places are also important for national economic performance;
  - Significant differences remain between urban and rural regions in their growth dynamics.
- Regional competitiveness is an important concept, and encourages elected officials and planners to think in productive ways about how to engage with the global economy.
  - Competitiveness benchmarking can be useful for cities, regions and communities when they target generally comparable centers, and use the exercise to both monitor their performance and improve their development processes.

## Discussion questions

- The OECD identifies the following factors to explain the growth of regions and cities: 1) the importance of human capital; 2) innovation; 3) infrastructure; 4) distance from markets; and 5) the advantages that arise from being close to fast-growing places. Consider three communities in your region and discuss the strengths and weaknesses on the factors.
- Business attraction, business retention and business development activities have been described as the three legs of an economic development stool. Is there a difference in how one would gauge a region's competitiveness when focused on any one these activities?
- Pick a publication that produces a 'best (places) to do business' list, such as Forbes, US News and World Report or another, and compare the factors used for these rankings versus the regional economic development competitive factors discussed in this chapter.

## References

Avraham, E. 2004 Media strategies for improving an unfavorable city image, *Cities*, 21:6, pp 471–479.

Beer, A. 2009 The theory and practice of developing locally, Chapter 4. In Rowe, J. (ed.) *Theories of Local Economic Development: Linking Theory to Practice*, Sage Publications, Thousand Oaks, CA.

Boschma, R. 2004 Competitiveness of regions from an evolutionary perspective, *Regional Studies*, 38:9, pp 1001–1014.

Bristow, G. 2005 Everyone's a winner: problematising the discourse of regional competitiveness, *Journal of Economic Geography*, 5, pp 285–304.

Bristow, G. 2010 *Critical Reflections on Regional Competitiveness*, Routledge, London.

Budd, L. and Hirmis, A. 2010 Conceptual framework for regional competitiveness, *Regional Studies*, 38:9, pp 1015–1028.

Desrochers, P. 2010 The wealth and poverty of regions. Why cities matter, *Regional Studies*, 44:8, pp 1097–1098.

Florida, R. 2003 Cities and the creative class, *City and Community*, 2:1, pp 3–19.

Glaeser, E. 2011 Cities, productivity, and quality of life, *Science*, 333:6042, pp 592–594.

Green Leigh, N. and Blakely, E. 2013 *Planning Local Economic Development: Theory and Practice.* 5th edition. Sage Publications, New York.

Huggins, R. 2009 Regional competitive intelligence: benchmarking and policy making, *Regional Studies*, 43:1, pp 1–20.

Huggins, R. 2010 Regional competitive intelligence: benchmarking and policy making, *Regional Studies*, 44:5, pp 639–658.

Kitson, M., Martin, R. and Tyler, P. 2010 Regional competitiveness: an elusive yet key concept? *Regional Studies*, 38:9, pp 991–999.

Krugman, P. 1991 *Geography and Trade,* MIT Press, Cambridge, MA.

Krugman, P. 1994 Competitiveness: a dangerous obsession, *Foreign Affairs*, 73, pp 28–44.

Krugman, P. 1996 Making sense of the competitiveness debate, *Oxford Review of Economic Policy*, 12, pp 17–35.

Lovering, J. 1999 Theory led by policy: the inadequacies of the 'new regionalism' (illustrated from the case of wales), *International Journal of Urban and Regional Research*, 23:2, pp 379–956.

Marshall, A. 1920 *Principles of Economics: An Introductory Volume*, Macmillan and Company, London.

McCann, E. 2013 Policy boosterism, policy mobilities, and the extrospective city, *Urban Geography*, 34:1, pp 5–29.

Myrdal, G. 1957 *Rich Lands and Poor*, Harper and Row, New York.

OECD 2009 *How Regions Grow: Trends and Analysis*, OECD, Paris.

OECD 2010 *Regions Matter*, OECD, Paris.

OECD 2012a *Promoting Growth in All Regions*, OECD, Paris.

OECD 2012b *Growth in All Regions*, OECD, Paris.

O'Farrell, P., Hitchens, D. and Moffat, A. 2006 The competitiveness of business service firms: a matched comparison between Scotland and the south east of England, *Regional Studies*, 26:6, pp 519–563.

Perry, M. 2010 *Controversies in Local Economic Development*, Routledge, London.

Polese, M. 2010 *The Wealth and Poverty of Regions: Why Cities Matter*, Chicago University Press, Chicago, IL.

Porter, M. 1990 *The Competitive Advantage of Nations*, The Free Press, New York.

Porter, M. 2010 The economic performance of regions, *Regional Studies*, 37:6, pp 549–578.

Rainnie, A. and Grobbelaar, M. 2005 *New Regionalism in Australia*, Ashgate, Aldershot.

Rodríguez-Pose, A. 2013 Do institutions matter for regional development? *Regional Studies*, 47:7, pp 1034–1047.

Rostow, W. 1960 *The Stages of Growth*, Cambridge University Press, Cambridge.

Saxenian, A. 1994 *Regional Advantage*, Harvard University Press, Cambridge, MA.

Solow, R. 1956 A contribution to the theory of economic growth, *The Quarterly Journal of Economics*, 70:1, pp 65–94.

Stimson, R., Stough, R. and Salazar, M. 2009 *Leadership and Institutions in Regional Endogenous Development*, Edward Elgar, Cheltenham.

Storper, M. 1997 *The Regional World: Territorial Development in a Global Economy*, Guilford Press, New York.

Storper, M. 2014 Regions and development clubs: a structural perspective from economic geography, presentation to the Regional Studies Association, Winter Conference, London, November.

World Bank 2009 *World Development Report 2009 – Reshaping Economic Geography*, World Bank, Washington, DC.

# 4 The components of local growth in the 21st century

This chapter:

▶ Addresses the importance for cities, regions and communities to be connected to the global economy;

▶ Looks at innovation, what it is, how it relates to economic development and business growth, and the strategies used to encourage innovation;

▶ Considers the advantages associated with agglomeration, and how smart specialization strategies can allow places to develop their own reputation for business and technological excellence;

▶ Discusses population growth processes and their impact on local economies;

▶ Examines the way local and national institutions establish the foundations for economic growth, either accelerating or impeding development;

▶ Outlines the part played by local leaders and leadership in bringing about positive change.

IN CHAPTER 3 we considered how we can understand growth at the local level and how the various components of development fit together to produce the complex outcomes we see today. That discussion emphasized both change over time and the fact that economic processes affect different locations in different ways. Some factors that accelerate or sustain the development and prosperity of one set of places slow the growth of other cities, communities and regions. Chapter 3 also looked at the policy recommendations resulting from the OECD's work on regional growth trajectories. The OECD (2009, 2010, 2012) argued that measures to encourage the growth of places – cities, regions, townships, communities – need to fit within a broader regional planning framework and should be implemented as a package of interventions, rather than one-off programs that may fail or generate perverse outcomes. While accepting this argument, it is important we understand in some detail each of the key drivers of growth so that later discussion of policy measures – examined in later chapters – is firmly grounded.

This chapter begins with a discussion of the importance of connectivity within a globalized economy. It then moves on to consider other pathways for growth, including human capital; policy, agglomeration economies, population processes – the role of institutions; the spillover of growth from other locations; and the quality of the business environment.

## ■ 4.1 Connectivity and the global economy

To a greater or lesser degree, globalization has been a feature of the world economy for a considerable period of time. Humanity has always exchanged goods, and even in ancient times trade routes spanned substantial borders including mountains, deserts and seas. Some of these trade routes – such as the Silk Road – were famous for crossing continents, but even in less well-known places such as pre-European North America and Australia, the movement of goods and knowledge was substantial. By the 1500s Basque fishermen were whaling and fishing for cod off Newfoundland, and the period of European colonization that followed saw a rapid expansion in trade networks and economic linkages. While acknowledging this history, academics and commentators alike discuss contemporary economies as being marked by a globalized world that is somehow different from earlier periods.

Many would argue that while global trade has a long history, we now live in a world that is undeniably different because of the speed of information and financial flows. Improvements in ICT have been critical in enabling the rise of global money and stock markets, but institutional reforms have, perhaps, been more critical, especially in the removal of regulatory barriers. Barca et al. (2012) argued that the contemporary era of globalization can be traced to the economic and financial transformations of the 1970s (Stilwell 1977), including the decline of the Bretton Woods Agreement and the emergence of global financial markets. Further institutional reform and technological innovation took place between 1988 and 1994, with the creation of the European Single Market, economic reform in China, Indonesia and India, the signing of the North American Free Trade Agreement (NAFTA) and the fall of the Berlin Wall. Barca et al. (2012 p 136) see contemporary globalization reshaping the geography of the global economy with:

- Slow income convergence between poorer and richer countries;
- An eastward shift in economic activity; the rise of three 'super regional areas of integration' – NAFTA, the EU and South and East Asia – where increasing shares of global economic activity are concentrated;
- The growing importance of global cities for trade and related activities;
- The ongoing significance of the economies of smaller metropolitan centers and nonmetropolitan regions.

The importance of the global economy for economic growth and prosperity is rarely – if ever – questioned. What is contestable, however, are the implications for individual cities, regions and communities. Some authors have argued ICTs have created a 'flatter' world, where distance no longer matters – or at least not to a significant degree (Friedmann 2008; Green Leigh and Blakely 2013) – and that business is now a truly global phenomenon. Others argue this perspective oversimplifies a complex set of processes and that location remains important.

Indeed, for a number of authors this significance has grown greater with the digital revolution exacerbating the differences between leading and lagging communities (McCann 2008; McCann and Acs 2011). And, 'The reason for this is that ICTs are complements for knowledge intensive activities requiring highly frequent face-to-face interactions (Gaspar and Glaeser 1998; McCann 2007), while at the same time they are substitutes for routinized activities.' (McCann and Ortega-Argilés 2015 p 4)

In a similar vein, Barca et al. (2012 p 136) contended that

> Globalization has made localities and their interaction more important for economic growth and their prosperity. . . . Space is becoming increasingly 'slippery' in the sense that capital goods, people and ideas travel more easily . . . but, at the same time, increasingly 'sticky' and 'thick' because capital, goods, people and ideas, despite being constantly on the move, tend to remain stuck in large agglomerations.

## ■ 4.2 Innovation and the knowledge economy

The importance of innovation and technological development for economic growth is now an accepted fact of contemporary life. When politicians, community members and government officials turn their attention to the future of their economies, they almost invariably look to technological success stories such as Silicon Valley in California or the Oresund in Denmark and Sweden as their models for growth. But innovation is complex. While anecdote and economic analysis alike underscore the importance of innovation in driving the performance of contemporary economies, stimulating innovation is not straightforward. A great deal of research and policy analysis has examined innovation and the knowledge economy and it is possible to draw out insights that can inform the development of places.

One of the most basic insights to emerge from research into innovation is that it is not simply a matter of knowledge; instead it is a question of *knowledge processes* (McCann and Ortega-Argilés 2015). The creation of new knowledge does not lead to innovation; instead innovation occurs when an invention is taken up commercially and 'it is the market which distinguishes innovation from invention, because innovation also implies commercially successful application; in the end it is the market that distinguishes an invention from an innovation.' (McCann and Ortega-Argilés 2015 p 190)

The World Bank and OECD (2012) put forward their view that innovation is a social process, and that innovation takes place in a variety of contexts and industries. In many respects, innovation in low technology industries is as important as those in cutting-edge fields. In combination, these observations explain why places that are knowledge rich are not necessarily strong in innovation. Innovation is not limited to the invention of new products or technologies. Service industries can be innovative, with the development of new financial products or new business models of equal importance in driving economic growth. McCann and Ortega-Argilés (2015 p 193) drew out key findings of the literature on innovation systems and concluded that:

- Firms operating internationally were 40–70 percent more likely to innovate than domestically focused firms;
- Collaboration between firms increases the likelihood of innovation by 20–50 percent;
- Funding from public sources increased innovation by 40–70 percent;
- Firms that innovate are more likely to survive and are more likely to grow;
- Businesses that are not at the cutting edge of technology invest less in innovation and receive lower returns when they innovate. On the other hand, public sector investment for innovation in low technology firms has a larger return;
- Innovation is concentrated in small and large businesses. Mid-sized businesses are less likely to innovate;
- Only a small number of firms account for most innovations;
- Venture capital has a strongly positive impact on firms seeking to bring new technologies to market.

Clearly, innovation occurs in very specific contexts and many researchers argue that place or location is an important element in driving innovation. There is very substantial literature on regional innovation systems (Cooke et al. 1997; Ashiem and Coenen 2005; Agrawal et al. 2014) and places that are more likely to be innovative and often already have characteristics that make it likely they will be successful: appropriate industry structures, strong entrepreneurial cultures, economies of scale, an appropriate workforce and an environment embedded with both technical knowledge and business 'know-how.' Boschma (2005) makes the point that geographical proximity does not generate automatic advantages for innovation; instead innovation is fostered by secondary factors including the culture of the locality, the presence of relevant institutions and access to cognate technologies – or technology 'relatedness.'

Globally, governments at all scales – national, provincial/state, city and local – have attempted to promote innovation, and indeed it is often the central principle of their economic development strategy. Some have been successful (e.g. Helsinki), while others have not, and in part this may reflect a confusion in the minds of some city and region officials between invention and innovation. McCann and Ortega-Argilés (2015) argue that it is possible to distinguish between the policies and strategies needed to sustain the advancement of places that are already world-leading centers for innovation, and those that should be implemented in places that aspire to achieve this status. In both instances key components include:

- Access to world-class labor;
- Business-to-business collaboration and business-to-government coordination;
- Fostering a culture of entrepreneurialism;
- Loan schemes and other funds for new startups;
- Business and technology incubators;
- Programs to encourage the internationalization of the activities of existing firms;
- Focusing on particular technologies and industries – for example, life sciences, ICT or pharmaceuticals.

Importantly, these basic building blocks need to be implemented in different ways depending upon the maturity of the innovation economy or ecosystem in each place. Where innovation is a less developed feature of the economy, there needs to be a greater emphasis on a limited number of sectors, effectively the building of new technologies that match existing industry strengths and the formation of relationships between businesses and the research community. There is also a need for greater government assistance with the financing of startups – as there may be little or no access to venture capital and the mentoring of fledgling entrepreneurs, which may take place in a business incubator (discussed in Chapter 6) or other environment.

In summary, innovation is an important driver of growth and has a strong regional component. While innovation doesn't directly benefit from proximity, the creation of an innovative environment – sometimes referred to as an innovative milieu (Aula and Harmaakorpi 2008) – has the capacity to generate long-run growth at the local scale.

Critically we need to remember that innovation is not invention:

- Places that are rich in the sorts of assets that make up the knowledge economy – universities, research institutes, et cetera – will not necessarily become hotbeds of innovation;
- Innovation is most likely to be found in small and large firms, and businesses that work in international markets, and it is a phenomenon that is highly concentrated;
- Governments can successfully foster innovation at the local or community level, but any action needs to be targeted at the most appropriate industries or sectors, firms and locations.

## 4.3  Agglomeration economies – does size matter in the 21st century?

As discussed in Chapter 1, there is a strong body of evidence and argument that cities now occupy a preeminent position in the advanced economies. Cities are seen to have distinct advantages relative to small towns and rural areas as:

- The more diversified economies of cities enable them to continue to grow even as the economy changes in new and unexpected ways;
- Their larger labor markets provide surety to businesses seeking to attract and retain workers and also provides the range of skills needed by the enterprise;
- Workers with specialized skills are concentrated in the cities, which in turn allows firms with tightly defined business models to prosper;
- Cities represent significant concentrations of infrastructure, including key 'linking' infrastructure such as international airports, major research institutions, government agencies and major hospitals;
- Higher average incomes result in greater disposable incomes which adds to both the volume of demand and the range of goods and services sought;

- Cities represent a substantial pool of consumers and in a world dominated by global production networks firms prioritize access to markets over proximity to their raw material inputs;
- There are higher levels of innovation in cities as they contain concentrations of specialist research bodies – including the research and development (R&D) units of major corporations – as well as the businesses able to bring these new technologies to market;
- Finally, cities contain major agglomerations of institutions – public sector, not-for-profit and private sector. As will be discussed later in this chapter, institutions play a long-term role in shaping growth and the most critical institutions, such as government agencies and major corporate headquarters, are concentrated in the major metropolitan regions.

In virtually all developed economies in the 21st century, therefore, major cities are primed for growth. It is simply the nature, direction and pace of development that is open to question. This does not rule out the growth of smaller cities or rural communities who can both grow through their own distinctive processes and replicate some of the advantages cities capitalize on. Growth overall is not limited to the large metropolitan areas and there are many ways smaller communities can bring forward the development of their economies.

The scale of the population and the diverse industry structure found in larger urban centers means they are able to capture or retain the economic benefits associated with their growth sectors. That is, the advantages of a vibrant export economy are able to be shared across the community as income earned through globally focused activities is spent locally. Economists refer to this as the 'multiplier effect' arising from an activity such as the establishment of a new factory or headquarters. An incoming firm may generate 1,000 jobs, but the local economy may grow by a further 1,600 jobs as the wages and salaries of these new employees spread through the community. In smaller places, a higher percentage of those earnings flow out of the region or community, and in extreme cases manufacturing plants or other facilities may have few links with the wider community, resulting in a form of 'enclave development.' Successful economic development strategies seek to overcome these hurdles by first ensuring incoming firms fit well with the existing economic base, and secondly by seeking to create a high degree of integration between the new firm and the region. Newly arrived firms can be embedded into the local economic structure though the inclusion of existing firms into the supply chain but it is clear this will be more easily accomplished in larger centers where the population of firms and capacities are greater.

## 4.3.1 Smart specialization

Communities often face difficult choices when planning their economic future. One of the most basic decisions they have to make is to find an appropriate balance between a specialized industrial structure on the one hand, and a diversified spread of industries on the other. This issue is not as straightforward as we might otherwise think: places with highly specialized industry structures are able to achieve economies of scale in production that boost their competitiveness on global and local markets, but their success means they are highly vulnerable to shifts in the fortunes of that industry. By contrast, places with a diverse industry base are highly resilient in the face of a downturn in one or two sectors, but do not generate the productivity benefits associated with agglomeration economies – clustering, knowledge spillover, effective use of costly infrastructure and the maximization of human capital (labor). The complexity of this issue is highlighted by research into the economic performance of Australia's regional cities between 1996 and 2001 (Beer and Clower 2009). The research found that, on average, cities that became more specialized in their industry mix over that five-year period *were more likely* to record population and job growth. However, the highest individual rates of growth were found in cities that shifted their industry structure over time, becoming, in aggregate, more diversified.

Recent thinking in the European Union has considered this challenge in some detail and has developed a perspective on planning for growth that offers the prospect of both the greater resilience and flexibility found in more diversified economies, and the efficiency of specialized production. Smart specialization is an idea that focuses on the ways entrepreneurs find new business opportunities, arguing they focus on opportunities to innovate and apply emerging technologies that are a good fit with their existing business (McCann and Ortega-Argilés 2015). For many entrepreneurs, the most attractive opportunities are close, and connected, to their existing businesses. From the perspective of a city or region, some of these new opportunities will be of smaller size, while others will be of considerable magnitude. Smart specialization suggests that cities and regions can best grow by focusing on those growth prospects that are linked to their existing industrial base; are based on the application of new technologies that will either open up new markets, or deliver significant productivity gains; and have the potential for large-scale benefit or 'uplift.' All other things being equal, of course, investments that generate larger returns will be more attractive.

Smart specialization is a tool for cities and regions that enables them to fine-tune their efforts. It suggests that radical industry diversification is less likely to be successful than a small-scale broadening of the employment and technical base, and that technology and the knowledge economy needs to feature in decision making. Smart specialization contains an element of 'picking winners' – deciding which technologies and industries to support or not support (McCann and Ortega-Argilés 2015). These risks can be managed by:

- Using local entrepreneurs as part of the search process;
- Considering industries that will be embedded within the region – that is, linked to, and dependent upon, already-established businesses;
- Focusing on those possibilities where there is the best chance to both learn about the nature of the opportunity and the magnitude of the potential impact.

## ■ 4.4 Population processes and human capital

As the case studies in Chapter 2 have shown, population plays a fundamental role in driving local growth. At its simplest, population growth adds to the demand for goods and services within a city or region, while also determining the stock of skills and abilities available to employers. Both are important considerations when firms seek new locations as their business changes (Chapter 5).

Populations change in a number of ways, all of which have implications for economic development at the local scale:

- Populations may grow through natural increase or migration, both of which have implications for the demand for goods and services and the prosperity of the community. High rates of natural increase can create additional stresses on education and other services, while potentially providing a more substantial workforce in the long term. Migration adds to the labor force, while also raising demand for housing, transport and related services. Some communities experience population growth because of their proximity to major metropolitan centers, effectively captured as a dormitory-center for the expanding region. In these places, growth may be inescapable and communities can only choose the type of development they experience with respect to urban form, locally based industries and accessibility to the urban center;
- In many parts of the developed world population decline is entrenched in communities, especially in rural areas where the processes of rural to urban migration continue to have an impact. Falling populations can result in the provision of fewer services by governments and private firms such as banks, and increased pressures on public sector budgets (Beer and Keane 2000). In many rural regions the absence of key services, such as health care or high-level education opportunities, encourages out-migration and discourages new arrivals. Populations may decline as a result of out-migration, natural decrease – where deaths exceed births – or the combination of both processes. In 2017 Japan's population fell by 0.2 percent – the continuation of a long-term trend – and nations such as Latvia and Lithuania are also affected by falling populations, with potential long-term impacts on economic development. This is not a challenge limited to those economies conventionally thought of as 'developed': in 2019 the Chinese Academy of Social Sciences announced that the nation's population would begin to decline from 2030, with a resultant fall in the workforce of 200 million persons (ABC 2019). Population loss presents significant challenges to sustaining economic growth at the community, city and national scale;
- Migration is a significant determinant of economic growth, and one which is often seen to reinforce growth trajectories. In general, migrants move to employment opportunities – or the expectation of job opportunities. Immigrants also tend to be younger than the general population, more highly educated and more entrepreneurial, which implies there are substantial benefits to be gained from attracting migrants, and that out-migration represents a significant loss to the community. Over recent decades new trends have emerged in a number of developed economies: first, the aging of national populations has resulted in a significant group of retirees with secure income and assets. This – large – cohort within the population is able to choose a place of residence independent of the need to find work, resulting in the significant relocation of many households to attractive coastal and

rural locations. These processes – often referred to as 'seachange' and 'treechange' – have driven substantial development in select locations, often with profound implications for the local economy. Second, highly skilled and highly educated individuals – Richard Florida's (2002) creative class – may decide upon their city or town of residence depending on cultural or environmental assets. There is increasing evidence (Østbye et al. 2018) that employment opportunities follow the location decisions of the creative class, with entrepreneurs moving to cities and regions that accommodate the skilled workforce they need;

- Many cities and regions seek to attract highly skilled workers because they exert a positive impact on regional incomes. For example, a study of US metropolitan regions found that a 1 percent increase in residents with a college degree resulted in a 2 percent increase in metropolitan gross regional product. Those working in producer services – banking, finance, management consulting, accounting, et cetera – as well as ICT were seen to have a substantial impact on economic growth (Abel and Gabe 2011). Other work suggests the quality of the workforce attracted into the region had a larger impact on productivity than research and development expenditures (Mannasoo et al. 2018) and that the ability of prosperous and productive places to attract immigrants boosts their export performance, thereby reinforcing growth (Ghosh and Mastromarco 2018);

- Some populations are relatively immobile, choosing to stay in low-income, slow-growth communities or regions because of family or other ties, the perception they lack the skills needed in other labor markets or for lifestyle reasons (Coulombe 2003). These resident populations represent an opportunity for development practitioners because of their potential to take on additional employment as the economy grows.

Overall, population change is a critical determinant of the growth and prosperity of a region, city or community. Strategies that result in a better educated and more highly skilled labor force, while also creating an attractive environment, will minimize the risks of population loss and maximize the chances of attracting new arrivals' labor force skills. Population growth in itself is not a guarantee of development – in any sense – but it does assist the further expansion of places with already vibrant economies. Well-targeted population policies that pay attention to skills matching, local growth sectors and urban development issues have a central role in economic development strategies in the 21st century.

## ■ 4.5 Institutions and institutional dynamics

There is growing recognition that institutions are central to delivering growth (Rodríguez-Pose 2013). This insight is not new, with North (1990) arguing for the importance of institutional determinants of growth three decades ago. For North (1990) the long-term economic performance of places was shaped by their institutional structure, while others have noted (Rodríguez-Pose 2013) that institutions are specific to places, both shaping their development and in turn being shaped by them. They potentially have far-reaching impacts as:

> They generate place-specific forms of trust amongst economic actors and reduce transaction costs . . . provide collective goods . . ., foster transparency . . ., promote entrepreneurship, grease the functioning of labor markets (Giddens 1990), adapt in the face of shocks in order to provide problem-solving arrangements (North 1990), and ultimately lead to greater economic efficiency (North 2005).
>
> (Rodríguez-Pose 2013 p 1037)

Institutions can take a variety of forms. North (1990 p 477) defined institutions as 'the rules of the game' while others have argued that it is possible to identify both formal and informal institutions, with Amin (1999 p 367) arguing for the need to recognize 'formal institutions such as rules, laws and organizations, as well as informal or tacit institutions such as individual habits, group routines and social norms and values.'

Property laws and the formal structures of government are recognized as formal or 'hard' institutions, while social capital – the trust and collaboration individuals display with others – can be thought of as an informal or 'soft' institution, as can expectations about models for working cooperatively and integrity within government. But this is a complex field, with commentators distinguishing between bonding social capital that can be seen to tie a small community or group together, and bridging social capital which reflects on the openness to deal with outsiders.

Analysis of the relationship between place-based growth and institutional factors shows a clear relationship between formal institutional arrangements and development. Put simply, places with inadequate property laws and governance arrangements either will not grow or grow slowly. However, evidence on the impact of informal institutions is less clear-cut. In part this reflects the challenge of measuring – and therefore assessing – the influence of factors such as trust, effective leadership and culture. Rodríguez-Pose (2013 p 1041) noted 'soft' institutions can exert a detrimental impact on the growth, as

> while informal institutions can facilitate opportunities for economic activity, they can also end up creating vicious cycles of suboptimal development trajectories through institutional lock in, which takes place in the presence of rigid institutions that can neither anticipate nor respond to changes in economic circumstances.

The OECD argued that the slow development of some regions in Mexico was an outcome of cultural factors, including the influence of long-established groups of wealthy landowners who prioritized the maintenance of their power over economic success. Clearly, 'soft' institutional factors cut both ways: propelling development in some places, and ruling it out elsewhere.

A number of theorists have discussed the idea of 'institutional thickness,' noting that places endowed with many institutions are more likely to grow because there is a greater number of entities – chambers of commerce, Main Street organizations, regional development agencies, business incubators, et cetera – working to promote the well-being of that place (Amin 1999; Beer and Lester 2015). This argument has been challenged by Rodríguez-Pose (2013), who argues instead that places grow when they have the 'right' mix of institutions, all of which are integrated and effective. Other research has come to similar conclusions, with Safford (2009) contrasting the fortunes of two manufacturing communities – Allentown, Pennsylvania and Youngstown, Ohio – over the period from the 1970s. In the case of Youngstown the institutions that set out to reshape its economy failed because they were inward-looking and focused on the past, while Allentown remade itself as it adopted new ideas and embraced the thinking of new arrivals. Others have attempted to empirically examine the 'institutional thickness' hypothesis (Raco 1998) and while the evidence to date is unclear, at least one study found the places with the greatest concentrations of institutions nationally had the strongest economies and growth rates (Beer and Lester 2015).

Rodríguez-Pose (2013) and Farole et al. (2011) concluded that it is difficult to draw firm conclusions about institutions because each city and community is distinctive, which means there cannot be a 'one size fits all' approach to reform. Institutions are also difficult to transform, and it may be more straightforward to create new sets of arrangements – business incubators, leadership networks, knowledge exchange precincts, relationships with universities and other research providers – rather than reshape bodies that are already well established. More broadly he has argued that good governance is the primary precondition for growth (Rodríguez-Pose and Tselios 2019) and that the way government is organized – a federal system or a unitary government – is largely immaterial. As the case studies in Chapter 2 showed, many places grow not because of a single government acting alone, but because a set of actors – government agencies, not-for-profit or community groups, private firms – came together to drive prosperity. This set of arrangements is referred to as governance, with governments seeking to 'steer not row' in order to achieve economic development (Jessop 1997).

Intuitively, the argument put forward by Rodríguez-Pose (2013) makes sense. We all know of places where the culture of one city or community varies greatly from that of its neighbor, and many of us have observed places that pay lip service to promoting growth locally, but make little real effort. So how can we bring about change? Culture, the 'lived memory' of towns and cities, and the attitudes of community officials are difficult things to shift. Rodríguez-Pose (2013) felt the answer lay in tailor-made solutions for each locality or region, which he acknowledged as being expensive and cumbersome. But his work was focused on regional policy, not practice. If we consider how local economic development is brought to life around the world, inevitably each city or community economic development strategy is crafted to the needs of that particular place, and is implemented by a dedicated staff member or agency. Tailor-made solutions are an embedded feature of local development and they are an appropriate, and practical, mechanism for building valuable institutional settings such as local leadership capacity, an entrepreneurial culture and an openness to sharing resources and information. How that can be undertaken is discussed below.

### 4.5.1 Leadership

Leadership is a phenomenon that everyone can agree is important, but at the same time struggle to define and/or identify in a meaningful way. While many argue that they 'know it when they see it,' few can speak to the precise process for recognizing and acknowledging leadership, let alone creating and then further developing leadership at the local scale. And this challenge is even greater when we consider the leadership of places – such as cities, regions or small rural communities – where leadership appears much more complex than in a hierarchical organization, such as a company, central government department or city administration.

We can distinguish between leadership *in* regions and cities, and the leadership *of* these communities (Collinge et al. 2010) as the leaders of places may not hold formal authority (Sotarauta 2016) while mayors and other elected officials may not – in any substantive sense – be effective leaders. There is a strong consensus among researchers (Stimson et al. 2009) and policymakers alike (McKinsey and Co 1994) that place-based leadership is important and that communities need to enhance their opportunities for leadership if they seek to maximize development. Importantly, while planners and economic development practitioners are unlikely to improve the performance of individual city mayors or the CEOs of the chambers of commerce, they help create the conditions under which local leadership flourishes.

Over the past decade a great deal of work has been published on the leadership of places (see, for example, Beer and Clower 2014; Sotarauta 2016; Bowden and Liddle 2017). This work has shown that broadly comparable local leadership processes are evident in many developed economies (Beer et al. 2018) and that effective leadership is critical when a city or region faces an economic shock (Horlings et al. 2018). A great deal has been written on leadership by authors from various perspectives and in response to a wide range of practical needs. Stimson et al. (2011) examined the question of leadership within endogenous growth models while Sotarauta (2009, 2010) considered the role of networks and professional officers in leading regions. He also examined the relationship between leadership and power within communities, and the tactics employed by leaders to achieve specified ends. Others have considered leadership in peripheral regions (Kroehn et al. 2010) and the contribution leadership makes to the achievement of better environmental outcomes (Sotarauta and Mustikkamaki 2012). Many academic discussions of the leadership of places are dominated by case studies (see, for example, Peters 2012; Raagma et al. 2012). There are, however, some clear lessons to be drawn from the literature that have the capacity to inform good practice and these include insights into:

- The leadership of places as a shared or community-based activity;
- The importance of vision setting and communication;
- The role of professionals as enablers within leadership structures;
- The relationship with formal government authority;
- The capacity for place leadership to deliver benefits for economies in transition.

The leadership of places is not the same as the leadership we see in other environments, such as a workplace, religious organizations or even a community group. An early definition was given by Stough et al. (2001 p 177) who argued that regional leadership is 'the tendency of the community to collaborate across sectors in a sustained, purposeful manner to enhance the economic performance or economic environment of its region.'

While Stimson et al. (2002 p 279) offered the following insight:

> leadership for regional economic development will not be based on traditional hierarchical relationships; rather it will be a collaborative relationship between institutional actors encompassing the public, private and community sectors – and it will be based on mutual trust and cooperation.

These definitions are helpful as they make explicit that the leadership of places:

- Is focused on improving economic – and potentially other – outcomes and is therefore achievement focused;
- Tends to be collaborative rather than hierarchical – that is, it involves collaboration across a number of institutions, individuals and firms;
- Has a distinct long-term perspective.

Place-based leadership is purpose-driven: its goal is to achieve the aspirations of its community or region and does not simply serve as a conduit for socialization or networking. It therefore follows that effective leadership will take a strong role in setting a vision for the future, implementing plans and processes that bring about change and monitor regional performance, and then adjusting strategies and plans as necessary (Stimson et al. 2011 p 1).

The leaders of places are not simply drawn from elected officials or other office holders. In a city, a group of leaders may well comprise individuals drawn from large businesses, local governments, one or more universities, local government representatives, small business owners and industry bodies – such as an organization representing retailers or manufacturers. In smaller communities, local governments and small businesses will be participants, but they are more likely to be joined by community members rather than representatives of big business. Each group of leaders will operate differently, but to be successful they will need to have the resources – and especially the time – to be successful. As a number of authors have argued, the effective leadership of places comes from having 'slack resources' in the region:

> 'excess' resources that may be manifest as sources of voluntary contributions to 'civic activities', or locally-based and focused community efforts by public, private and non-profit organizations and foundations. Such allocation of excess resources to those types of organizations and activities may be seen as enhancing both the leadership potential and institutional capacity of a region.
>
> (Stimson et al. 2009 p 27)

Good leadership therefore comes from having both uncommitted resources and high-quality individuals willing to take on responsibility, while working closely with others. Place leadership needs to be a collaborative effort, because – unlike a workplace or other hierarchy – there is no capacity to compel action or compliance (Sotarauta 2016). Instead, achievement depends on persuading others.

In many places effective place leadership often includes professional staff who may well create the preconditions for elected officials and others within the community to be successful. A study examining the ways in which regions in six nations responded to major economic change (Beer et al. 2018) found that in many nations local government officials drove the process of transformation, with mayors and senior government representatives providing oversight of the process (Sotarauta 2009). Place-based leadership commonly comes into conflict with central governments – opposing government proposals, lobbying for additional services or infrastructure, et cetera – but such disagreement is an inevitable part of leading through advocacy.

Regions, cities and communities often have their greatest need for effective leadership when confronted by major changes, especially adverse events such as the closure of a major plant or headquarters. Under these circumstances leaders may be called upon to:

- Consult with a range of stakeholders including community members, local businesses and central government departments;
- Articulate a new vision for the economic growth of the community, city or region;
- Communicate the nature and shape of the new economy to the community and discuss ways to bring about that change;
- Lobby governments to provide the resources needed to achieve a new economic future, and leverage those assets with community-provided resources;
- Monitor progress and adjust the strategic vision as both the local and wider economy continues to evolve.

Finally we would argue that economic development practitioners need to acknowledge the importance of adequate leadership in the places in which they work and seek to develop. In some places there will be leadership deficits and these gaps need to be filled regardless of whether the community's economy is performing strongly or poorly.

 ## 4.6 Conclusion

In the 21st century, being connected to the global economy is virtually a precondition for economic development. Places that can improve their physical accessibility and their profile among potential customers and investors are more likely to prosper than those that are seen to be remote or unknown. Encouraging innovation is one way places can raise their standing on national and global stages, as their programs – and the businesses they foster – receive recognition from policymakers, markets and the mass media. Promoting innovation speaks to a future orientation and helps future-proof a city or regional economy from the unknowns of economic disruption. Innovation is often associated with the larger cities and metropolitan areas, but well-planned innovation programs in rural areas can be of benefit to the wider rural economy. Finally, it is important to reflect upon both the importance of population growth and having the right mix of institutions. Larger places with more substantial populations find it easier to carve out a role in the globalized economy, while the task of reviewing and reshaping institutions – including leadership – helps future-proof the local economy.

## Key messages

- Places are much more likely to grow if they are able to access global markets. Strategies and investments that encourage such connectedness will result in growth;
- Innovation is central to growth in today's economy, and some firms and some places are more likely to be innovative. Communities can encourage innovation by building on their areas of strength and focusing their entrepreneurial activity, providing grants to support startups and technology transfer, focusing on the translation of new knowledge into the world of commerce rather than the creation of new knowledge, and supporting small businesses to explore new opportunities;
- Population processes are a key determinant of local and regional economic growth, and attracting migrants – especially skilled immigrants – can be a critical first step in reshaping a city or community's economy;
- Local leaders are central to starting and sustaining growth at the community or city level. Ideally, leadership comes from those responsible – e.g. the city mayor, state and local government political representatives and business leaders, but also individuals working as a group to achieve growth.

## Discussion questions

- Innovation is seen to be one of the keys to unlocking the development of cities and regions, but many localities find it difficult to create an environment that fosters the emergence of new ideas and their successful commercialization. As a class, discuss:
  - o How universities could better promote innovation in the local community through programs and partnerships. (Think back on the San Diego case study.)
  - o The role of economic development professionals in promoting a more innovative culture. How could they help entrepreneurs emerge, and what could they do to assist newly graduated university students start their own businesses?
- There is much talk in the economic development community about cities having an *innovation ecosystem*. What does this mean and what does it take to have such an ecosystem?

## References

Abel, J. and Gabe, T. 2011 Human capital and economic activity in urban America, *Regional Studies*, 45:8, pp 1079–1090.

Agrawal, A., Cockburn, I., Glasso, A. and Oetti, A. 2014 Why are some regions more innovative than others? *Journal of Urban Economics*, 81, pp 149–165.

Amin, A. 1999 An institutionalist perspective on regional development, *International Journal of Urban and Regional Research*, 23, pp 365–378.

Ashiem, B. and Coenen, L. 2005 Knowledge bases and regional innovation systems, *Research Policy*, 34, pp 1173–1190.

Aula, P. and Harmaakorpi, V. 2008 An innovative milieu – a review of regional reputation building, *Regional Studies*, 24:4, pp 5233–5258.

Australian Broadcasting Corporation (ABC) 2019 China's ageing population, low birth rate to cause 'unstoppable' population decline, experts say. Available at https://www.abc.net.au/news/2019-01-06/chinese-declining-population-going-into-overdrive/10687996, accessed January 7, 2019.

Barca, F., McCann, P. and Rodríguez-Pose, A. 2012 The case for regional development interventions: place based versus place neutral approaches, *Journal of Regional Science*, 52:1, pp 134–152.

Beer, A., Ayres, S., Clower, T., Faller, F., Sancino, A. and Sotarauta, M. 2018 Place leadership and regional economic development: a framework for cross-regional analysis, *Regional Studies*. DOI: 10.1080/00343404.2018.1447662.

Beer, A. and Clower, T. 2009 Specialisation and growth: evidence from Australia's regional cities, *Urban Studies*, 46, pp 369–389.

Beer, A. and Clower, T. 2014 Mobilising leadership in cities and regions, *Regional Studies, Regional Science*, 1:1, pp 4–18.

Beer, A. and Keane, R. 2000 Population decline and service provision in regional Australia: a case study of rural and remote South Australia, *People and Place*, 8:2, pp 69–76.

Beer, A. and Lester, L. 2015 Institutional thickness and institutional effectiveness: developing regional indices for policy and practice in Australia, *Regional Studies, Regional Science*, 2:1, pp 204–227.

Boschma, R. 2005 Proximity and innovation: a critical assessment, *Regional Studies*, 39, pp 61–74.

Bowden, A. and Liddle, J. 2017 Evolving public sector roles in the leadership of place-based partnerships, *Regional Studies*, 52:1, pp 145–155.

Collinge, C., Gibney, J. and Mabey, C. 2010 Leadership and place, *Policy Studies*, 31:4, pp 367–378.

Cooke, P., Uranga, M. and Etxebarria, G. 1997 Regional innovation systems: institutional and organisational dimensions, *Research Policy*, 26, pp 475–491.

Coulombe, S. 2003 Human capital, urbanization and Canadian provincial growth, *Regional Studies*, 37:3, pp 239–250.

Farole, T., Rodríguez-Pose, A. and Storper, M. 2011 Cohesion policy in the European Union: growth, geography, institutions, *Journal of Common Market Studies*, 49:5, pp 1089–1111.

Florida, R. 2002 *The Rise of the Creative Class*, Basic Books, New York.

Friedmann. T. 2008 *Hot, Flat and Crowded*, Farrar, Strauss and Giroux, New York.

Gaspar, J. and Glaeser, E. 1998 Information technology and the future of cities, *Journal of Urban Economics*, 43:1, pp 136–156.

Ghosh, S. and Mastromarco, C. 2018 Exports, immigration and human capital in US states, *Regional Studies*, 52:6, pp 840–852.

Giddens, A. 1990 *The Consequences of Modernity*, Polity Press, Cambridge.

Green Leigh, N. and Blakely, E. 2013 *Planning Local Economic Development: Theory and Practice*. 5th edition. Sage Publications, New York.

Horlings, L., Roep, D. and Wellbrock, W. 2018 The role of leadership in place-based development and building institutional arrangements, *Local Economy*, 33:3, pp 245–268.

Jessop, B. 1997 The entrepreneurial city: re-imaging localities, redesigning economic governance, or restructuring capital? In Jewson, N. and MacGregor, S. (eds) *Transforming Cities: Contested Governance and New Spatial Divisions*. Routledge, London, pp 28–41.

Kroehn, M., Maude, A. and Beer, A. 2010 Leadership of place in the rural periphery: lessons from Australia's agricultural margins. In Collinge, C., Gibney, J. and Mabey, J. (eds) *Leadership and Place*, Routledge, London, pp 125–138.

Mannasoo, K., Hein, H. and Ruubel, R. 2018 The contributions of human capital, R&D spending and convergence to total factor productivity, *Regional Studies*, 52:2, pp 1598–1611.

McCann, P. 2007 Sketching out a model of innovation, face-to-face interaction and economic geography, *Spatial Economic Analysis*, 2:2, pp 117–134.

McCann, P. 2008 Globalisation and economic geography: the world is curved not flat, *Cambridge Journal of Regions, Economy and Society*, 1:3, pp 351–370.

McCann, P. and Acs, Z. 2011 Globalization: countries, cities and multinationals, *Regional Studies*, 45:1, pp 17–32.

McCann, P. and Ortega-Argilés, R. 2015 Smart specialization, regional growth and applications to European Union cohesion policy, *Regional Studies*, 49:8, pp 1291–1302. DOI: 10.1080/00343404.2013.799769.

McKinsey and Co 1994 *Lead Local, Compete Global*, McKinsey and Co, Boston.

North, D. 1990 *Institutions, Institutional Change and Economic Performance*, Cambridge University Press, Princeton, NJ.

OECD 2009 *How Regions Grow: Trends and Analysis*, OECD, Paris.

OECD 2010 *Regions Matter*, OECD, Paris.

OECD 2012 *Growth in All Regions*, OECD, Paris.

Østbye, S., Moilanen, M., Tervo, H. and Westerlund, O. 2018 The creative class: do jobs follow people or do people follow jobs? *Regional Studies*, 52:6, pp 745–755. DOI: 10.1080/00343404.2016.1254765.

Peters, K. 2012 Socially embedded leadership. In Sotarauta, M., Horlings, L. and Liddle, M. (eds) *Leadership and change in sustainable regional development*, Routledge, London, pp 145–163.

Raagma, G., Kindel, G. and Lusi, M. 2012 Leadership and institutional change: economic restructuring, sense of place and social capital in Emmanste, Estonia. In Sotarauta, M., Horlings, L. and Liddle, M. (eds) *Leadership and Change in Sustainable Regional Development*, Routledge, London, pp 164–189.

Raco, M. 1998 Assessing 'institutional thickness' in the local context: a comparison of Cardiff and Sheffield, *Environment and Planning D*, 30, pp 975–996.

Rodríguez-Pose, A. 2013 Do institutions matter for regional development? *Regional Studies*, 47:7, pp 1034–1047.

Rodríguez-Pose, A. and Tselios, V. 2019 Wellbeing, political decentralisation and governance quality in Europe, *Journal of Human Development and Capabilities*. Available at https://www.tandfonline.com/doi/full/10.1080/19452829.2018.1563773.

Safford, S. 2009 *Why the Garden Club Couldn't Save Youngstown: The Transformation of the Rust Belt*, Harvard University Press, Cambridge, MA.

Sotarauta, M. 2009 Power and influence tactics in the promotion of regional development: an empirical analysis of the work of Finnish regional development officers, *Geoforum*, 400, pp 895–905.

Sotarauta, M. 2010 Regional development and regional networks: the role of regional development officers in Finland, *European Urban and Regional Studies*, 17:4, pp 387–400.

Sotarauta, M. 2016 *Leadership and the City*, Routledge, London.

Sotarauta, M. and Mustikkamaki, N. 2012 Strategic leadership relay: how to keep regional innovation journeys in motion. In Sotarauta, M., Horlings, L. and Liddle, M. (eds) *Leadership and Change in Sustainable Regional Development*, Routledge, London, pp 190–211.

Stilwell, F. 1977 *Regional Economic Policy*, Macmillan, London.

Stimson, R., Stough, R. and Roberts, B. 2002 *Regional Economic Development: Analysis and Planning Strategy*, Springer, Berlin.

Stimson, R., Stough, R. and Salazar, M. 2009 *Leadership and Institutions in Regional Endogenous Development*, Edward Elgar, Cheltenham.

Stimson, R., Nijkamp, P. and Stough, R. 2011 *Modelling Endogenous Regional Development*, Edward Elgar, Cheltenham.

Stough, R., DeSantis, M., Stimson, R. and Roberts, B. 2001 Leadership in regional economic development strategic planning. In Edgington, A., Fernandez, C. and Hoshino, C. (eds) *New Regional Development Paradigms*, 2, Greenwood, London.

World Bank and OECD 2012 *Promoting Inclusive Growth: Challenges and Policies*. OECD, Paris, and the World Bank, Washington, DC.

# 5 Exogenous development: fast-tracking growth

This chapter:

▶ Defines exogenous development and identifies both the strength and weaknesses of endogenous development approaches;

▶ Looks at the relationship between exogenous and endogenous growth strategies;

▶ Considers the range of factors modern corporations use when selecting a new site for a production or other facility;

▶ Considers which site location factors fall under the direct control of communities, and which can only be influenced through lobbying or other action;

▶ Examines foreign direct investment (FDI) as a subset of the broader set of inward investment strategies, and considers its capacity to link communities to global production networks.

HOW CAN COMMUNITIES encourage growth? Should their focus be on developing entrepreneurs and businesses already within their region – *endogenous development* – or should they look to attract new firms from other parts of the national economy or from other countries – *exogenous development*? To express this more simply, what can local or regional economic development bodies do to help their economies develop and their businesses prosper? Which strategies and actions offer the best prospects for success, and why do some communities rely upon approaches with a poor record? Answering these questions calls for an examination of what businesses need in order to flourish, including:

- Knowledge – on how to achieve success in business, as well as information on market opportunities and risks;
- Capital for establishment and growth;
- Access to markets, which entails physical access, information technology capabilities and the absence of regulatory barriers that impede participation in established and emerging markets;
- Appropriately skilled and productive labor;

- Material inputs/supplies;
- Land for production, distribution and retail activities;
- An appropriate regulatory framework;
- Services that support business – including generalist services such as accounting or financial advice, as well as more specialist services that may be unique to an industry or sector;
- Innovative capacities, to improve their businesses and adapt to changing conditions.

As a first step, addressing these needs, either by themselves or as part of a wider set of actions, will contribute to local development. However, if we think more broadly and consider groups of businesses at any scale – the city, the region or a small rural community – additional needs emerge:

- An entrepreneurial culture that embraces change and acknowledges opportunities within local, national and global markets:
  - This culture may be supported by a spectrum of intangible assets such as the tacit knowledge embedded within the labor force, a locality's reputation or 'brand,' or the benefits associated with either the agglomeration of industries or the co-location of individual firms – clustering or smart specialization.
- An educated population that is adaptable to shifting conditions.

It is important to acknowledge that many of the actions and strategies that can assist both individual businesses and groups of businesses within a locality are either not amenable to action by individual enterprises, or more efficiently provided at a community level. For example, it is not practicable for individual firms to finance and build major transport or telecommunications infrastructure, nor is there a strong business case for them to look to build synergies with other businesses in their region. There is therefore a degree of inevitability to government engagement with local development.

## ▌ 5.1  Exogenous or endogenous development?

Researchers working across the globe have identified a range of economic development strategies. In the US and elsewhere, and as introduced in Chapter 1, research has identified somewhere between three and five waves or approaches to economic development strategy, with each reflecting a distinct perspective on what drives economies, and how communities can bring about growth. The evolution of these waves can be traced from the 1920s to the current era (Tietz 1994; Blakely and Green Leigh 2010):

- *Wave 1:* industrial recruitment through the provision of relocation incentives;
- *Wave 2:* business retention and expansion;
- *Wave 3:* responding to the global marketplace – including the use of clusters and the improvement of human capital;

- *Wave 4:* sustainable development – a policy direction and set of programs which emerged in response to heightened environmental concerns in the 1990s following publication of the Brundtland Report (1987). Such strategies focus on enhancing the environmental sustainability of local economies;
- *Wave 5:* regeneration of disadvantaged areas and the mobilization of both local demand and existing resources within these communities.

In many communities, economic development is planned and implemented using a mix of strategies that draw from the various 'waves' in economic development, and on the ground it can be difficult to distinguish the implementation of one from the others. In addition, not all parts of the world have adopted the full set of strategies. For example, regeneration activities were highly visible and well funded in the UK under the Blair and Brown Labour Governments (1997–2010), but were largely unexplored in Australia, and used to a much more modest degree in the US and Canada. In broad terms, we continue to distinguish between those actions that look to encourage growth by bringing in a stimulus from outside the region – exogenous development – and those that look to enhance local growth dynamics – endogenous development.

There is an ongoing debate about the relative merits of exogenous versus endogenous development strategies, with many critical of the former because of a perception of high costs and modest long-term returns. This issue is discussed in greater depth later, but it is worth reflecting upon the fact that recent evidence continues to furnish mixed outcomes. Jarmon et al. (2012) examined both the economic outcomes and strategies employed by 304 economic development corporations in Texas. The authors concluded that the presence of such corporations was associated with a lower level of unemployment, and that those that focused on direct industrial development – including firm recruitment – were more likely to be successful. Broader strategies – which include human capital and lifestyle elements and are commonly associated with Waves 3, 4 and 5 – were rated less favorably and were associated with higher rates of unemployment. Osgood et al. (2012) reported that cities across the US are making greater use of industrial incentives. However, the authors also noted higher levels of competition, especially among places with few advantages relative to their peers. At a practical level, we must conclude that both exogenous and endogenous strategies have a place in economic development, and that their appropriateness will vary from one location to the next. While Jarmon et al. (2012) reported positive outcomes for exogenous development in Texas, it may be a special case as this state's economy has distinctive advantages and a growing industrial base.

Finally, it is important to acknowledge that while we need to make a conceptual distinction between endogenous and exogenous growth processes, in reality most places develop through a mix of the two, and measures intended to foster one often work to the benefit of the other. For example, some localities work to attract a particular type of business because it complements the already established industrial ecology of its community, adding greatly to local productive capacity and efficiency (Lowe 2014). Additionally, a region with highly attractive endogenous conditions will likely attract FDI because of the potential for higher returns on investment. Economic planning development efforts have many and complex impacts.

## 5.2 Industrial recruitment and retention

Not all economic growth comes about through the further development of existing enterprises. Growth in communities is commonly driven by the entry of a new business or industry into the region. This fact has long been recognized by analysts, with a number of influential models of economic development – including Solow's growth model – demonstrating growth at the regional level is driven by external processes, notably technological change. Bringing new businesses into a region or community is seen to have a number of benefits, including:

- The injection of much-needed capital into a city or town with a weak economy;
- Stronger integration with the global economy as new firms introduced into the community export into national or foreign markets;
- The injection of new skills as incoming firms bring in qualified staff to perform technical work and other key roles;
- Raising the profile of the community or region;
- Accelerating job growth as investment creates direct and indirect jobs.

Moving to a new site offers advantages to firms, including better access to markets and the labor force it needs, the opportunity to modernize production, expansion of production, increased productivity, and attracting of government subsidies (incentives).

The provision of subsidies to both recruit and retain businesses in a region or community has a very long history. The practice has been – and remains – widespread in the US (Tietz 1994; Loveridge 1996) but it is evident at one scale or another in most other developed economies and is badged under various labels including 'smokestack chasing,' business retention, selective assistance and corporate welfare. The practice of 'smokestack chasing' persists even when agreements between governments, or other arrangements, are put in place to rule out this activity.

Industrial recruitment takes a number of forms including cash handouts, the supply of land or buildings, reduced cost loans, customized worker training, tax breaks or subsidies for production costs. Some enterprises clearly have a corporate culture focused on such payments, and as Tietz (1994 p 101) observed more than 20 years ago 'the lure of industrial attraction, with its lottery-like huge jackpots and uncertain probabilities, continues to exert an enormous impact.'

In some parts of the world, including the US, industrial relocation firms collect and sell information on the subsidies made available by communities to firms seeking to relocate.

Industrial recruitment carries with it risks for communities and their governments:

- First, subsidies alone are only likely to influence the decisions of 'footloose' industries that are not necessarily tied to a particular region or community. They are likely to move to a new donor region once the current suite of subsidies expire. The community then needs to renew the subsidy or face the prospect of the firm leaving;

- Second, the provision of a relocation incentive to some businesses encourages other firms – including those already in place – to seek them also. Communities end up paying to retain a business that was likely to stay anyway;
- Third, providing assistance to businesses erodes the local government or state/province tax base, imposing additional costs on other tax payers. Subsidy-providing jurisdictions may find that they lose smaller businesses, as they are too small to attract a recruitment or retention subsidy themselves, but higher local taxes either make them uncompetitive or attracted to lower-tax communities nearby;
- Fourth, the 'footloose' industries attracted by subsidies are unlikely to become embedded in the local economy. That is, they are less likely to develop links with other businesses in the region, thereby limiting their contribution to local growth;
- Fifth, in many instances assistance packages simply do not deliver the anticipated outcomes, even when the provision of further financial support is dependent upon achieving specified targets with respect to job numbers or investment. Firms often miss out on payments because they cannot meet their contracted obligations, and while many companies are aware of this likelihood, they continue to seek retention or attraction payments:
  - In the US, the Governmental Accountability Standards Board (GASB) established a Tax Abatement Disclosure Statement in August 2015 that calls on state and local government agencies that provide tax relief to businesses to disclose agreements that reduce tax revenues. There is now an increased emphasis on reviewing such agreements and reporting on progress towards contracted targets – such as the number of jobs created, the value of investment, et cetera.
- Sixth, there is always a community or region willing to offer even greater incentives. Companies amenable to being influenced by the provision of incentives will demonstrate no loyalty to a host community. Subsidies may therefore offer only short-term benefits and come at a high cost to public budgets.

Others have noted incentives are relatively unimportant for re-locating firms, with the economic fundamentals – including the adequacy of infrastructure and the workforce – determining the choice of site (Jolley et al. 2015). Communities may therefore provide incentives that are unnecessary.

Despite the highly visible risks for communities, industrial recruitment remains an important feature of the landscape of local economic development, and a key consideration in the planning of communities and their development. Loveridge (1996) suggested these policies persist through a combination of political, economic and social drivers, arguing that governments continue to engage in industrial recruitment and attraction because:

- They have a *tradition* of such activities. Having established recruitment policies and programs for industry attraction, large and small governments alike find it difficult to develop an alternative approach. Many businesses actively seek out subsidies and elected officials and senior managers find it difficult to turn away these apparent opportunities. Many have little knowledge of other ways of doing business;

- *The expected value* of firm recruitment is high, communities believe the arrival of a new business will have substantial benefits;
- There is a *substantial political benefit* from firm recruitment activities. Even unsuccessful bids to lure new businesses demonstrate a commitment to growth;
- The *high discount rate* for most economic development strategies drives communities and their governments to seek short-term gains. The policy and political landscape changes rapidly and elected officials and practitioners alike need to demonstrate progress in the short term;
- Even *weak communities* can offer business incentives. Economic development activities take a considerable period to mature and require substantial resources. Poorer communities lack both the resources and the capacity to wait for growth, and business recruitment is seen to be quick and relatively inexpensive;
- Industrial recruitment can be used to *diversify* the community's economic structure. Communities seeking to establish a particular local industrial ecology may target individual businesses that complement their current set of firms;
- Industrial recruitment is accessible to all communities and localities, it does not call for specialist skills or abilities and can be pursued at any scale – from modest incentives to substantial payouts;
- Industrial recruitment may be *appropriate* in some instances, especially where existing facilities would otherwise go unused. Cities do not wish to be left with stranded assets and communities may recruit new enterprises where they will complement existing businesses, adding to the production process locally by taking the outputs of local firms or acting as an additional source of inputs;
- Some communities are already growing, and industrial recruitment gives them the chance to determine the type of economic structure that develops. Examples include small communities on the fringe of an expanding metropolitan area. In the absence of firm recruitment, they may experience substantial population growth, but few additional jobs.

Industrial recruitment and retention carries with it both risks and benefits. On the one hand, communities have to carry the cost of subsidies or incentives provided; on the other, they need to actively shape their futures. Academic commentators – and especially economists – have been highly critical of this pathway to growth, but economic development practitioners and planners cannot escape the reality that firm recruitment persists and is a prominent feature of the landscape they work within.

Firm recruitment is easily understood by nonexperts and helps garner political support for broader-scale economic development planning and action, both internally and externally. Warner and Zheng (2013) found additional justification for such incentives in the fact that communities providing incentives had a strong focus on the accountability of their expenditures, which suggests a sharply focused economic development strategy.

**TABLE 5.1**  Comparison of site selection factors ranked important or very important, US, 1986–2015

|  | 2015 | 2010 | 2005 | 2000 | 1995 | 1990 | 1986 |
|---|---|---|---|---|---|---|---|
| Availability of skilled labor | 92.9 | 85.9 | 87.2 | 87.7 | 87.9 | 87.1 | 84.8 |
| Availability of unskilled labor | 47.8 | 45.4 | 50.6 | 65.5 | 64.9 | 73.6 | 54.4 |
| Training programs | 68.7 | 56.7 | 59.6 | 57.2 | 58.6 | 49.6 | 50.9 |
| Labor costs | 80.8 | 91 | 87.9 | 91.6 | 94.2 | 92.1 | 96.6 |
| Low union profile | 66.3 | 75.4 | 77 | 79.7 | 82.8 | 78.7 | 79 |
| Right-to-work state | 67.7 | 67.9 | 69.7 | 72.9 | 77.8 | 71.3 | n/a |
| Highway accessibility | 88 | 97.3 | 91.4 | 95.9 | 93.6 | 92.3 | 91.3 |
| Railroad service | 32.4 | 36 | 28.9 | 29.8 | 28.7 | 32.2 | 25.8 |
| Access to major airport | 58.6 | 50 | 50.7 | 53.2 | 59.5 | 55.5 | 61 |
| Waterway or ocean port access | 24 | 21.9 | 20.2 | 21 | 20.7 | 16.2 | 15.3 |

*Source:* Crawford 2016.

The website areadevelopment.com provides insights into the priorities of firms seeking to establish new facilities, as well as their priorities in making decisions (Table 5.1).

The data in Table 5.1 present a clear picture of the most critical factors for US firms looking to either establish a new business or relocate. It is also evident that the key site selection factors have changed over time. Under current economic conditions the most important factors affecting where a firm relocates or establishes a new facility include:

- The availability of skilled labor;
- Highway accessibility;
- Labor costs.

Twenty years earlier the top three factors were the same, but in a different order, with labor costs ranked first, highway accessibility second, and access to skilled labor placed third. Since 1986 workforce skills – and the availability of training – has become more important, while, in contrast, access to unskilled labor, the presence of labor unions and overall employment costs have become less influential. Access to skilled labor is often seen to be a product of the quality of life a location offers, and is especially important in recruiting younger workers in technology and related industries.

The factors that influence the investment decisions of firms vary by industry and by the type of activity. The 2016 Area Development survey reported that to a growing degree large firms are looking to relocate headquarters in the downtown or central business districts of major cities. This trend reflects a desire to attract the best young talent, who are in turn drawn to urban lifestyles and opportunities. At an industry level, other patterns are evident, some of which operate at a global scale: in 2015 the accounting and services firm PwC released its *Aerospace*

*Manufacturing Attractiveness Rankings* (PwC 2015). The top ten countries for aerospace manufacturing were:

- the US;
- Canada;
- the UK;
- Singapore;
- Switzerland;
- Denmark;
- Hong Kong;
- the Netherlands;
- Ireland;
- Finland.

The use of this one industry as an example underscores the global scale at which many sectors operate, and the highly competitive nature of the race to secure investment. Within the US, the top ten states for the aerospace industry were Arizona, Florida, Georgia, Missouri, Indiana, Texas, Michigan, Ohio, Pennsylvania and Washington. The outcomes of such ranking exercises vary from industry to industry. A ranking of 'top states for doing business' generally in the US produced the following order: Georgia, South Carolina, Texas, Tennessee, Louisiana, Alabama, Florida, Indiana, North Carolina and Mississippi (Crawford 2016).

KPMG has produced a comparable index of competitiveness internationally (KPMG 2016) and concluded the ten countries with the lowest business costs for a broad portfolio of industries were Mexico, Canada, Netherlands, Italy, Australia, France, the UK, Germany, Japan and the US. They found the ten most competitive cities – by rank order – were Monterrey (Mexico), Mexico City, Montreal, Toronto, Vancouver, Manchester, Rotterdam, Amsterdam, Melbourne and Rome. Interestingly, fluctuations in the value of a nation's currency have a substantial impact on where they, and their cities, place in international rankings.

Data from the surveys of site selection consultants help in understanding the decisions firms make as they relocate or select a location for a new facility. Importantly, we can analyze which factors fall under the direct control of communities, which factors they can influence but not control, and which site selection considerations are beyond their scope of influence. First, we can see in Table 5.2 that communities and local governments have relatively few of the key decision influencers under their direct control. And while some of these factors are highly influential, others are only modestly important in shaping firm location. Second, places can exert an influence over a slightly larger set of factors, many of which are highly ranked in terms of the decisions businesses make. Localities, therefore, need to look to how they can get the best possible outcomes for their community by lobbying other agencies or tiers of government, by working in partnership with others or by running advocacy programs. Third, the largest group of considerations that shape where businesses invest falls outside the sphere of influence of communities and their governments. Factors such as energy availability and cost are decided at a much larger scale, while corporate tax rates are set by state and/or national governments. However, communities can take action where they have a

**TABLE 5.2**  Assessment of importance of site selection factors by capacity of localities to control or influence them, 2015

| Factors within local control | % Reporting as very important or important | Factors that can be influenced but not controlled locally | % Reporting as very important or important | Factors outside local control | % Reporting factor is very important or important |
|---|---|---|---|---|---|
| Highway accessibility | 88 | Availability of skilled labor | 92.9 | Labor costs | 80.8 |
| Available buildings | 83.7 | Quality of life | 87.6 | Corporate tax rate | 78.8 |
| State and local incentives | 75.8 | Occupancy or construction costs | 85.4 | Proximity to major markets | 76.3 |
| Tax exemptions | 74.7 | Training programs/colleges | 68.7 | Energy availability and costs | 75.3 |
| Expedited permitting | 74.2 | Water availability | 54.6 | Availability of long-term financing | 67.7 |
| Available land | 73.9 | Availability of advanced ICT services | 53.6 | Right to work state | 67.7 |
| | | Proximity to innovation centers | 48.4 | Low union profile | 66.3 |
| | | | | Inbound/outbound shipping costs | 64.6 |
| | | | | Proximity to suppliers | 64.3 |
| | | | | Accessibility to major airport | 58.6 |
| | | | | Raw material availability | 52.6 |
| | | | | Availability of unskilled labor | 47.8 |
| | | | | Railroad service | 32.4 |
| | | | | Waterway or ocean port access | 24 |

*Source*: Crawford 2016.

natural advantage – say, in access to major markets; they can actively promote and market their advantages to firms and should do so as part of their broader economic development efforts. They could also promote their relative advantage as a right-to-work state, or because of the proximity they offer to key suppliers in an industry or a major airport.

Importantly, the Area Development data on firm relocations – which is based on surveys of major corporations – found almost half of all respondents expected to establish new facilities within the next five years domestically, and one quarter in another nation. The demand for new sites for facilities is therefore an enormous opportunity, and actions that address the key needs of corporations will have an impact. The incentives offered by a city or community are only one factor in the decision to relocate, a point acknowledged by those working in the site location industry:

> Although incentives can add up into an attractive package, they can be a bit distracting from fully evaluating other key site selection factors. Most site consultants agree that incentives shouldn't be considered until there is a short list of three to five final potential locations. At this point these locations all look very similar in terms of key factors such as human capital, tax liability, real estate, infrastructure – it is at this juncture that incentives can help offset project and operating costs and make a significant impact in the final decision.
>
> (Crawford 2016)

How then should planners and economic developers respond? What strategies and actions are likely to result in the best possible outcomes for public sector expenditures? Five key strategies are central:

- First, communities need to incorporate firm recruitment into land use planning, corporate strategy and economic development strategy. They should identify the type and size of firms sought, and plan for their location and other needs so that the benefits can be maximized for their communities. Planning in this way reduces the shock of having to accommodate a firm unexpectedly recruited into the community;
- Second, communities need to benchmark themselves – what they offer incoming firms, or those seeking to be retained – relative to their peers. This evaluation ensures the community remains competitive, and it can be used to increase their competitiveness if weaknesses are identified;
- Third, planners and economic development practitioners need to network with industrial relocation consultants in order to develop their understanding of what firms seek, and to ensure they are abreast with current trends. The data from Area Development presented above makes it clear that firm relocation and plant establishment isn't solely focused on tax incentives:
  - Tax abatements or grants are an important part of the relocation equation, but they need to be matched by strategies that deliver the workforce businesses need, as well as the highway access and staff training that makes for a competitive business. Crawford (2016) noted that increasingly communities are funding training partnerships with incoming businesses to close any skill gaps in the local area.
- Fourth, communities can collaborate with their peers to make themselves a globally attractive investment location (Jacobs 2012). Cities can work together to create the conditions that attract investors in aggregate, while remaining competitive with respect to individual bids;

- Fifth, communities should use industrial recruitment strategically, and target industries and businesses that complement existing industries. Business recruitment can further complement other economic development strategies, such as cluster building or technology transfer strategies, and should be viewed as part of this broader whole.

## ▊ 5.3 Foreign direct investment

From the perspective of individual communities and cities, foreign direct investment (FDI) is simply a subset, or special set of conditions, associated with inward investment by already established enterprises. Commonly we think of FDI as linked to the establishment of large manufacturing facilities – such as the investment of Mercedes Benz in Alabama in the 1990s – but FDI can include many industries – including tourism and hospitality, the services sector, research and development (R&D), as well as agriculture.

Foreign direct investment is defined by the World Bank (2017) as

> the net inflows of investment to acquire a lasting management interest (10 per cent or more of voting stock) in an enterprise operating in an economy other than that of the investor. It is the sum of the equity capital, reinvestment of earnings, other long-term capital, and short-term capital as shown in the balance of payments.
>
> (World Bank 2017)

Businesses invest in other countries for a number of reasons, including to:

- Take advantage of lower labor costs, or access to raw materials which may be expensive to transport;
- Enter markets that are protected by tariff and/or nontariff barriers. The car industry in Australia, for example, was established by multinational firms investing in local subsidiaries in order to overcome very high tariffs. Much of Ireland's growth in the 1990s can be attributed to American investment in that nation as firms eager to enter the European market established plants in an environment that offered a highly educated, English-speaking workforce within the eurozone and with a lower taxation regime compared with other nations of the European Union;
- Find new buyers for their products as the business recognizes their products are competitive with those currently available in that market. Firms may also be encouraged to look oversees if they have saturated their home market. Some 20 years ago Mullins and Sutherland (1998) noted many high technology goods now have a minimum market size needed to support the development of new technologies that is greater than the largest national market. In these instances, global engagement is essential;
- Build the profile of the firm by entering new markets and establishing a presence globally;
- Respond to broader economic changes such as the introduction of a free trade agreement – or its suspension – or shifts in the relative taxation rates between nations;

- Gain low-cost, easy-to-access markets;
- Draw on labor pools that have skills or knowledge not found in their home base. This may be formal knowledge – such as technical capacities – or tacit knowledge, including insights into local market conditions and the cultural norms associated with doing business within an economy.

Foreign direct investment has become a more important part of the global economy over recent decades, and therefore of greater significance for communities everywhere. This growth has reflected advances in ICT that make it possible for head offices and their subsidiaries to communicate seamlessly. The removal or reduction of tariff barriers has been a second, highly influential factor, with many nations establishing free trade agreements, or taking advantage of broader economic liberalization under the General Agreement on Trade and Tariffs (GATT). Buoyant economic conditions in some developing economies – including the 'tiger economies' of China, South Korea, Thailand and others from the mid-1990s – encouraged firms to invest in new markets, starting a trend that has continued. The World Investment Report (UNCTAD 2015) noted that total FDI stood at just over $1 trillion in 2014, with China the largest single recipient ($129 billion), Hong Kong second at $103 billion and the US third at $92 billion; the UK was ranked fourth at $72 billion. Five of the top ten FDI recipient nations could be classified as developing economies, with the remainder already developed.

FDI is not wholly comparable with investment from a national firm as conditions may apply that shape the performance of a foreign investor. First, there may be regulations that affect the entry and operation of overseas investors and there may be limitations on the repatriation of profits or other payments. Overseas-based headquarters may also impose limitations on the operations of their international entity, for example, in reserving research and development functions for the head office, limiting access to markets or determining which market segments are pursued.

FDI is a valuable source of capital for the creation of productive facilities and employment and is therefore attractive to many communities and regions. In some industries it brings with it other benefits; for example, foreign investors in tourism and hospitality will market their new resorts and hotels in their home market, as well as the other markets in which they operate. Foreign investment in agricultural production helps break through tariff and other barriers as the investor's knowledge of home-market expectations and government regulatory structures increases market access. FDI may also attract further investment into the region as other firms seek to co-locate with that facility and as production expands beyond the capacity of the initial site.

### 5.3.1 FDI as a driver of local growth?

The use and attraction of FDI to propel growth at the local or community level has both advocates and detractors. It is an important question in planning for development, as awareness of both opportunities and shortfalls should shape strategy.

Many argue FDI is an important pathway to growth: injecting much-needed capital into businesses and the local economy; helping establish a presence in the global market; introducing high-level business expertise into the community; and assisting in the process of technology transfer (Borensztein et al. 1998). Li and Liu (2004) compared 84 nations and concluded FDI is a clear driver of growth, both through its direct impacts – construction employment, contribution to the local tax base, long-term employment, et cetera – but also via indirect influences, including improvements to the quality of the workforce, technology transfer and exposure to global markets. Others have been more reserved in their assessment of FDI and its impacts, noting that there are a range of practical challenges that can result in limited benefits for communities.

The OECD (2005) noted that governments have sought FDI as a mechanism for creating employment, but also generating spillovers that assist local businesses connect with local markets and become more globally competitive. However, in many instances the outcomes have been disappointing: with few productivity gains among firms within the region; the establishment of branch plants weakly connected to other parts of the regional economy; few supplier linkages; little innovation locally; and R&D activities firmly grounded in the home country (OECD 2005 p 21). Hayter and Han (1998) argued that FDI is especially limited in transferring technological capacity, with branch plants typically performing low-value, mass production activities, while high-value product, research, development and control remains headquartered in the place of origin. Schwartz et al. (2008) analyzed FDI in Puerto Rico and Israel and concluded that while such investments generated short-term employment, they did little to address the long-term difficulties within an economy. This conclusion replicates earlier findings in Canada (Britton 1980) where FDI was seen to negatively affect technological development. It also presents outcomes similar to Rugraff's (2010) analysis of the Czech automotive industry, which saw few linkages between foreign-owned firms and local businesses. Other research has noted the 'footloose' nature of FDI and the potential for relocation at a later date (Bilbao-Ubillos and Camino-Beldarrain 2008).

## BOX 5.1  BUILDING A BIOTECH INDUSTRY – FDI VERSUS LOCAL GROWTH

From the year 2000 both Singapore and South Korea sought to create dynamic biotechnology sectors. South Korea looked to develop from within its own nation, creating new government institutions (the Genetic Engineering Center and the Korea Research Institute for Bioscience and Biotechnology) while also providing tax breaks for local firms, establishing clusters and strengthening education. The Singaporean approach was based on FDI, and relied on attracting foreign firms by establishing offices in other nations, by providing tax incentives to globally significant pharmaceutical companies, and by recruiting foreign experts with specific skills.

Both strategies could report success, but while South Korea had more firms than Singapore and approximately 40 percent more employees in the biotech sector after five years, the output of the Singaporean biotech sector was four times larger than its Korean comparator. The biotechnology sector in Singapore is globally focused and engaged, whereas firms in South Korea tend to be 'characterized by low-tech and low-value-added elements.' (Lee et al. 2009)

There is clear evidence that FDI has fueled development in a number of nations, including Spain since the 1960s (Bajo-Rubio et al. 2010) and China since the 1980s (Hayter and Han 1998). Much of China's rapid economic growth since the late 1980s has been underpinned by FDI, with the nation adopting an 'open door' stance to such investment, while still exercising a relatively high degree of control (Hayter and Han 1998). Part of this regulation has included limiting the location of FDI, as well as requirements for joint ventures with local partners and oversight of labor markets. Some places have grown rapidly as a consequence of FDI, with Shenzen an archetypical case, with its population growing from 30,000 in 1977 to more than 2 million by 1992. Bajo-Rubio et al. (2010) present a similarly positive picture of FDI and regional economic growth in Spain, arguing that it contributed to productivity growth and technology transfer. Torau and Goss (2004) found that FDI resulted in higher rates of growth in manufacturing in the US over the period 1995 to 1999. Critically, FDI in other sectors did not make an equally positive contribution to economic development. Giblin and Ryan (2012) reported substantial knowledge spillovers associated with FDI in Galway, Ireland, resulting in the formation of industry clusters. Other research has shown that FDI can have *either* positive or negative impacts, and that the detail of FDI investment and its relationship with local industrial structures is important (Markusen and Venables 1999) and that the relationship changes over time (Barrios et al. 2005). Overall we can conclude that FDI has complex impacts, and in part its relative value to a community needs to be assessed against a number of measures (Box 5.1).

Halvorsen's (2012) analysis of FDI in the US led him to draw out the implications for localities:

- Large-scale FDI projects were less evident in more urbanized places, where the presence of existing firms within that industry appeared to discourage large-scale foreign investment;
- FDI projects are affected by distance. That is, foreign investment is more likely to come from neighboring nations;
- Rural localities were more likely to attract larger FDI projects, partly because of lower land costs;
- Communities with strong R&D activities appeared less reliant on FDI, partly because their university and research institutions supported local business growth. Other research, however, has noted that the presence of research institutions helps in attracting FDI in some advanced sectors (Pelegrin and Bolance 2008), while Huang et al. (2012) concluded that innovation spillovers from FDI only occur once the region has developed sufficient capacity within the knowledge economy.

The analysis above has clear lessons for planning and economic development at the local level. FDI can accelerate economic development, but it is better targeted at manufacturing industries and in sectors where the region or community has both the skills and related firms to generate spin-off benefits. Larger urban centers are better served by targeting smaller FDI projects, and placing greater emphasis on local, knowledge-led development. Rural communities with larger tracts of land will be more likely to offer larger FDI projects the conditions they require. In large measure this is a land use planning issue.

In all instances, localities need a strategy to ensure the spread of benefits from the presence of foreign investment, especially the diffusion of technological capacity and innovation.

### 5.3.2 Global production networks

Over the past 20 years the way we think about transnational business has changed, with key commentators (see, for example, Henderson et al. 2002; Yeung and Coe 2015) highlighting the important role of global production networks in the global economy.

Global production networks 'integrate firms (and parts of firms) into structures which blur traditional organizational boundaries – through diverse forms of equity and non-equity relationships – but also integrate national economies (or parts of national economies).' (Henderson et al. 2002 pp 445–446)

This concept highlights:

- The interrelationship between firms involved in product development, the production process and the marketing of a good or service, and how these are arranged at the local and global scales;
- Where corporate power sits within these networks and how the center of influence can change over time;
- The role of labor in creating value within the production network and how that value is transferred around the world;
- The part played by national and local institutions in shaping the behavior of firms participating in the network;
- Technology as a determinant of change within the network and a source of value adding and capture.

Global production networks are a significant part of world's economy and a pervasive influence in social and economic development. Yeung and Coe (2015) estimate that 40 percent of world trade consists of 'intermediate goods,' that is, the components, software, et cetera that are then assembled or transformed elsewhere for sale.

As Box 5.2 demonstrates, global production networks are complex, dynamic and look to take advantage of local assets and capacities – access to raw material, skilled labor, an innovative environment for technology development, et cetera – to maximize the competitiveness of their product and the value created for the business and its shareholders. Critically, many components may be sourced from more than one supplier – thereby reducing dependence on that firm – and product innovation is embedded into all parts of the production process.

Many high-technology production chains illustrate this new business environment, but similar practices are evident in more traditional industries. Inditex is the world's largest fashion group with more than 7,000 stores across the globe and a range of brands, including Zara, as well as Massimo Dutti. The business is located in the small town Artexio, in the relatively remote region of Galicia in north-west Spain. The business has a truly global reach in terms of its retailing but also in the development and production of fashion. New fashion is released on an ongoing cycle – every six weeks or so – with designers creating and selecting new fabrics that are produced in China and then flown – often on specially chartered fights – to Spain and Portugal to be made into garments. From there the finished products are distributed around the globe.

## BOX 5.2 GLOBAL PRODUCTION NETWORKS AS PART OF OUR DAILY LIVES – THE IPHONE

In practical terms we accept the reality of global production networks in our daily lives. For example, if we look at recent production of iPhones we see a very complex set of relationships creating different parts of the final handset.

- The accelerometer is produced by Bosch Sensortech, which is based in Germany, with locations in the US, South Korea, Japan and Taiwan;
- Audiochips come from Cirrus Logic which is based in the US, with locations in the UK, China, South Korea, Taiwan, Japan and Singapore;
- The battery is sourced from Samsung which is based in South Korea, with locations in 80 countries, or from Sunwoda Electronic located in China;
- The camera is produced by Qualcomm which is based in the US, with locations in Australia, Brazil, China, India, Indonesia, Japan, South Korea and more than a dozen locations through Europe and Latin America, or by Sony, which is located in Japan and with a presence in dozens of countries;
- The chips are produced by Qualcomm which is headquartered in San Diego and has sites globally;
- The compass comes from AKM Semiconductor, with locations in Japan, as well as in the US, France, England, China, South Korea and Taiwan;
- The glass screen comes from Corning out of the US, with plants and facilities in Australia, Belgium, Brazil, China, Denmark, France, Germany, Hong Kong, India, Israel, Italy, Japan, South Korea, Malaysia, Mexico, Philippines, Poland, Russia, Singapore, South Africa, Spain, Taiwan, the Netherlands, Turkey, the UK and the United Arab Emirates.

This is only a partial inventory of the components of an iPhone, with assembly undertaken by Foxconn and Pegatron, both of which are sited in Taiwan. We also need to acknowledge that the software is produced in California's Silicon Valley, which hosts the firm's headquarters.

Source: https://www.lifewire.com/where-is-the-iphone-made-1999503.

Global production networks are important for the growth of communities and the work of economic developers and planners. Cities and regions can engage in a process of 'strategic coupling' (Coe et al. 2004) to link their local growth aspirations to the identifiable needs of transnational production. Regions that don't participate in global production networks are effectively excluded from an important part of the global economy. In consequence, they may become invisible to key corporations making substantial investments in new facilities. Research has shown that regions and communities participating in global production networks benefit as technology and 'know-how' is diffused into the wider business community (Ernst 2002). This diffusion is essential, as global firms require their suppliers to improve their technical and managerial skills in order to meet their specific requirements. This provides an opportunity for the transfer of both explicit and tacit knowledge as personnel move and as supplier firms apply their new-found competencies to other products and markets.

Global production networks are without doubt a significant feature of the world and national economies. They represent a substantial challenge for planners and economic development practitioners working at the local scale, but strategies to consider include:

* Prioritizing participants in global production networks when recruiting firms;
* Working with other tiers of government and major corporations to identify what the opportunities may be to attract network members;
* Establishing a relationship with firms within these networks in order to attract them, or others within their network, at a later date.

## ■ 5.4  Assessing externally led growth

Investment attraction or firm recruitment strategies remain a core part of the economic development landscape in virtually all nations. They bring with them significant risks, including the potential for firms attracted to the region to move to other places once subsidies or other assistance is withdrawn, the failure of firms to achieve agreed targets with respect to employment or investment, and the potential to undermine government revenues. Conversely, they are an economic development strategy easily understood by outside observers and stakeholders – including political leaders – and represent an opportunity to achieve economic development gains within a short time frame, and without risking public sector capital in long-term projects.

In the contemporary era, exogenous development is best considered one part of a 'package' of measures. Communities seeking to develop are confronted by considerable uncertainty – what will the economy look like in ten years' time, which industries will grow and which ones decline – and evidence on the effectiveness and appropriateness of particular strategies may not be available. Economic development efforts that embrace a number of strategies and include inward investment as one part are more likely to succeed and will be better positioned to take advantage of opportunities as they arise. Indeed, many of the actions needed to deliver investment attraction – such as the zoning of land, the provision of transport infrastructure – also serve an endogenous growth agenda.

Both exogenous and endogenous development strategies are important at the scale of communities, cities and regions, and a focus on the needs of local businesses is critical in establishing priorities for action. Exogenous strategies – including firm recruitment – can assist less developed communities to grow quickly and deliver higher incomes, and greater job security, for workers. Targeted firm recruitment can also have benefits for other firms in the region, bringing complementary capacities with respect to the overall supply chain, and the skill sets of the workforce. Attracting the branch plants of transnational corporations may also be an essential step in ensuring a position in global supply chains – and potentially in the future global economy. FDI is one form of inward investment or firm recruitment, and should be recognized as involving more than simply the movement of mass production capacities to low-wage nations. Instead it includes a variety of sectors – some of which are emerging industries, others of which are long-established sectors – across primary, secondary and tertiary activities. Many high-value activities – such as R&D – may be attracted by inward investment measures, and firms making FDI decisions are likely to be motivated by a range of factors, of which labor and other production costs are only one consideration.

## 5.5 Conclusion

Many cities and regions in developed and developing economies have grown in response to an external stimulus, such as the demand for resources that has encouraged investment in major plants or the decision of a major corporation to base additional production capacity in a new market. This outward orientation remains important for economic development efforts at the global scale, and there are now many 'tools' and approaches used to bring in new investment. Foreign direct investment is an important subset of this suite of approaches, and for both FDI and investment from domestic sources, it is important to always acknowledge the accompanying risks. This includes the risk of investment brought into the region departing as quickly as it entered, and of few connections developing between the new firm and established businesses. But all growth pathways carry some form of risk, and the challenge for economic development professionals is to manage these risks effectively.

## *Key messages*

- Industrial recruitment remains prominent in economic development efforts in some parts of the world, with a resurgence in the US after the 2008 Great Recession;
- While industrial recruitment and retention strategies have been much criticized, they remain a key part of economic development strategies;
- To be effective, industrial recruitment needs to be integrated with land use planning and strategic planning;
- Access to skilled labor is increasingly shaping the location decisions of businesses, and community funding for training programs is one way of attracting businesses;
- Global production networks represent an opportunity for communities to improve their competitiveness in the global marketplace and upgrade their local or regional innovation system, thereby enhancing the competitiveness of local businesses;
- Foreign direct investment can play an important part in the development of cities and localities, but FDI strategies need to target particular industries and enterprises and include mechanisms to maximize benefits for the local region.

## Discussion questions

- This chapter has considered exogenous development strategies, the programs and actions that look to bring investment into the region in order to fast-track growth and build the productive capacity of a region or community. These investment attraction programs have been criticized by many – including academics and government officials – but they remain an important feature of the economic development landscape in most countries. As a class, develop a list of the ten key strengths or benefits of exogenous strategies and ten important deficits or failings.
- How would exogenous-focused development strategies be different in these three types of regions?
  - A manufacturing region specializing in metals production;
  - A coastal tourism center that relies on domestic and international visitors;
  - A state capital with strong government sector employment.

## References

Bajo-Rubio, O., Diaz-Mora, C. and Diaz-Roldan, C. 2010 Foreign direct investment and regional growth: an analysis of the Spanish case, *Regional Studies*, 44:3, pp 373–382.

Barrios, S., Görg, H. and Strobl, E. 2005 Foreign direct investment, competition and industrial development in the host country, *European Economic Review*, 49:7, pp 1761–1784.

Bilbao-Ubillos, J. and Camino-Beldarrain, V. 2008 Proximity matters? European Union enlargement and relocation of activities: the case of the Spanish automotive industry, *Economic Development Quarterly*, 22:2, pp 149–166.

Blakely, E. and Green Leigh, N. 2010 *Planning Local Economic Development: Theory and Practice*, Sage Publications, Thousand Oaks, CA.

Borensztein, E., DeGregorio, J. and Lee, J. 1998 How does foreign direct investment affect economic growth? *Journal of International Economics*, 45, pp 115–135.

Britton, J. 1980 Industrial dependence and technological underdevelopment: Canadian consequences of foreign direct investment, *Regional Studies*, 14:3, pp 181–199. DOI: 10.1080/09595238000185181.

Coe, N., Hess, M., Yeung, H., Dicken, P. and Henderson, J. 2004 Globalizing regional development: a global production networks perspective, *Transactions of the Institute of British Geographers*, 29:4, pp 468–484.

Crawford, M. 2016 Critical site selection factor #9: state and local incentives. Available at http://www.areadevelopment.com/taxesIncentives/q4-2016/state-local-incentives-critical-site-selection-factors.shtml, accessed January 10, 2017.

Ernst, D. 2002 Global production networks and the changing geography of innovation systems. Implications for developing countries, *Economics of Innovation and Technology*, 11:6, pp 497–523.

Giblin, M. and Ryan, P. 2012 Tight clusters or loose networks? The critical role of inward foreign direct investment in cluster creation, *Regional Studies*, 46:2, pp 245–258.

Halvorsen, T. 2012 Size, location and agglomeration of inward foreign direct investment (FDI) in the United States, *Regional Studies*, 46:5, pp 669–682.

Hayter, R. and Han, S. 1998 Reflections on China's open policy towards foreign direct investment, *Regional Studies*, 32:1, pp 1–16.

Henderson, J., Dicken, P., Hess, M., Coe, N. and Yeung, H. 2002 Global production networks and the analysis of economic development, *Review of International Political Economy*, 9:3, pp 436–464.

Huang, L., Liu, X. and Xu, L. 2012 Regional innovation and spillover effects of foreign direct investment in China: a threshold approach, *Regional Studies*, 46:5, pp 583–596.

Jacobs, J. 2012 Collaborative regionalism and foreign direct investment: the case of the Southeast automotive core and the "new domestics," *Economic Development Quarterly*, 26:3, pp 199–219.

Jarmon, C., Vanderleeuw, J., Pennington, M. and Sowers, T. 2012 The Role of Economic Development Corporations in Local Development: Evidence from Texas cities, *Economic Development Quarterly*, 26:2, pp 124–137.

Jolley, G., Lancaster, M. and Gao, J. 2015 Tax incentives and business climate: executive perceptions from incented and nonincented firms, *Economic Development Quarterly*, 29:2, pp 180–186.

KPMG 2016 Competitive alternatives, KPMG. Available at https://home.kpmg/ content/dam/kpmg/pdf/2016/03/competitive-alternatives-2016-full-report. pdf.

Lee, Y., Tee, Y. and Kim, D. 2009 Endogenous versus exogenous development: a comparative study of biotechnology industry cluster policies in South Korea and Singapore, *Environment and Planning C: Government and Policy*, 27, pp 612–631.

Li, X. and Liu, X. 2004 Foreign direct investment and economic growth: an increasingly endogenous relationship, *World Development*, 33:3, pp 393–407.

Loveridge, S. 1996 On the continuing popularity of industrial recruitment, *Economic Development Quarterly*, 10:2. DOI: https://doi. org/10.1177/089124249601000202.

Lowe, J. 2014 Beyond the deal: using industrial recruitment as a strategic tool for manufacturing development, *Economic Development Quarterly*, 28:4, pp 287–299.

Markusen, J. and Venables, A. 1999 Foreign direct investment as a catalyst for industrial development, *European Economic Review*, 43, pp 335–356.

Mullins, J. and Sutherland, D. 1998 New product development in rapidly changing markets: an exploratory study, *Journal of Product Innovation Management*, 15:3, pp 224–236. DOI: 10.1016/S0737–6782(97)00081–7.

OECD 2005 *Building Competitive Regions: Strategies and Governance*, OECD, Paris.

Osgood, J. Jr., Opp, S. and Bernotsky, R. 2012 Yesterday's gains versus today's realities: lessons from 10 years of economic development practice, *Economic Development Quarterly*, 26:4, pp 334–350.

Pelegrin, A. and Bolance, C. 2008 Regional foreign direct investment in manufacturing. Do agglomeration economies matter? *Regional Studies*, 42:4, pp 505–522.

PwC 2015 *Aerospace Manufacturing Attractiveness Rankings*, PwC, New York.

Rugraff, E. 2010 Strengths and weaknesses of the outward FDI paths of the Central European countries, *Post-Communist Economies*, 22:1, pp 1–17.

Schwartz, D., Pelzman, J. and Keren, M. 2008 The ineffectiveness of location incentive programs: evidence from Puerto Rico and Israel, *Economic Development Quarterly*, 22:2, pp 167–179.

Tietz, M. 1994 Changes in economic development theory and practice, *International Regional Science Review*, 16:1, pp 101–106.

Torau, M. and Goss, E. 2004 The effects of foreign capital on state economic growth, *Economic Development Quarterly*, 18:3, pp 255–268. DOI: 0.1177/0891242404265994.

United Nations Conference on Trade and Development (UNCTAD) *2015 World Investment Report*, United Nations, New York and Geneva.

Warner, M. and Zheng, L. 2013 Business incentive adoption in the recession, *Economic Development Quarterly*, 27:2, pp 90–101.

World Bank 2017 Available at https://tcdata360.worldbank.org/indicators/BX. KLT.DINV.WD.GD.ZS.

World Commission on Environment and Development 1987 (Brundtland Report) *Our Common Future*, Oxford University Press, Oxford.

Yeung, H. and Coe, N. 2015 Toward a dynamic theory of global production networks, *Economic Geography*, 91:1, pp 29–58.

# 6 Endogenous development: building the economy from the ground up

This chapter:

▶ Builds on the discussion in the earlier chapters, mapping out how our understanding of contemporary growth translates into action;

▶ Sets out the five basic approaches available to economic developers as they work to encourage the growth of existing firms within their region or community;

▶ Discusses commonly used programs and policies to encourage growth;

▶ Reviews the evidence on which endogenous development strategies are effective.

T HE PREVIOUS CHAPTER considered the advantages and disadvantages of bringing new businesses into a city, region or community in order to stimulate growth. The chapter also examined some of the ways new entrants can be brought into a local economy, via the provision of infrastructure, through tax abatements of cash subsidies or with the delivery of a workforce development scheme that ensures incoming firms have the labor force they need. The recruitment of new firms into a region is not the only mechanism for growth: local economies also prosper when the firms already present become more successful and employ additional staff. Part of that equation may include a rise in the number of new businesses established and the development of an entrepreneurial culture that elevates the number of 'startups,' while enhancing their success rate. This chapter considers the ways in which planners and economic development practitioners can ensure that firms within their community have every chance of success, with their development in turn adding to the prosperity of the city or region.

## ▪ 6.1 Encouraging endogenous development

Endogenous development strategies aim to encourage the growth and profitability of businesses already established locally while also encouraging new firm formation. There are potentially multiple strategies and programs that can be deployed to stimulate local business activities, and we can identify five fundamental approaches to encouraging endogenous development. Within each of these we can then nominate numerous strategies and actions potentially available to communities:

- The first approach is to make your community *a better place to do business*. This means taking steps to enhance the attractiveness of your town or community in order to make it a more profitable place for manufacturers, a better proposition for running a corporate headquarters, and the preferred location for retailing or managing a distribution network. In effect, these are *supply side measures* that address some of the issues that confront local businesses. Some of the ways communities can improve the productive capacity of their businesses include the building or upgrading of infrastructure, further developing the skills of the local labor force, streamlining development approvals or offering assistance through the provision of business advice.
- The second approach is to *find new markets* or opportunities for the goods and services already produced within the region, or able to be produced if markets could be found. Strategies informed by this perspective are *demand side measures* that work by boosting demand for the community's products.
- The third approach involves *the creation of institutions that work to encourage further economic growth* locally. This *institutional approach* has been discussed in earlier chapters and accepts that organizations such as professional associations, chambers of commerce, business networks, tourism associations and related organizations have a positive impact on the economic performance of a region or community.
- The fourth approach works to *encourage new firm success*. Small businesses employ the major portion of the workforce in most economies and each year every community or region witnesses the establishment of many new enterprises. This entrepreneurial approach recognizes that the overwhelming majority of new firms fail within five years, and strategies that can both increase the number of new businesses established and enhance their survival rate will deliver growth. The development of one or more of these enterprises into a major enterprise will deliver substantial growth.
- The fifth – *transformational approach* – to endogenous development combines elements of supply and demand side measures to find ways *to transform existing local products – goods and services – into higher-value goods*. Such change may call for the provision of new specific-purpose infrastructure, an assessment of likely demand, and perhaps most importantly, new knowledge. To take simple examples, a region or community that produces grains for global commodity markets can increase its returns through the transformation of that raw material into flour, beverages or other higher-value products. A wine-producing region could shift its focus from large-scale production to the delivery of bespoke experiences, for which individuals are willing to pay a premium. Alternatively, a region that has supported the automotive industry could transform its production facilities to support the plant needed to generate renewable energy.

## 6.1.1 Supply side strategies

There are a number of strategies cities, regions and communities can use to create a more productive environment, which assists the growth of existing businesses and is attractive to incoming firms. These actions can be grouped into a number of major themes:

- Land use planning:
  - Orienting land use planning for economic growth is one of the most basic ways cities can improve the productive potential of their landscape. Key actions include:
    - Ensuring an adequate supply of land is zoned for development, including industrial, commercial and residential development;
    - Offering flexibility in the range of lots available;
    - Planning to ensure good access to transport networks. The City of Weatherford in Texas, for instance, planned for, and built, access roads adjacent to the interstate highway in order to give developing firms rapid access to markets;
    - Developing industrial estates in anticipation of demand.
- Infrastructure provision:
  - Infrastructure is often central for boosting local growth. This includes transport networks, water supply, telecommunications, water treatment and related services;
  - A number of studies have shown the building of transport infrastructure has a positive impact on the growth of communities in the long term. However, costs are high. Telecommunications offers the prospect of uplift but at a much lower cost.
- Skills acquisition and training:
  - Offering tailored training to incoming firms or firms already within the region;
  - The provision of subsidies for workers seeking to increase their skills;
  - Assisting the movement of key workers into a region to facilitate the development of an industry;
  - Enhancing education within the region, through further development of local educational facilities and the possible tailoring of curriculum to better reflect the regional economy.

The provision of loans or other assistance to gain access to finance is a supply side measure employed in many nations. The US has used such instruments since Lyndon Johnson's War on Poverty, with the Economic Opportunity Loan scheme established in 1964 (Bates et al. 2011). Other schemes have included the Minority Enterprise Small Business Investment Company program created in 1970 and the Micro-Loan Programs generated in the 1980s. Despite their popularity, Bates et al. (2011) caution that many loan programs are ineffective as they are poorly targeted and relatively expensive, which suggests that effective policies and programs need to address both these challenges.

Venture capital – where an investor takes a share of an emerging business in the expectation of growth in the value of their stock – is one solution to the challenge of financing the growth of small enterprises. However, as Zhang (2007) observed, this form of finance is unevenly distributed even within the US, and certainly at the global scale. In the US a number of government programs have attempted to provide venture capital in communities and cities where none currently exist (Bates 2002). Similar initiatives are present in many parts of the world, though not on the scale evident in the venture capital market of Silicon Valley, the region most commonly associated with this form of finance. In the US, and some other nations, access to business capital is an issue of social justice, with minority business enterprises adversely affected by restricted access to finance (Bates and Robb 2013). Strategies that enhance the ability of small businesses to secure finance will result in more viable businesses that are more resilient to change and more likely to grow (Burgess and Coker 2001).

## 6.1.2 Demand side strategies

Shifts in global markets and production networks (Yeung and Coe 2015) can leave some communities stranded without easily identifiable markets for their established and potential products. This phenomenon can be evident at a number of scales, with communities within individual urban areas affected as well as whole cities. Restructuring can take place quickly or unfold relatively slowly, but in all instances communities and regions need to work to generate new demand for their products. To a substantial degree the marketing and branding strategies that will be discussed in Chapter 7 directly address this question. All regions need to create and sustain their own 'brand.' Brands are important for marketing the goods and services cities, regions and communities produce, but are also central in attracting investment.

## 6.1.3 Institutional strategies

Researchers have emphasized the importance of the creation of new organizations – institutions – as a grassroots strategy for bringing forward development. For example, Loukaitou-Sideris (2000) noted that the formation of merchants' associations in strip malls (shopping centers) in Los Angeles was key to encouraging revitalization. The associations brought businesses together to talk about common issues, identify solutions and develop suggestions about other businesses that could be attracted into the region. This is similar to San Diego's MIT Enterprise Forum noted in Chapter 2. Sutton (2010 p 364) concluded that African American business owners in the Fort Greene community of Brooklyn, New York created a new future for their neighborhood through the establishment of the Bogolan Merchants Association that served as 'an institutional voice for Fort Greene small businesses routinely excluded from the planning and development decision-making process.' The Association set out to 'build' its community and encourage creativity and entrepreneurship by helping existing businesses grow and attracting new firms into the region.

The examples provided above are typical of institution building around the globe. Governments, practitioners and planners have found one of the most effective ways to encourage development is to create a specific purpose organization dedicated to economic development. As discussed in Chapter 4, institutions are fundamental to economic growth, but they should not be considered abstract entities of theoretical significance only. Such organizations are frequently at the cutting edge of economic development planning and practice: mobilizing local resources, identifying needs and working with other communities and tiers of government to find solutions. They need to be tailored to meet local needs and cultures:

- Public–private partnerships are often identified as critical to the success of economic development efforts. Both business improvement districts (BIDs) and Main Street programs are examples of public–private partnerships at the community or locality level, and generate sizeable benefits;
- Special purpose agencies can be created within government to provide a focus for economic development planning, and better coordination both within governments and with the private sector;
- Research suggests such organizations perform better when they have both a clear mandate and a relatively narrow focus on economic development issues (Beer et al. 2003). Agencies may struggle to clearly articulate their priorities in places where agencies have a wider focus, potentially embracing issues such as social inclusion, or environmental protection;
- Institutional arrangements need to match the geography of the problem. Local solutions are often the best answer to community level challenges, but some issues are genuinely regional in character, and call for collaboration on a wider scale;
- The management of such bodies needs to be inclusive and reflect the broader community. Diversity in boards of management creates further opportunities to tap into new markets and better understand the range of economic opportunities on the horizon.

## 6.1.4 New firm development

Strategies focused on the development of new firms acknowledge that business formation is fundamental to the economies of many regions, and central to their prospects for growth (Lichtenstein and Lyons 2001; Derbyshire 2012). Henderson and Weiler (2010 p 23) argue that entrepreneurial development policies call for a fresh perspective on economic development, one that asks 'how well can a region foster entrepreneurs and grow them into successful drivers of regional growth?' There are two fundamental challenges for economic planning at the local or regional scale: encouraging new business startups, and ensuring their prosperity. The first challenge is substantial, with Botham and Graves (2011) concluding that the 'job creation problem' in the United Kingdom's less prosperous regions was a shortage of business startups. However, the formation of new firms is not the sole issue: many new enterprises do not survive more than five years, with estimates suggesting 55 percent of new firms in the UK and 50 percent in the US fail in the first five years (Headd et al. 2010). Importantly, new firms have higher rates of failure, but all enterprises are potentially at risk. The economic development task therefore has

**FIGURE 6.1**  New firm formation: from a pipeline to a funnel

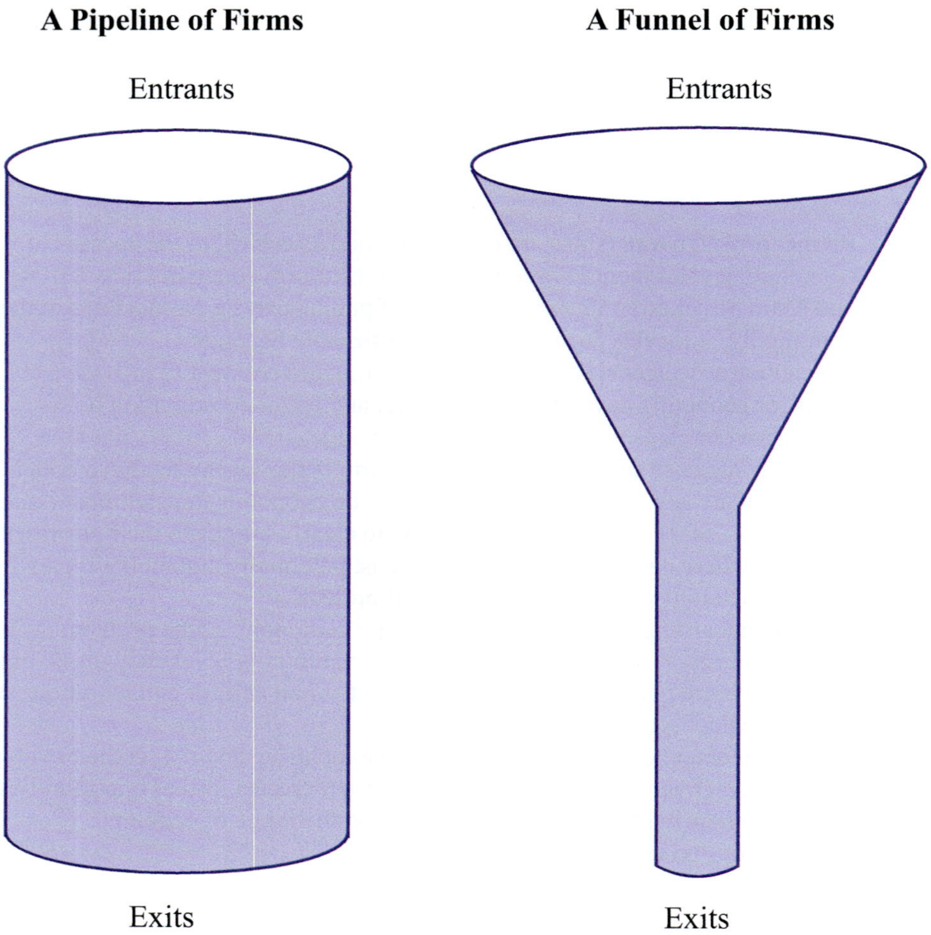

## A Pipeline of Firms                          A Funnel of Firms

Entrants                                      Entrants

Exits                                         Exits

two dimensions: first, places need to increase the number of new firms established in their community, and second, they must improve survival rates amongst new entrants in commercial and industrial activity. Conceptually, the challenge is to move from a 'pipeline' of active small businesses, to a 'funnel' with many new entrants, few exits and a rapidly increasing 'bulge' within the small business sector (Figure 6.1).

The establishment of new businesses is acknowledged as resulting in significant job creation, although Li et al. (2011) note that outcomes vary profoundly between urban and rural localities, and between different parts of the nation. Loveridge and Nizalov (2007) found regions with a higher proportion of smaller businesses had better rates of employment growth, although this impact was dependent on the mix of businesses in the region.

How can economic development planning and action ensure a higher percentage of firm startups survive? Some of the most common strategies are listed below in order of increasing complexity and expense, and include:

- The provision of management advice to either new entrants or those considering the creation of a new commercial enterprise;
- Information services – including seminars and general advice, but also the tailored gathering of information on market opportunities, planning requirements for the proposed new business, et cetera;
- Formal mentoring programs or 'economic gardening' initiatives;
- The formation of business 'clubs' where firms learn from each other, and ideally, new entrepreneurs are tutored by experienced business owners or managers;
- The establishment of business incubators or managed workspaces.

## 6.1.4.1  Management advice and information services

The provision of management advice to potential and existing businesses is central to economic development efforts at the local or community scale. Such roles are commonly reported in a range of nations, including the US, Australia, England and Northern Ireland (Beer et al. 2003), as well as in South Africa (Nel and McQuaid 2002) and continental Europe (Halkier and Danson 1998). Economic developers seek to encourage growth by helping individuals establish a new business and sustain that enterprise in the longer term. For Lichtenstein and Lyons (2001 p 5), 'The primary mission of enterprise development must be to develop entrepreneurs.' They recognize that knowledge – human capital – is a key ingredient for success in new business formation (Bates et al. 2011). Typically, advice covers a range of issues:

- Grant access;
- Taxation obligations;
- Market conditions and opportunities, including opportunities to promote their product;
- Professional associations;
- Training opportunities;
- Real estate availability.

Wu and Young (2003) reviewed the experience of a large-scale business advice service in the US and concluded that marketing was the greatest challenge for most small businesses, followed by record keeping and accounting, and then human resource management and ways to ensure cash liquidity. Advice in all these areas was likely to be beneficial, with some challenges emerging over time and then becoming less severe. Marketing and human resource management problems, however, appeared as a constant.

## 6.1.4.2  Mentoring and economic gardening

Mentoring programs provide startups with access to a senior business leader, in the expectation that the sharing of business advice and knowledge will assist the fledgling firm. Such programs can be highly effective, mirroring initiatives within large corporations and helping new entrepreneurs adjust to the challenges of small business management. Mentoring, however, is a relatively unstructured activity and is limited by the strength of the relationship between the individuals and the fact that knowledge exchange is unscripted and informal. Kutzhanova et al. (2009) reported that the Advantage Valley Enterprise Development Scheme in central Appalachia was successful because it used a mix of professional and peer coaches. They reported that through this mentoring scheme entrepreneurs learned how to learn, they acquired specific skills, and became more motivated to achieve success.

Economic gardening is an approach to encouraging the growth of small and medium-sized enterprises (SMEs) developed in Colorado (Gibbons 2010) that focuses on stimulating entrepreneurial activity as new businesses approach their potentially most productive phase. As Braun et al. (2014) note, the reference to 'gardening' seeks to draw out the distinctions between this place-based approach to growth and the more established strategy of 'hunting' down business opportunities.

Economic gardening is distinguished by its focus on firms that have progressed beyond the startup phase of business and have the potential for substantial growth – they are referred to as *gazelles*. This group of high-growth-potential firms is small – estimated at less than 5 percent of businesses in a region or community – and typically employ between 10 and 100 people (Braun et al. 2014). The aim of economic gardening is to expedite their growth through the provision of information about the markets they are working in; developing links with key sources of intellectual capital; building connections with other firms; and fostering product innovation. Ideally economic gardening programs result in the rapid growth of one or more of the participant firms into a very substantial entity employing hundreds or thousands of workers. Under the best-case scenario they would enable the development of a 'unicorn' – a technology firm with a market value in excess of US$1 billion.

Economic gardening programs are relatively common in the US and are also found in Japan and Australia. Braun et al. (2014) note that there is mixed evidence on the effectiveness of economic gardening programs because *gazelles* are rare and few programs are of sufficient size or maturity to allow evaluation. However, Braun et al.'s (2014) research found that an economic gardening program in Victoria, Australia was viewed favorably by both participants and external stakeholders.

## 6.1.4.3 Business clubs

In many cities and regions economic development planners and developers have established 'clubs' for local businesses that offer an opportunity to share experiences, learn from each other and develop joint initiatives. In many places, this role is not led by an economic development agency, but is associated with a local chamber of commerce or similar agency. Kearins (2002) found that an exporters club established in southern Adelaide, Australia stimulated export activity, enhanced profitability, improved knowledge of business opportunities and enhanced business management.

## 6.1.4.4 Business incubation

Business incubators gained widespread acceptance in the 1990s and typify the 'third wave' approaches discussed above. They are now an accepted part of the economic development landscape and can be found in most cities – and many rural communities – within developed (France, Sweden and Canada) and developing (e.g. Kerala, India) economies. Qian et al (2011) noted the number of business incubators in the US rose from 12 in 1980 to 1,100 in 2006. We also consider business accelerators, small business development centers, extension services and shared workspace arrangements as other forms of business incubation activities.

Conventionally, business incubators take the form of a building owned by a specialist agency that rents out work spaces – office accommodation, small manufacturing spaces, et cetera – to new businesses. The incubator is distinguished from other commercial space by the fact that the facility is managed by a small business specialist who is available to provide advice to the fledgling companies and assist them in establishing themselves in the marketplace. Commonly business incubators have time-limited tenancies (Allen 1988), with the expectation that firms will be successful after a fixed period and graduate to larger premises. Alternatively, they are likely to fail and their space in the incubator needs to be taken by another firm with better prospects. Business incubators can take a number of forms:

- Some business incubators have a specific focus on one industry sector – for example, startups in ICT, furniture manufacture or the life sciences. Some are developed as light manufacturing spaces, with attention given to fostering manufacturers rather than office-based work;
- Incubators can be publicly or privately owned, or they can be owned by a not-for-profit organization or a university (Campbell and Allen 1987). Qian et al. (2011) noted many are linked to a university;
- They may provide additional support services to startups, including business skills training, market briefings and assistance in gaining access to grants;
- Incubators can either charge rent or not, and there is a lively debate on this issue. Some contend that startups need a 'rent holiday' as they establish, while others argue that business ideas that are viable will have the capacity to pay rent at all stages. The discipline of market rents will ensure an efficient and profitable business model from inception;
- They may be formally linked to a university or other research institution. Some are developed to serve both the desire for growth within the community and to provide an opportunity for new graduates to test the commercial value of their ideas.

Business incubators operate on the assumption that new entrepreneurs will learn from the manager of the incubator, but also from each other. That one of the drivers of business success will be the unscheduled, informal discussions between new proprietors as they are confronted by problems and are offered solutions by their peers previously confronted by similar issues. Some sparsely populated regions have experimented with 'virtual incubators' but the evidence as to their success is unclear. Choi (2010) discussed how some religious and social groups serve as an informal incubator, with the Korean church in Los Angeles held up as an example of a religious group with a 'hands on' approach to assisting its members.

The majority of business incubators are developed to assist with job creation (Markley and McNamara 1995), with Qian et al. (2011) noting that the geography of business incubators in the US reflects a 'push' from communities seeking to stimulate growth, rather than an evident demand from businesses. Incubators have a record of success that remains in debate, with the sector in the US arguing that it created 27,000 startups in 2005, and 100,000 jobs. Bearse (1998), however, questions the validity of such claims in the absence of more reliable data. Wynarczyk and Raine (2005) argued that incubators have been effective in the UK and suggested they are most valuable when located close to a city center, contain a mix of businesses, offer a wide variety of supports to tenants, provide accommodation that ranges from very small spaces to relatively large properties, and are owned by a not-for-profit company.

Business accelerators are more limited than formal incubator programs. Business owners typically apply to join an accelerator program, either sponsored or for a fee, which gives the owner access to mentors, enhanced visibility to funding networks (angel investors and venture capital firms), and other services. Companies entering accelerators have usually passed the startup phase and can more accurately be thought of as young firms. Hathaway (2016) lists four distinguishing characteristics of accelerators:

- They use a cohort model – with groups of firms passing through the program together;
- Participation is for a fixed term;
- Mentorship is a driving resource;
- Graduation includes a demo day and/or pitch for funding.

Beyond the business support outcomes, which have not been widely studied, Hathaway concluded that the presence of accelerators help regions attract more seed and early-stage financing, as well as additional investors.

The Manufacturing Extension Partnership (MEP) program in the US is a special case of small business support. These programs, which have operations in all 50 states plus Puerto Rico, are funded primarily through the National Institute of Standards and Technology of the US Department of Commerce. They provide technical assistance, management guidance, and other services to small manufacturers. They have become especially important in helping startups through the processes of commercializing inventions. Additional materials on MEPs can be found on the textbook website (www.gpaled.com).

Small Business Development Centers (SBDC) are partially federally supported resource centers based at universities, community colleges and/or state economic development agencies to provide training and advice, and serve as liaisons between small businesses and financiers, including Small Business Administration-supported loan programs. Their roles include helping prospective entrepreneurs with business planning, import–export training and support, market research assistance, and disaster planning and recovery among other services at more than 900 service locations across the US and its territories. The trade association for SBDCs reports that between 2015 and 2016, more than 17,000 businesses were started by SBDC client entrepreneurs.[1] For many communities, the local/regional SBDC is *the* small business component of their economic development efforts.

Managed workspaces represent a less formal approach to fostering economic activity and represent a real estate solution to the challenges of encouraging growth (Green and Strange 1999). Typically, they provide flexible accommodation for businesses, without some of the restrictions associated with conventional office space – such as fixed-term leases. They differ from incubators in not providing overt management assistance and do not target startups. Managed workspaces have been popular in many parts of the UK, including Huddersfield in West Yorkshire (Wood and Taylor 2004) and London (Levy 2006). Co-working spaces represent the next step in this field, and are a rapidly growing real estate market trend through companies such as WeWork and Impact Hub. Statista estimates that in 2017 there were more than 4,000 co-working spaces in the US hosting almost 1.2 million workers, and there were over 15,000 such spaces in the global market.[2] This business model, which evolved from the executive suite short term office rental market, is both a form of on-demand space and a set of collaboration hubs that support innovation among small, especially technology-focused, businesses. The companies providing co-working spaces have created a private sector response to growing entrepreneurial demand that has emerged as a local economic development asset.

## BOX 6.1 MANAGED WORKSPACES AND VIRTUAL OFFICES, CITY OF HULL, ENGLAND

There are seven managed workspace centers spread across the City of Hull. Each center is different from the other, with a variance to suit your business needs. Managed by the council's economic development and regeneration service, the program provides ideal accommodation for all businesses, ranging from small startup businesses and businesses looking to expand. Hull City Council also works closely with a variety of partners – with factory estates as progression property offering larger units, with numerous sites across the city. Not only are all the centers unique, but the managed workspace centers are competitively priced and suitable for industrial and commercial use up to 7,400 square feet in size.

With easy in, easy out terms, the premises are offered on a monthly rolling contractual basis – ideal for those just starting up a business wanting to keep costs and expenditure as low as possible. Each center has a vast range of services and facilities at their disposal. All centers have meeting rooms, conference rooms, photocopying, laminating, binding and many more. All facilities are available at little or no extra cost. Each center has 24-hour access giving businesses the flexibility to meet their client's needs.

Source: City of Hull, 2015.

The challenge of supporting new businesses is complicated by the need to allow the market to work. Some business models are not sustainable and some business owners do not possess the qualities needed for long-term success. Additionally, lifestyle entrepreneurs measure success in different ways – they have limited desire for growth beyond being a 'mom-and-pop shop.'[3] Dedicating resources to these firms will not result in meaningful economic development. Entrepreneurial support programs typically have screening requirements, which can even include personality testing for business owners, to limit this risk.

## 6.1.5 Transformational strategies

Transformational strategies seek to reshape local economic dynamics, bringing together supply, demand and institutional processes to drive growth. In the contemporary era, transformational strategies commonly have a technology or technology application focus. Transformational strategies may challenge land use planning processes in new ways, as they seek to use the physical development of urban areas to achieve economic goals, or they may be implemented without significant consequence for how a city or region is planned and developed. However, in most instances they have considerable implications for land use planning, through the redevelopment of sites or the co-location of activities.

The OECD (2005) observed that three frequently applied strategies seek to transform local economies: first, programs to encourage technology development located in special-purpose land developments – such as technology parks or business parks; second, cluster policies; and third, efforts to link research and industry. The OECD (2005), however, cautions that these approaches are not suitable for all places. Measures to encourage the development of industry via innovation assume that regions have some degree of technological competence and that local businesses have a capacity for innovation (OECD 2005 p 9). This is not always the case in rural communities or disadvantaged regions, which in turn suggests those working in these areas need to consider alternative strategies.

## 6.1.5.1 Technology parks or business parks

Technology or science parks have a long-established tradition in economic development, and they are intended to provide a supportive environment for innovative firms. As the OECD (2005) acknowledges, their emergence has arisen out of a desire to emulate well-known success stories such as Route 128 (Boston) and Silicon Valley (Saxenian 1994). These initiatives assume that a sharing of space will, inevitably, result in the cross-fertilization of ideas and the spread of innovation. However, experience shows that they are not always successful. Dynamic technology hubs arise at particular times and in specific locations in response to unique factors, which may not easily be replicated by government policy or the efforts of a community. They work best when they build on existing technological strengths – in research, advanced manufacturing, et cetera – and even then they may require considerable public resources over an extended period. The OECD (2005) suggests that technology parks appear to have been most successful in three types of location:

- Old industrial regions already undergoing change, and seeking to reposition themselves;
- Urban economies offering economies of scale;
- Some new industrial regions where technology park formation has been able to take advantage of the dynamism of fast-growing companies.

## 6.1.5.2 Clusters

Much industry development in the 21st century continues to be based on Michael Porter's highly influential research on industry clusters (Porter 1990, 1994). He argued that in the contemporary era regions compete to provide the most conducive environment for growth and that the conditions found within cities, regions and communities generate *competitive advantage*, which sustains industries and businesses at both a national and global scale.

Porter's cluster concept emphasized three key drivers of growth: geographic proximity between firms; the presence of linkages across sectors within a region's economy; and the degree to which industries use related technologies and approaches (Ketels 2013). He further differentiated between businesses which were essentially local in approach (retailing), those that were concentrated in trade-exposed industries (manufacturing, financial services, et cetera), and natural resource-driven industries (coal mining, forestry).

For both analysis and policy development, Porter placed the greatest importance on traded industries as they are concentrated spatially, and unlike natural resource-driven industries, their location can be shaped by human action and planning. Parker and Beedell (2010) noted that many natural resource-based industries – including wine production, horse racing and horticulture – are sufficiently embedded within the traded-goods sector to benefit from the application of cluster thinking. Critically, the success of cluster initiatives should be judged on what happens in the traded sector, rather than across all parts of the economy (Ketels 2013). Porter (1990) argued that a region's competitiveness is based upon four key factors, which he presented as the four points of a diamond:

1. A supportive environment for firm strategy and rivalry;
2. Robust demand conditions for the goods and services produced by firms;
3. Related and supporting industries;
4. Sound conditions for production, including infrastructure and human capital (Figure 6.2).

Porter's work acknowledged that similar businesses will often co-locate – or cluster – to each other and that such agglomeration meant that individual firms were able to benefit from a skilled or specialized workforce, access to both common suppliers and markets (forward and backward linkages), shared infrastructure and the spillover of knowledge. The fact that businesses tend to agglomerate spatially has long been understood, with most commentators acknowledging the scholarship of Alfred Marshall in the 19th century (Marshall 1890). Porter (1990), however, gave new impetus to this set of ideas by drawing out and popularizing the implications for policy.

**FIGURE 6.2**   Adapted from Michael Porter's Diamond of Competitive Advantage

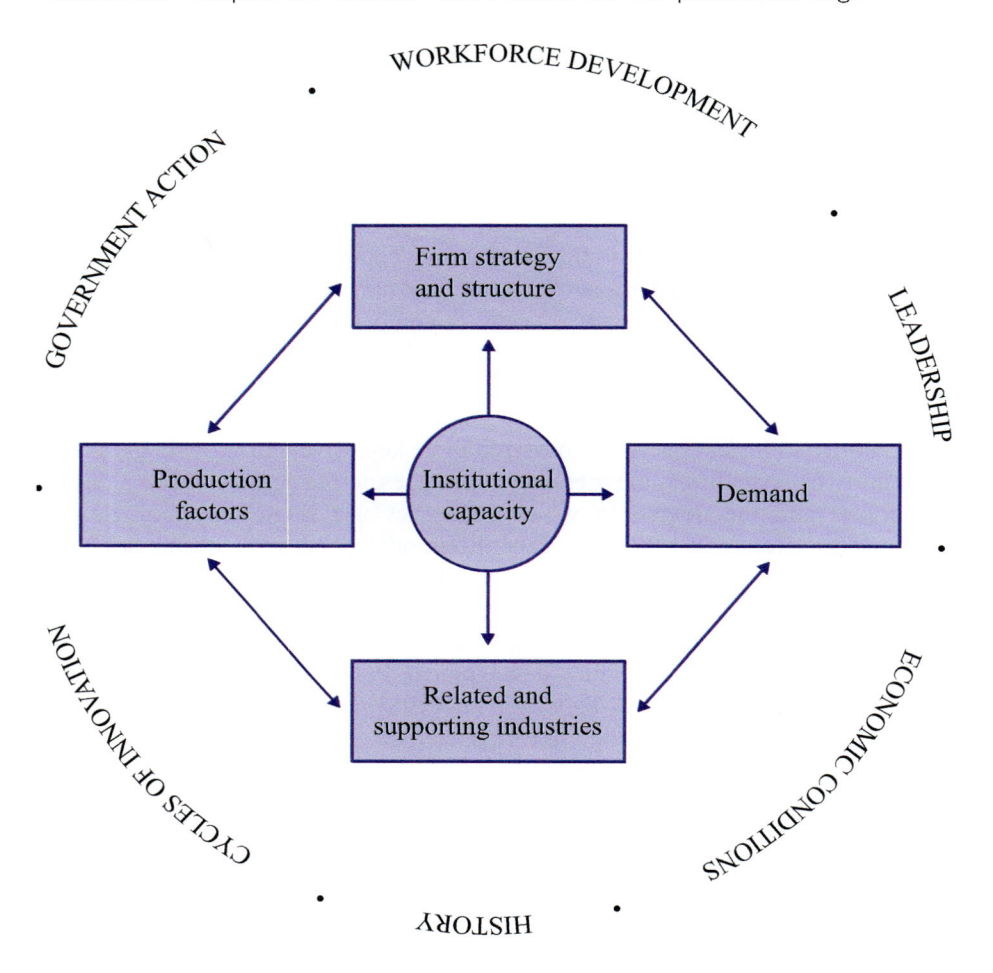

Perhaps most importantly, Porter's diamond suggests that governments can, and should, intervene at the local or regional scale to bring about growth. As the OECD (2005 p 33) noted:

> Advocates of clusters argue that they promote specialization in a complex array of related activities demanding diverse and highly market-oriented skills. Interest in clusters arises, therefore, because of the potential of innovative clusters to offer the benefits of specialization at the regional level with flexibility and resistance to adverse changes.

The OECD (2005) cited successful clusters including the original example of the 'Third Italy,' as well as Helsinki (public policy led) and the TAMA network cluster in Japan. Brackman and van Marrewijk (2013) noted a wide array of actions can be justified on the basis of 'cluster building,' including the further development of human resources in the region, investment in infrastructure, marketing and other activities to strengthen demand, and the provision of subsidies to firms that would complement existing enterprises. Ffowcs-Williams (2004) considered cluster development to be the 'focused lens' through which governments could tackle multiple economic challenges.

Some commentators have been critical of clusters, with Brackman and van Marrewijk (2013) suggesting many researchers are dismissive because of four major failings:

1. First, the definition of an industry cluster is not clear. While it is understood they are related firms proximate to each other, how close in structure and function do they need to be?
2. Second, what is the geographic scale of a cluster? Are they very local or are they regional or national in scale, and what is their relationship with global production chains?
3. Third, the concept of a cluster implies an immobility that may be illusory. Businesses within a cluster may simultaneously consolidate some operations in one location while sending other elements of their business elsewhere.
4. Fourth, cluster theory highlights the advantages of concentration, while overlooking the negative impacts of such agglomeration – including rising house prices, congestion, et cetera.

These criticisms need to be taken seriously. Parker and Beedell (2010) noted that there was a 'lack of definitional focus' in the discussion of clusters but felt that this breadth added to the value of the concept by not allowing it to become too narrowly focused. They also noted Rosenfeld's (1995 p 12) definition that clusters were a 'loose, geographically bounded agglomeration of similar, related firms that together are able to achieve synergy. Firms "self-select" into clusters based on their mutual interdependencies in order to increase economic activity and facilitate business transactions.'

Similarly, Hill and Brennan (2000) argued that clusters could be identified on four characteristics: a concentration of firms in the same industry; close buying and selling relationships between firms; shared technologies; and the use of specialist labor.

Despite limitations, cluster development has remained popular among policymakers. Ketels (2013) found:

- Naturally occurring clusters were positively identified with a range of desirable regional outcomes, including higher average wages, elevated employment growth, higher rates of new business startups and growth in patenting;
- Positive impacts on job creation don't come from within the tightly defined industries within the cluster, but instead employment growth takes place in related industries where the potential for further growth and development is considerable;
- Cluster policies are more appropriately considered to be strategies to enhance the competitiveness of clusters, not increase their size;

- There are mixed outcomes with respect to the performance of cluster programs, with a majority of studies finding 'positive returns for the participants and an expanded capacity for joint action. . . . [and] they find that companies active in cluster projects register better performance in subsequent years' (p 276);
- Cluster initiatives work best when the underlying cluster is already strong.

The OECD (2005 p 38) used their evaluations to recommend the following actions that are likely to generate cluster success:

- Initial regional economic analysis and benchmarking to understand the local economy;
- Engaging with the collective needs of institutions and employers;
- Delivering services that meet collective needs;
- Building a specialized workforce;
- Allocating resources to maximize impacts on the economy – e.g. funding for multi-firm projects;
- Stimulating innovation and entrepreneurship;
- Marketing and branding the region.

Importantly, most cluster programs focus on further developing existing strengths, with relatively few attempts – and even fewer successful attempts – at building clusters from the ground up (Ketels 2013).

Perhaps most critically, many of those who criticize the concept of industry clusters do so from a perspective where they are willing to accept growth in some places and no growth elsewhere. This viewpoint is not attractive if you are a location marked for little or no development. Cluster building makes sense in communities and cities committed to change, offering the prospect of more effective and integrated measures than would otherwise be the case. It is a policy suite that is not limited to one set of actions, and which seeks to build upon the strengths already evident in a city, region or community. But cluster building is not necessarily straightforward, or inexpensive. The OECD (2005) observed that cluster policies require relatively little capital investment when compared with many other programs such as the development of science parks, but instead they require substantial resources for personnel – largely to drive the processes of facilitation and build links between firms.

Ffowcs-Williams (2004) sees cluster development taking place in five phases and through 12 relatively simple steps (Box 6.2):

Other authors present variations on this method, but all approaches are broadly similar. Importantly, the formation of a cluster is predicated on the creation of 'soft infrastructure' for development, including local leadership. Ultimately it also requires the establishment of a dedicated entity to facilitate the cluster's ongoing success. In many respects the greatest practical challenge lies in sustaining the cluster and the cluster formation process, because while it is straightforward to generate initial interest, the ongoing demands on firms and governments can be considerable. Ffowcs-Williams (2004 p 32) summarized this challenge nicely in this comment that 'the reality is that many clusters are more dysfunctional clumps than pro-active,

## BOX 6.2  ESTABLISHING A CLUSTER

**Phase one – gather support** for the initiative.

**Step one – demonstrate the relevance** of the concept to key stakeholders.
**Step two – identify clusters** in the region, and then establish priorities among them. Clusters serving markets beyond the region are to be considered more important.

**Phase two – build the base.**

**Step three – analyze** the performance and drivers of the priority clusters.
**Step four – establish a leadership group** within the cluster to direct the process of change and improvement.

**Phase three – create momentum.**

**Step five – outline a vision** for a preferred future.
**Step six – identify the stepping stones** that need to be taken to achieve that vision.
**Step seven – develop an implementation agenda** that specifies short-term goals and actions.

**Phase four – extend the base.**

**Step eight – launch the cluster**, and use the associated publicity to recruit additional supporters.
**Step nine – formalize** the cluster by establishing an industry-supported organization to service the cluster's needs over time.

**Phase five – sustain the momentum.**

**Step ten – revise** and upgrade the strategic agenda.
**Step eleven – review** the process of cluster formation to date and identify areas for improvement.
**Step twelve – link the cluster** to other clusters locally and globally, as well as other economic development initiatives.

densely networked clusters.' Another long-term advocate for clusters explicitly acknowledges that clusters require a considerable commitment and the long-term efforts of a wide array of staff and external supporters. The Swedish Government, he notes, provides a minimum of ten years of support for the clusters they establish and support. In his words, 'it takes a whole village to make a cluster work' and 'this is patient, hard work . . . the hard yards, day in, day out.' (Genoff 2015)

Overall, the available evidence suggests clusters can be successful with respect to employment, investment and, most importantly, the ongoing competitiveness of the industry participants. Success appears limited to existing concentrations and there is little or no evidence to suggest that attempts to start new clusters have stimulated new jobs, firm startups or other investments.

### 6.1.5.3 Innovation and learning – linking research and business

Across the globe, Silicon Valley is an acknowledged leader in technological development, business success and innovation. Silicon Valley is also acknowledged as an important model of local or community economic development, and Stanford University's role in driving that growth is both well documented and understood. Other examples include Tucson, Arizona (Wright 2004) and the M4 motorway region in the UK (Cooke and Morgan 2000). A great deal has been written on the role of universities in driving regional or city growth, with Henderson and Weiler (2010) commenting that innovation and entrepreneurial policy are becoming an increasing focus of regional policy. The WK Kellogg Foundation (2002) was more reserved in its assessment of the interaction between universities and their local communities, noting that genuine partnership between the two is rarely achieved.

Cabalu et al. (2000) recognized universities as having three major impacts on regions:

- The income and employment generated locally through research and teaching;
- The enhancement of human capital through the education of graduates;
- The creation of wealth through the spillover effects to the public and private sectors as a consequence of research and development (R&D) activities.

Of these three, Cabalu et al. (2000) considered the second – skills formation – to be the most significant.

Universities and research institutions are seen to be pivotal because they are a source of innovation, which may either arise out of fundamental research or is jointly developed with industry. Universities in particular are an important source of skills for the workforce, adding greatly to local human capital. Similarly, technical colleges are 'acknowledged as a vital ingredient in regional technology and innovation strategies – retraining in the wake of technological change and ensuring a sufficient flow of technically proficient workers into the region to meet needs.' (OECD 2005 p 49)

Potentially there are benefits for regions associated with the development of new technologies, but at the same time it is important to acknowledge that universities working at the leading-edge of research will operate on a global scale. Such institutions commonly work in partnership with other institutions around the globe and in conjunction with multinational corporations with the budgets needed to support substantial research programs. It is therefore naïve to assume that the presence of a large and successful university will automatically engender technological innovation among local enterprises.

Places that aim to benefit from the research and development efforts of their universities need to acknowledge the strengths of each, and develop programs that facilitate commercialization. One example is the emergence of the life sciences sector in San Diego, California which was discussed in Chapter 2, and as Box 6.3 shows, success has been the product of commitments by the university, governments and businesses within the region:

## BOX 6.3 THE LIFE SCIENCES IN SAN DIEGO, CALIFORNIA

San Diego has emerged as a high technology center and hosts headquarters and research facilities for numerous biotechnology companies. Major biotechnology enterprises such as Neurocrine Biosciences and Nventa Biopharmaceuticals are headquartered in San Diego, while biotech and pharmaceutical companies, such as BD Biosciences, Biogen Idec, Merck, Pfizer, Élan, Genzyme, Celgene and Vertex, have offices or research facilities in San Diego. There are also several nonprofit biotechnology institutes, such as the Salk Institute for Biological Studies, the Scripps Research Institute and the Burnham Institute.

The presence of University of California, San Diego and other research institutions has fueled biotechnology growth. In June 2004, San Diego was ranked the top biotech cluster in the US by the Milken Institute and 8 percent of all biotechnology firms in the US are headquartered in San Diego.

The University of California San Diego (UCSD) is an active participant in encouraging innovation and new firm formation within the region. The SREDC works in partnership with the UCSD's CONNECT program that seeks to nurture high technology entrepreneurship and facilitate interaction with the university. The program is funded through the university's Extended Studies and Public Programs area. Other agencies that seek to foster the growth of high technology companies in the region include:

- BIOCOM San Diego – a regional association for biotechnology, medical device and bio-agriculture companies;
- Centers for Applied Competitive Technologies – one of 12 state-funded advanced technology centers designed to help manufacturers modernize their manufacturing and production technologies;
- San Diego MIT Forum – events and workshops to address business challenges facing San Diego entrepreneurs;
- EvoNexus – technology incubator and hub;
- San Diego Software Industry Council – which fosters networking and communications between its members.

Wu (2005) attributed much of San Diego's success to academics, local business and political interests coming together to create a productive environment. The University of California San Diego and its CONNECT program is seen as central to this growth, though the Scripps Institute and the Salk Institute are also important. Walcott (2002) argued that San Diego's growth as a bioscience center is a function of outstanding research at UCSD and the links between that institution's own spin-off companies and other firms working in the life sciences.

## 6.1.5.4 Smart specialization

Smart specialization has been discussed in some depth in Chapter 4, but it is important to reflect upon its implementation. The OECD (2013 p 11) notes that

> What distinguishes smart specialization from traditional industrial and innovation policies is mainly the process defined as 'entrepreneurial discovery' – an interactive process in which market forces and the private sector are

> discovering and producing information about new activities and the government assesses the outcomes and empowers those actors most capable of realizing the potential . . . Hence, smart specialization strategies are much more bottom-up than traditional industrial policies . . . the focus is on the 'enabling knowledge based assets'. . . . This more upstream approach gives more of a margin for the market to determine and lead on downstream choices.

A focus on activities rather than industries is critical to the way smart specialization strategies are put into effect. Whereas many conventional economic development strategies, including land use planning, focus on the needs of individual employment sectors, smart specialization strategies provide support that ranges across individual industries and businesses. They also encourage 'strategic diversification,' with localities encouraged to think about the ways in which new technologies can help broaden their economic base. In this sense, policies are intended to help entrepreneurs explore the possibilities arising out of innovation, rather than support individual projects or investments. Smart specialization focuses on the role of local government in facilitating the take-up of new technologies, rather than supporting the development of individual businesses. The OCED (2013) emphasizes the importance of regional profiling in smart specialization strategies, noting that the technologies to be explored for further commercialization should match the actual and potential comparative advantage of each region or community.

Smart specialization has been accepted in many parts of Europe, and has been adopted as a major platform for regional and city development by the European Union (EU), and in parts of other nations such as Australia. The European Union Cohesion Policy for 2014–2020 firmly placed smart specialization at the center of regional and city development, linking national research and innovation strategies to the EU's goal of becoming a 'smart, sustainable and inclusive economy.' Specific goals attached to this strategy include:

- Making innovation a focus for all regions;
- Focusing investment at the local scale;
- Improving the innovation process;
- Improving governance – that is, public sector processes – to include stakeholders;
- Using place-based strategies to transform local and regional economies;
- Making regions more visible to international investors;
- Improving international and external connections;
- Streamlining the development planning process;
- Accumulating a critical mass of resources in innovation;
- Promoting knowledge spillover and technological diversification (European Commission 2014b).

The way in which smart specialization is presented by the EU suggests an aggregation of many of the themes covered in this chapter: the focus on innovation and new firm formation, achieving economies of scale in economic development, attracting foreign investment and working more effectively with stakeholders.

In many respects, smart specialization is seen as a complement to, or a refinement of, already established economic development strategies. Industry clusters, for example, are seen to be central to smart specialization strategies within Europe (European Commission 2013). Universities and research organizations are also considered fundamental to the EU's approach to smart specialization (European Commission 2014a and b). For the EU, one of the key innovations within smart specialization is the greater focus on 'entrepreneurial actors' – i.e. business leaders – when compared with previous policies that were largely focused on governments and infrastructure. They bring businesses rather than public policymakers into the center of economic development planning and implementation, and they seek to encourage innovation by avoiding the 'valley of death' that often confronts new technologies as they move from invention in a university or research facility to market commercialization (European Commission 2013).

In conclusion, smart specialization strategies can be thought of as a way of encouraging ongoing technological innovation in regions, cities and communities. They acknowledge that many technologies are transferrable from one industry to the next, and mechanisms are needed to both bring forward innovations and encourage businesses in a range of industries to test their value. Regional profiling simply ensures that limited resources are concentrated in the areas most likely to generate a positive outcome, and the role of public sector agencies – at the national, state or city scale – is to facilitate this process.

##  6.2 Conclusion

In many respects encouraging the growth of firms already within the city or region has emerged as the 'new orthodoxy' in the practice of economic development globally. Strategies to develop clusters, operate business incubators, encourage the formation of supply chain networks, diffuse technology into new sectors and provide work spaces that enable new firm formation have proliferated over the past two decades. This activity reflects both the level of documented achievement for these programs and community interest in measures to assist local businesses, and the task of economic development practitioners is to select the right mix of programs for their city, region or community.

## *Key messages*

- Both exogenous and endogenous development strategies have a place in economic development strategies, and that the appropriateness of each will vary from one location to the next;
- Planning and building business incubators and managed work places improves the rate of new firm formation and survival, and encourages a more entrepreneurial culture;
- Clusters take advantage of the agglomeration economies by creating an environment that fosters ongoing innovation in both business processes and technological advancement. Specialist infrastructure, R&D and labor markets are central to cluster formation and policies;
- Clusters have relatively low capital costs, but high recurrent costs and may impose considerable burdens – time and money – on participating enterprises;

- The processes for establishing formal clusters are relatively straightforward and well understood;
- The rise of the knowledge economy has emphasized the importance of universities in local economies. While the development and transfer of new technologies is important, the development of a skilled and educated workforce is the most important contribution most universities make to their region;

## Discussion questions

Endogenous development strategies often include programming that provides direct assistance to individual businesses to promote sales and employment growth. This chapter has introduced several of these programs including industry cluster development, business clubs, business incubation, mentoring and economic gardening, as well as technology parks and smart specialization.

As a class, identify three types of programs you would choose to implement if you were asked to take responsibility for the development of your region. You need to:

- Review and agree on the three programs;
- Identify which types of firms (size, industry sector) will be targeted;
- Determine how the three programs would be integrated into a singly coherent strategy.

## Notes

1 See https://americassbdc.org/about-us/economic-impact/.
2 See www.statista.com.
3 Mom-and-pop shops can be important for quality of life by providing the community with unique options in retail and services.

## References

Allen, D. 1988 Business incubator life cycles, research and practice, *Economic Development Quarterly*, 2:1, pp 19–29.

Bates, T. 2002 Government as venture capital catalyst: pitfalls and promising approaches, *Economic Development Quarterly*, 16:1, pp 49–59.

Bates, T., Lofstrom, M. and Servon, L. 2011 Why have lending programs targeting disadvantaged small business borrowers achieved so little success in the United States? *Economic Development Quarterly*, 25:3, pp 255–266.

Bates, T. and Robb, A. 2013 Greater access to capital is needed to unleash the local economic development potential of minority-owned businesses, *Economic Development Quarterly*, 27:3, pp 250–259.

Bearse, P. 1998 A question of evaluation: NBIA's impact assessment of business incubators, *Economic Development Quarterly*, 112:4, pp 322–333.

Beer, A., Haughton, G. and Maude, A. 2003 *Developing Locally*, Policy Press, Bristol.

Botham, R. and Graves, A. 2011 Regional variations in new firm job creation: the contribution of high growth start-ups, *Local Economy*, 26:2, pp 95–107.

Brackman, S. and van Marrewijk, C. 2013 Reflections on cluster policies, *Cambridge Journal of Regions, Economy and Society*, 6, pp 217–231.

Braun, P., Harman, J. and Paton, F. 2014 Economic gardening: capacity building for stronger regions, *Journal of Economic and Social Policy*, 16:1, Article 8.

Burgess, R. and Coker, P. 2001 How to help regions help themselves . . . the capital regional agribusiness fund, *Sustaining Regions*, 1:1, pp 43–47.

Cabalu, H., Kenyon, P. and Koshy, P. 2000 *Of Dollars and Cents: Valuing the Economic Contribution of Universities to the Australian Economy*, BHERT, Melbourne.

Campbell, C. and Allen, D. 1987 The small business incubator industry: micro-level economic development, *Economic Development Quarterly*, 1:2, pp 178–191.

Choi, H. 2010 Religious institutions and ethnic entrepreneurship: the Korean ethnic church as a small business incubator, *Economic Development Quarterly*, 24:4, pp 372–383.

City of Hull 2015 Managed workspaces and virtual offices. Available at http://www.hullcc.gov.uk/pls/portal/url/page/HULL_MEANS_BUSINESS/HMB_BUSINESS/HMB_PREMISES/HMB_MAN_WORK/, accessed April 24, 2015.

Cooke, P. and Morgan, K. 2000 *The Associational Economy*, Oxford University Press, Oxford.

Derbyshire, J. 2012 High-growth firms: a new policy paradigm or a need for caution? *Local Economy*, 27:4, pp 326–328.

European Commission 2013 *The Role of Clusters in Smart Specialisation Strategies*, Report.

European Commission 2014a *The Role of Universities and Research Organisations as Drivers for Smart Specialisation at Regional Level*, Report.

European Commission 2014b *National/Regional Innovation Strategies for Smart Specialisation, Cohesion Policy 2014–2020*, Fact Sheet.

Ffowcs-Williams, I. 2004 Cluster development: red lights and green lights, *Sustaining Regions*, 4:2, pp 24–32.

Genoff, R. 2015 Presentation to the City of Playford, Unpublished, April 10, Adelaide.

Gibbons, C. 2010 Economic gardening, *Economic Development Journal*, 9:3, p 5.

Green, H. and Strange, A. 1999 Managed workspace: do tenants stay too long? *Local Economy*, November.

Halkier, H. and Danson, M. 1998 Regional development agencies in Western Europe: a survey of key characteristics and trends. In Halkier, H., Danson, M. and Damborg, M. *Regional Development Agencies in Europe*, Jessica Kingsley/Regional Studies Association, London.

Hathaway, I. 2016 *Accelerating Growth: Startup Accelerator Programs in the United States.* The Brookings Institution, Washington, DC. Available at https://www.brookings.edu/research/accelerating-growth-startup-accelerator-programs-in-the-united-states/.

Headd, B., Nucii, A. and Boden, R. 2010 What matters more: business exit rates or business survival rates? US Census Bureau, Business Dynamics Statistics.

Available at https://www.census.gov/ces/pdf/BDS_StatBrief4_Exit_Survival.pdf, accessed April 24, 2015.

Henderson, J. and Weiler, S. 2010 Entrepreneurs and job growth: probing the boundaries of time and space, *Economic Development Quarterly*, 24:1, pp 23–32.

Hill, E. and Brennan, J. 2000 A methodology for identifying the drivers of regional clusters, *Economic Development Quarterly*, 14:1, pp 65–96.

Kearins, B. 2002 Exporting locally: a strategy for regional small business growth, *Sustaining Regions*, 2:1, pp 17–28.

Ketels, C. 2013 Recent research on competitiveness and clusters: what are the implications for regional policy? *Cambridge Journal of Regions, Economy and Society*, 6, pp 269–284.

Kutzhanova, N., Lyons, T. and Lichtenstein, G. 2009 Skill-based development of entrepreneurs and the role of personal and peer group coaching in enterprise development, *Economic Development Quarterly*, 23:3, pp 193–210.

Levy, D. 2006 Building a better future for generations in Barking and Dagenham, *Local Economy*, 21:3, pp 333–338.

Li, H., Cheng, S. and Haynes, K. 2011 The employment effects of new business formation: a regional perspective, *Economic Development Quarterly*, 25:3, pp 282–292.

Lichtenstein, G. and Lyons, T. 2001 The entrepreneurial development system: transforming business talent and community economies, *Economic Development Quarterly*, 15:1, pp 3–20.

Loukaitou-Sideris, A. 2000 Revisiting inner-city strips: a framework for community and economic development, *Economic Development Quarterly*, 14:2, pp 165–181.

Loveridge, S. and Nizalov, D. 2007 Operationalizing the entrepreneurial pipeline theory: an empirical assessment of the optimal size distribution of local firms, *Economic Development Quarterly*, 21:3, pp 244–262.

Markley, D. and McNamara, K. 1995 Economic and fiscal impacts of a business incubator, research and opinion, *Economic Development Quarterly*, 9:3, pp 273–278.

Marshall, A. 1890 *Principles of Economics*. 8th edition, 1920. Macmillan, London.

Nel, E. and McQuaid, R. 2002 The evolution of local economic development in South Africa: the case of Stutterheim and social capital, research & practice, *Economic Development Quarterly*, 16:1, pp 60–74.

OECD 2005 *Building Competitive Regions: Strategies and Governance*, OECD, Paris.

OECD 2013 *Innovation-Driven Growth in Regions: The Role of Smart Specialization*, OECD, Paris.

Parker, G. and Beedell, J. 2010 Land based economic clusters and their sustainability: the case of the horse racing industry, *Local Economy*, 25, pp 220–233.

Porter, M. 1990 The competitive advantage of nations, *Harvard Business Review*, March–April, pp 73–91.

Porter, M. 1994 The role of location in competition, *International Journal of the Economics of Business*, 1:1, pp 35–40.

Qian, H., Haynes, K. and Riggle, J. 2011 Incubation push or business pull? Investigating the geography of US business incubators, *Economic Development Quarterly*, 25:1, pp 79–90.

Rosenfeld, S. 1995 *Industrial Strength Strategies: Business Clusters and Public Policy*, Aspen Institute, Washington, DC.

Saxenian, A. 1994 *Regional Advantage*, Harvard University Press, Cambridge, MA.

Sutton, S. 2010 Rethinking commercial revitalization: a neighborhood small business perspective, *Economic Development Quarterly*, 24:4, pp 352–371.

Walcott, S. 2002 Analyzing an innovative environment: San Diego as a bioscience beachhead, *Economic Development Quarterly*, 16:2, pp 99–114.

WK Kellogg Foundation 2002 *Home Grown: Community-University Partnerships Can Create the Workforce of the Future*. Available at http://www.wkkf.org, accessed May 12, 2015.

Wood, P. and Taylor, C. 2004 Big ideas for a small town: the Huddersfield creative town initiative, *Local Economy*, 19:4, pp 380–395.

Wright, B. 2004 *The University of Arizona Science and Technology Park: A Case Study in the Creation, Development and Growth of a University Research Park*. Paper presented to the Western Regional Science Association Annual Conference, Maui, February 25, Unpublished.

Wu, C. and Young, A. 2003 Factors resulting in successes and failures for small businesses in the Small Business Institute Program at Syracuse University, *Economic Development Quarterly*, 17:2, pp 205–211.

Wu, W. 2005 *Dynamic Cities and Creative Clusters*, World Bank Policy Research Working Paper 3509.

Wynarczyk, P. and Raine, A. 2005 The performance of business incubators and their potential development in the north-east region of England, *Local Economy*, 20:2, pp 205–220.

Yeung, H. and Coe, N. 2015 Toward a dynamic theory of global production networks, *Economic Geography*, 91:1, pp 29–58.

Zhang, J. 2007 Access to venture capital and the performance of venture-backed start-ups in Silicon Valley, *Economic Development Quarterly*, 21:2, pp 124–147.

# 7     Amenity, branding and economic growth

This chapter:

▶ Examines the argument that amenity increasingly drives local economic development;

▶ Introduces the concept of the 'creative class' and its capacity to drive growth in urban and rural areas;

▶ Considers how the 'attractiveness' of places has been discussed and understood in both popular debate and in the research literature;

▶ Discusses the advantages and disadvantages of urban regeneration strategies;

▶ Looks at the capacity to develop smaller-scale regeneration strategies, and notes the importance of clear goals and targets;

▶ Considers place branding and place marketing, and considers how cities, regions and communities can attract tourists, residents and business;

▶ Considers the Main Street program and is contribution to retailing in many communities;

▶ Examines the differences between the marketing of consumer goods and the promotion of places and discusses the need to include local stake-holders in the development and implementation of these strategies.

OVER THE LAST 30 years economic developers, governments and research-ers have come to realize that the growth of cities, regions and communities is increasingly driven by their attractiveness – the amenities they offer, the quality of their natural environments, and their cultural and historical legacies. Where once analysis and policy focused solely on how to make localities more attractive – through the provision of infrastructure or subsidies – for investment that would result in direct employment gains, economic development professionals now acknowledge that people do not necessarily move to jobs; instead employment opportunities follow people.

A focus on amenity makes us consider how places promote their lifestyle, natural beauty, human-created or environmental assets. The 'branding' or marketing of places raises questions about the degree to which it is possible to follow the strategies used in promoting other products, or whether the very nature of places demands a different set of techniques. It also pushes us to consider, who is the target market, and what sort of strategy will be effective for each segment? Places are often 'multisold' as 'products to different groups of consumers for different purposes.' (Rainisto 2004 p 38) At least three types of 'consumer' are identifiable. First, promoting a city, region or community's amenity is one way of bringing in businesses who are attracted by the lifestyle advantages offered to key staff and the workforce more broadly. Some industries and businesses in all sectors are more likely to be relatively 'footloose' in terms of their locational needs, and therefore more able to choose an attractive location. Second, place branding can be an effective strategy for drawing in tourists, raising demand and effectively increasing earnings from outside the region. Third, many places use their natural beauty or the opportunities they provide for outdoor sports to attract highly qualified individuals, knowing that they in turn will either generate economic opportunities through business startups or lure businesses seeking to tap into their skills. All three target audiences are considered here, as branding strategies focused on one segment also raise awareness in the other two, with these spillover effects creating a positive feedback loop that drives growth.

## ■ 7.1 Amenity and the creative class

Approximately 20 years ago a great deal of attention was paid to the question of amenity and its impact on the growth of cities, towns and regions. This focus was kicked off by the work of Richard Florida, and his book, *The Rise of the Creative Class* (2002), which was followed by *The Flight of the Creative Class* in 2005. Florida used the analysis of growth rates for cities in the US to argue that metropolitan areas with concentrations of high technology workers, gays and 'bohemians' working in creative industries experienced higher rates of growth than comparable centers dominated by traditional blue- or white-collar employees. He referred to these types of workers as the 'creative class,' which he further divided into subgroups, including the 'super creatives' and 'creative professionals.' Importantly, Florida (2002) argued that cities that encouraged creativity were tolerant of different lifestyles – including alternative sexualities and immigrants – were attractive to young people. This attractiveness meant that they were more likely to reap benefits from the restructuring of the economies of the developed world. As Florida (2002, 2005) noted, many cities and regions do not attract the creative class, and in many cases members of the creative class migrate from those regions to more attractive environments. Florida (2002) measured how attractive individual cities are to the creative class, and developed a series of indices, including a bohemian index and a diversity index.

Florida's (2002) work was presented as directly relevant to the practice of developing locally because he argued that in the 21st century cities and regions need to foster a creative environment or culture. He argued that instead of adding infrastructure such as highways, cities needed to promote a café culture, introduce social reforms that emphasized tolerance, promote cultural events and reshape their urban environments to bring this pivotal group into the local labor market. His ideas around the importance of creativity was supported by research that found creativity was positively associated with higher levels of new firm formation (Lee 2014; Florida et al. 2017). In large measure Florida's ideas resonated with the arguments of earlier authors, including Robert Reich's (1991) writing on the economic importance of 'symbolic analysts,' Sharon Zukin's (1995) work on culture and economic development, and even Jane Jacobs' (1961) seminal book on the *Death and Life of Great American Cities*. In part Florida's (2002) work was taken up by many political leaders and other key decision makers because it had a strong quantitative foundation that provided easily understood evidence and provided a fresh perspective on how to encourage economic development.

In many ways Florida's (2002) ideas, and associated policy actions, challenged long established notions on how to encourage economic growth. He called into question the impact of accepted economic development strategies, including many of the policies and programs discussed in other chapters of this book, such as infrastructure investment as a strategy for fueling development (Chapter 3), and the use of inward investment strategies (Chapter 5). His perspective also forced a reevaluation of endogenous approaches: business incubators, for example, will be more successful if creative individuals populate them, and therefore strategies to attract this new labor force should be a first step in developing a startup economy. Florida's reading of contemporary growth processes has been disputed by some academics who have questioned his analysis (Nichols Clark 2003; Markusen 2006), while others have cast doubt on the relevance of his work for smaller communities (Rainnie 2005) or the political context within which his ideas have been adopted (Peck 2005).

There is no doubt that careful thought needs to be directed at the question of whether attracting the creative class is sufficient, or indeed the best approach, for any locality. It is likely that the fit between a city's or community's needs and creative class approaches will vary greatly, because in many instances conventional factors continue to determine economic growth. For example, Jarmon et al. (2012) examined the range of economic development strategies used by 304 cities in Texas and were able to relate rates of economic growth to specific sets of growth strategies. They concluded that cities that maintained a conventional focus on industrial recruitment and business assistance measures recorded – on average – higher rates of growth than those that addressed lifestyle issues. These results are robust but may reflect the particular circumstances of the Texas economy at that point in time. Texas led the US economy out of the recession that commenced in 2008–2009, with a strong focus on offering cost-competitive locations for industry and commerce. Other places have industry structures that are less dependent on low production costs, and their growth is more likely to be driven by amenity factors.

Florida's work has had a major influence on the practice of developing locally and it is worthwhile reflecting on the nature of that impact. Florida's (2002) prominence in economic development programs cannot be denied: over the last two decades cities in developed economies around the globe have been convinced they need to establish themselves as 'creative' cities in order to attract a skilled and innovative generation of new workers. Places as diverse as Sheffield in northern England, Charlotte in North Carolina and Adelaide in South Australia have attempted to establish their 'creativity' or bohemian credentials, while at the same time measuring their performance against one or more of Florida's metrics. Governments have hired consultants to assess their 'creative city' potential and advise them how to become more creative.

But what does the creative class – a concept designed to shed light on the growth of metropolitan areas – mean for rural areas or smaller cities? Fortunately, there is evidence that helps us understand the value of Florida's concept for rural or small urban areas and allows us to draw out policy insights. First, Florida's own work has shown that aesthetically attractive places have higher levels of community engagement and a more strongly developed sense of ownership of the community and its outcomes. This in turn contributes to a number of developmental benefits, including the retention of the population, higher levels of civic engagement and advocacy, and social cohesion (Florida et al. 2011). Second, Mcgranahan and Wojan (2007) looked at the growth rates of rural and urban counties across the US and concluded that patterns of development were related to the presence or absence of the creative class. Rural places that could offer an attractive lifestyle – including outdoor activities such as biking, hunting, water sports, fishing and hiking – were more likely to grow than those that could not offer similar opportunities. The authors noted that previously economic development practitioners sought to create growth from an attractive physical environment by attracting more tourists, but in an era of advanced communications and technology, even greater levels of growth can be achieved by permanently attracting creative individuals as residents and workers.

The OECD (2005) also supports the view that making better use of existing amenities, and further developing latent potential, can be a major catalyst for growth in rural regions, especially in tourism-related activities. Amenity-based development can be an important focus for small business development and the cultivation of a culture of entrepreneurship. Practical strateies for rural communities include:

- Creating additional recreational opportunities;
- Ensuring that places offer the retail opportunities – cafés, restaurants, sports and bike stores – that the creative class seek;
- Promoting cultural activities, such as artisinal communities or galleries;
- Creating networks or forums for creative class members already living within the community to provide advice on how to attract others.

The available evidence suggests that urban centers – regardless of size – should promote their urbanity and diversity, as well as the lifestyle savings associated with their location, if they are to develop (Zenker 2009).

Fundamentally, Florida's argument around the creative class can be seen to be a sharpening of the long-standing acknowledgment that human capital – the quality and skill set of the workforce – is a fundamental determinant of growth. More recently public debate has tended to look at this argument in terms of the workforce decisions of 'millennials,' that generation following Generation X that entered the workforce in the 21st century. There are also planning implications of how millennials, at least so far, view amenities. Where retail shopping is often at the core of community development efforts, Fromm (2017 p 1) observes: '[millennials] desire less stuff and more meaningful and tailored experiences.' (See additional material on The Experience Economy at the textbook website www.gpaled.com.) Flexibility in the amenities that a locality has on offer for its workforce, and how it is offered, will be key to long-run success since change itself is seen as desirable for emerging generations. Despite the change in labeling, the dynamics ascribed to millennials are exactly those documented by Florida – a more footloose, highly educated population, for whom quality of life is important.

## ■ 7.2 Urban regeneration

Urban, city or neighborhood regeneration is one way of ensuring that communities remain economically engaged. It is a strategy that has been used in many parts of the world, including the UK, Europe, New Zealand, Australia, Canada, the US and South America, as one way to boost demand and establish jobs. Famous examples of urban regeneration projects include the London Docklands, the Bull Ring development in Birmingham in England, the redevelopment of Barcelona in Spain, and Boston and Baltimore's Inner Harbor redevelopments on the US east coast. In many instances urban regeneration projects have arisen through the efforts of local or state/provincial governments, but in some instances national policies have fueled their adoption. The Blair Labour Government in the UK supported a substantial number of regeneration initiatives outside England's south east, while the Docklands redevelopment in London was a centerpiece of the Thatcher Government's planning. Neumann et al. (2011), for example, observed that in the 1990s urban policy in Germany adopted a comprehensive, business-oriented approach to urban regeneration which resulted in a range of social and economic benefits for these cities and communities.

In major cities urban regeneration strategies often represent a substantial investment in an old industrial district, riverfront or canal neighborhood or seaport, with many examples evident throughout the US, Canada, Europe and many parts of Asia. Many have a specific goal of improving the quality of the physical environment, with the HafenCity development in Hamburg, Germany established to transform an unused warehouse district into an extension of the inner city. It was developed to include a range of public benefits such as new affordable housing, cultural flagship facilities and open space, while providing an exemplar of environmentally sustainable development. Such broad-ranging ambitions are common with urban regeneration programs and reflect the scale of investment required. The OECD (2005) argues that regeneration is often undertaken with a view to achieving an idealized chain of benefits:

1.  Regeneration results in households increasingly placing a high value on living or visiting historic areas;
2.  The number of visitors and residents increases, raising the commercial value of these locations;
3.  Increasing property values and activity draws in additional investment to develop even more commercial and residential opportunities.

In one sense, regeneration is seen to 'kick-start' a regional or neighborhood economy, while simultaneously removing physically unattractive or redundant stock, addressing social disadvantage and boosting the broader regional or national economy. Commonly these projects are undertaken as partnerships between the public and private sectors, with governments more likely to contribute land and capital, while the private sector brings to the table new investment in properties, as well as marketing and development expertise.

Urban regeneration as an economic development strategy carries a degree of risk, with some of the potential failings including:

- Not contributing to the growth of the wider city or region because development is limited to the nominated target area, resulting in limited spillover benefits for the central business district as a whole;
- The regeneration area capturing all new investment in the wider region, with investment otherwise targeted for other parts of the city drawn into the regeneration zone;
- Too great a focus on commercial and residential development, with few additional employment opportunities created. Urban regeneration projects may create little net employment in sectors such as manufacturing, financial, tourism or professional services, and instead refocus retail and residential development from other parts of the city;
- Regeneration can result in the gentrification of old inner-city industrial areas, resulting in the displacement of low-income and working-class households. Previously identified problems of social and economic disadvantage may simply be moved to other parts of the metropolitan area.

In the light of these potential challenges, urban regeneration strategies need to both undertake property redevelopment and reshape local social and economic dynamics if they are to achieve their broad objectives.

Urban regeneration often takes place on a substantial scale and in the early 2000s Sheffield One – one of the City of Sheffield's economic development agencies – invested more than £1 billion in the physical revival of the city center. As discussed in Chapter 2, in the past San Diego in California addressed regeneration in other ways, with most of the central city nominated as a Renewal Community. Renewal Community status resulted in federal income tax savings to businesses that locate or expand in that area. In addition, the Redevelopment Agency of San Diego was established by the city council in 1958 to alleviate blight in older urban areas. The budget for this authority was $406 million for 2008, of which $150 million was for capital works and $145 million for affordable housing. In 2012 California closed all 900 redevelopment agencies in the state, with obligations incurred by these authorities handled by 'successor' boards, most of which have begun to end their activities. Elsewhere, the State of Washington created the authority for localities to engage in the redevelopment of blighted properties in 1957 with subsequent updates to statutes in 1965 and 2002. The intent was to revitalize distressed properties and make infrastructure improvements in targeted areas, with substantial community engagement in the renewal planning process.[1] Regeneration can take place with a specific focus – such as sports stadia development (Davies 2008), the redevelopment of run-down housing stock – or in order to achieve a range of social and economic objectives (Singhal et al. 2009; Mooney et al. 2015), including the creation of a new image (Harris 2015). These initiatives can be tied to international partnerships – such as Birmingham, UK's Frankfurt Christmas market (Bloomfield 2010) and frequently involve collaboration between governments, not-for-profit organizations and the private sector.

Regeneration does not have to take place on a substantial scale to offer benefits to communities. The City of Garland, Texas, has sustained a relatively modest program of revitalization that has generated valuable outcomes (Box 7.1). Such programs have applicability in many urban and rural communities.

## BOX 7.1 CITY OF GARLAND – REGENERATION AND REVITALIZATION OF OLDER NEIGHBORHOODS

The City of Garland is part of the Dallas–Fort Worth metroplex and 13th largest city – by population – in Texas. It is an established urban area, with a long history of manufacturing and associated activities. Its neighborhoods are fully developed, with several showing the signs of age and there are many residents on low incomes. The city has two challenges with its housing stock: it can be difficult to attract and recruit professionals and skilled workers as the area lacks the high-quality housing they seek, and there is degradation in some neighborhoods.

The City of Garland has taken an active approach to addressing these issues. It established a Home Infill program that promotes the revitalization of Garland's neighborhoods and communities while working to increase the rate of homeownership among low- to moderate-income families. This program supports new energy-efficient family homes within the city, with eligible applicants having incomes between 51 percent and 80 percent of the area median income. In addition, down payment assistance is available through the First Time Home Buyer Program, providing $10,000 of assistance to eligible households. This help takes the form of a forgivable loan that is due and payable upon the sale, home equity loan, lease or transfer of title within the first five years of ownership.

The City of Garland has given priority to the further development of housing quality in order to make its neighborhoods more vibrant places. The city established its GREAT homes initiative which encourages the construction of new homes, renovates existing homes and revitalizes infrastructure. The program uses federal funding and since 2011 it has developed more than 25 houses alongside the private and nonprofit sectors.

The GREAT homes program provides funding for both upgrading the existing stock of dwellings and also supporting aesthetic upgrades that maintain the architectural integrity and aesthetic charm of the city's more mature residential districts. It uses creative financing terms to help homeowners renovate their properties, while simultaneously returning funds to the city.

The City of Garland's housing programs are more than just an attempt to beautify a handful of neighborhoods. They work to turn around residential areas at risk of decline and thereby support dynamic communities. The initiatives assist in attracting skilled professionals into the businesses shaping the city's economic success. Finally, these programs generate local demand, with homebuyers purchasing goods and services locally – thereby providing a fillip to the local retail and construction sectors.

Business improvement districts (BIDs) are a second approach to the regeneration of city centers and have been credited with the regeneration of inner-city areas in Philadelphia, Milwaukee, Cleveland, San Diego and Washington, DC (Mitchell 2001). Business improvement districts rely upon commercial property owners agreeing to additional taxes or fees, and in return they receive higher amenities such as additional investment in streetscaping, security, cleaning, marketing, et cetera. In the US, BIDs are established by local governments, with the resources then redirected to a specific-purpose organization charged with the implementation of commercial regeneration. Survey research by Mitchell (2001) found most BID organizations were active in marketing, in the promotion of 'clean and safe' programs, policy advocacy and, to a lesser degree, the management of open spaces.

## ■ 7.3 Main Street and the activation of retailing

In many parts of the world, including Canada, the UK, Australia and the US, older commercial shopping centers, such as shopping strips or conventional town squares, are at risk of decay despite being considered important by nearby residents (Loukaitou-Sideris 2000; Tually 2006). Main Street programs look to generate vibrancy and increased commercial activity in older – usually strip – shopping centers that have declined or are at risk of decline. Often this reflects increased competition from shopping malls or other new retail developments that may be more attractive to customers because of ease of parking, a greater range of goods or other factors. Main Street programs have a long history in many parts of the world, especially in the US, and conventionally they take the form of a partnership between local governments and the targeted business community (Tually 2006). They are found in rural townships, suburban developments and in older inner-city areas. Robertson (2004) reported that more than 1,000 communities across the US are members of the National Main Street Center (NMSC). In the US, the NMSC advocates a four-point approach:

- **Organization** – establishes consensus and cooperation by building partnerships among the various groups that have a stake in the commercial district;
- **Promotion** – creates a positive image that will renew community pride and tell your Main Street story to the surrounding region;
- **Design** – getting the Main Street into good condition and creating a safe, inviting environment for shoppers, workers and visitors. Successful Main Streets take advantage of the visual opportunities inherent in a commercial district by directing attention to its physical elements: public and private buildings, storefronts, signs, public spaces, parking areas, street furniture, public art, landscaping, merchandising, window displays and promotional materials;
- **Economic** restructuring strengthening the community's economic assets while diversifying its economic base. Communities accomplish this by evaluating how to retain and expand successful businesses to provide a balanced commercial mix, sharpening the competitiveness and merchandising skills of business owners, and attracting new businesses (National Main Street Center 2019).

The NMSC claims that since 1980 it has triggered reinvestment in almost 277,000 buildings across the US, generated $74.7 billion in investment and created over 600,000 jobs (NMSC 2019).

Main Street programs place a strong focus on reinvesting in traditional shopping centers and using landscape architecture and planning to attract consumers. They acknowledge the architectural heritage of many of these shopping strips, and the sense of community they can engender, which helps distinguish them from shopping malls and other retail developments. Robertson (2004) suggested there has been relatively little independent evaluation of Main Street programs and concluded that the key to success was a successful public–private partnership. He also noted that economic restructuring appeared to be the weakest of the four elements to the NMSC program, with relatively few Main Streets commissioning active restructuring programs. Renew Programs (Box 7.2) present a

## BOX 7.2  RENEW ADELAIDE – WORKING TO KEEP INNER-CITY RETAILING STRONG

Around the globe, retailers in inner-city and central business district (CBD) locations often struggle to compete with suburban developments which offer easier access to those with a car, lower prices because space is cheaper, larger stores with a greater range of goods and a sense of convenience. Over the last decades the challenge has become even greater due to increasing competition from Internet sales and shifts in consumer demand.

Renew Adelaide was established in 2010 to breathe vibrancy back into Adelaide retailing. With support from the City of Adelaide, the state government as well as the private sector, Renew Adelaide was established as a not-for-profit organization to link emerging retail entrepreneurs and property owners. The establishment of Renew Adelaide acknowledged some shops had been left empty and that vacancies have strong spillover effects, signaling a locality is in decline and lacking the 'buzz' of leading-edge retailing.

Renew Adelaide set out an innovative approach to dealing with empty shops. It offers a 30-day rent-free rolling lease to potential retailers in the creative industries – arts, crafts, music, et cetera – giving individuals the opportunity to test their ideas prior to committing to a commercial lease. Property owners benefit as they are able to activate their building and regenerate them socially and economically. The Renew Adelaide model is unlike a conventional lease arrangement; when a vacant space is offered, Renew Adelaide calls for applications from people with ideas. Those with the most viable and creative ideas are then invited to interview.

The program seeks out creative retail opportunities, those looking for studio spaces or galleries, and projects that combine these elements. Proposals have a creative element and their products need to be made or sourced locally. Renew Adelaide looks for 'activity that is new, interesting, unique; things that generate foot traffic, encourage people to visit, develop communities and networks.' (Renew Adelaide 2015)

Property owners benefit because a space at risk of long-term vacancy is occupied by an enterprise that attracts new foot traffic, securing the future of existing tenants. Property owners benefit as the program encourages retail startups, with a number of businesses establishing permanently and taking out commercial leases.

refreshed perspective on the Main Street concept, with a specific focus on startup firms, rent holidays as businesses establish and a desire to maintain the occupancy of retail real estate.

##  7.4  Place marketing or place branding

Promoting a city, town or region as a place to visit, invest in, or buy products from, directly addresses the challenge of stimulating demand for a community's products. Place branding or marketing is both a well-developed field in economic development and near-universal in its coverage. Place marketing programs have been documented in the UK (Page and Hardyman 1996); Australia (Gibson and Davidson 2004); South Africa (Rogerson, 1999; Nel and Binns 2002); Europe (Luque-Martinez et al. 2007); the United States (Haider 1992); Sweden and Denmark (Hospers 2004); and many other nations. Page and Hardyman (1996) argued that it was now central to economic development efforts, with the resultant need to find new ways of managing and organizing these activities.

Place marketing is an exercise far larger than simply conducting an advertising campaign; it frequently involves ensuring existing assets – physical infrastructure, tourist attractions, natural resources – are at an appropriate standard; adding to the appeal of a place through the development or recruitment of additional attractors; an effective communication strategy; and its need to secure support from local leaders, business and the community (Rainisto 2004). To add to this complexity, place branding is not simply targeted at one audience or set of economic priorities; instead it is used to achieve multiple goals including the attraction of:

- Visitors;
- Residents and workers;
- Business and industry;
- Export markets (Zenker 2009).

Haider (1992 p 128) distinguished the marketing activities of places from those actions he labeled sloganeering, imaging or advertising and which can be generically thought of as 'boosterism.' (Kavaratzis and Ashworth 2008) Place marketing, he argued, was a substantial managerial and social process that required places to think and act commercially.

> All places have assets (actual or potential), but they may not have much value without a customer, which a place must attract and retain. All places have something to sell, but for selling to be effective it should be preceded by various marketing activities such as needs assessment, marketing research, market segmentation, product development, pricing, and distribution. A company does not usually build a widget without some understanding of who wants it, how to produce, sell, price, promote and distribute it, but this is precisely what places do in constructing their economic development programs.
>
> (Haider 1992 p 128)

However, not everyone agrees with this view, with some arguing that there is a substantial difference between marketing a product and marketing a place. Kavaratzis and Ashworth (2008 p 159) noted that places are not a corporation, and that they lack a single center for strategy development and a network of outlets through which to implement branding. Nevertheless, both perspectives deserve consideration, as each offers valuable insights for those planning and implementing the promotion of a city, region or community.

Fundamentally, place marketing and place promotion is important because most places are relatively substitutable (Bramwell and Rawding 1996). That is, they have few – if any – features or benefits that cannot be found in other places, and they therefore have to build an image of distinctive advantage based on those attributes that are unique or distinctive. Luque-Martinez et al. (2007) and Haider (1992) have commented on the significance of city image. It is important in attracting businesses, visitors, demand for goods and new investment, but it is also relatively transitory – with many cities and regions undergoing periods of both positive and negative perception. Haider (1992) suggests a focus on *place positioning* is a better way to engage with the challenges of marketing a place, as it calls on economic development planners and developers to craft both the image of a place, and the value it offers customers. Bradley et al. (2002) noted that such 'positioning' was evident in the efforts of many cities to attract large conventions, with long-term strategies needed to secure the convention market.

Place marketing can have unexpected outcomes: the Chinese government encouraged the development of speciality towns (*tese xiaozhen*) (The Economist 2017) as a way of stimulating the growth of smaller urban centers. Local officials were asked to identify features that make their locality distinctive – cultural assets, industry structure, et cetera – and then promote them as a focus for development. This has resulted in a number of innovative developments including a 'nuclear-power town,' a 'happy town' (based on adult industries) and a number of centers focused on e-sports/interactive games. From June 2016 to December 2017 some 403 speciality towns were approved by the central government, with a goal of having 1,000 by 2020 (The Economist 2017). The large-scale roll out of place marketing in China highlights a challenge: there are a limited number of ways in which a city, region or other place can present itself as distinctive. Often localities select strategies that reflect their current or anticipated strengths, without acknowledging that other places have already positioned themselves in this market segment. In China, for example, the town of Zhongxian sought to position itself as a hub for e-sports/interactive games, and built a 6,000-seat stadium for competitions, even though three other Chinese cities were in the process of developing comparable facilities (The Economist 2017).

Kavaratzis and Ashworth (2008) suggest place marketing has evolved to parallel corporate branding, where the objective is to associate a broad spectrum of positive perceptions to a place that are communicated in multiple ways and spill into a number of areas of enterprise. A region with a 'clean and green' image, for example, will be an attractive source of foodstuffs, but may also benefit in terms of tourism and recreation. A city or community able to present itself as a regional hub will be more attractive as both a shopping destination and as a location for business. These perceptions are supported by investment in the physical fabric – street beautification, investment in transport systems, et cetera, conventional marketing and trade, and other promotions. Critically, new forms of communication, including social media (see Box 7.3), have opened up new possibilities for place branding.

## BOX 7.3  A NEW MARKET, A NEW BRAND, A NEW PLATFORM: THE STORY OF SEA LAKE, VICTORIA

Tourism has long been one of the targets of place branding, but on occasion success comes in unexpected ways.

Sea Lake is a small town in northern Victoria, four hours by vehicle from Melbourne, the nearest major urban center and international airport. It is a wheat-growing community and has shrunk considerably over the last 20 years because of drought and increased economies of scale in on-farm production.

It has always been a quiet town, but from 2013 it started to see an influx of Chinese tourists attracted to the nearby Lake Tyrell because it was listed on a number of Chinese websites as one of the 'best things to do' in Australia. It also featured in innumerable posts on Weibo and WeChat.

The Chinese are attracted because Sea Lake has clear skies, and the thin layer of water found in some parts of Lake Tyrell provide a reflection that allows visitors to appear to be walking on stars.

It also provides sunsets that stand as a highlight in many holiday photos.

Lake Tyrell's fame in China defies the expectations of the local residents and the wider Australian population alike, with many visitors traveling directly from Asia to see the lake in the evening.

Sea Lakes' success was unexpected; the locals had not previously heard of the Chinese social media platforms, and were completely unaware of the promotion they received. But having had success granted to them, they have taken steps to ensure that Lake Tyrell was not adversely affected by its influx of visitors, while also commercializing the opportunities now available to them. For example, helicopter flights over the lake are now offered and the town has boosted its catering and range of souvenirs to cater for this new market (Grindlay 2016).

Place branding may have some of the features of corporate marketing, but when we look at the findings of contemporary marketing researchers, we quickly appreciate there is a world of difference between the ways in which places are currently marketed compared with household groceries such as toothpaste, food or laundry detergent. These differences should give all those involved in economic development pause for thought, as they suggest that there are further opportunities to improve programs and boost the economies of cities and regions.

The marketing researcher Byron Sharp argued that good practice in marketing comes down to making use of a small number of insights into how consumers buy. His three key insights, and associated strategies are:

- You achieve growth in market share by increasing the popularity of the product and by gaining market share, with most individuals consuming the brand occasionally;
- Most products are unique, but 'mainly compete as if they are near lookalikes' (Sharp 2010 p xiii). These products vary in popularity and therefore turnover, even if the points of difference between themselves and their competitors are relatively minor;
- Brands need to build two assets – physical availability and mental availability (whether consumers think about that product), and the easier they are for the consumer to recall the larger the number of individuals that will purchase them (Sharp 2010 p xiii).

These points are important because they show that too often places have been positioning themselves incorrectly: for example, the focus on building assets with potential to attract tourists or businesses is of little value if potential visitors are unaware of your city or town, or cannot travel there easily. The money previously spent on street beautification would be better spent improving road access or boosting the number of flights to the local airport, while also advertising across a range of markets.

Most marketing researchers would argue that places simply do not advertise enough. When asked what would make for a more effective advertising campaign, marketing researchers simply argue there needs to be more. Advertising works by 'refreshing, and occasionally building memory structures. . . . by consistently using the brand's distinctive assets' (Sharp 2010 p xiv). It is effective when it:

- Is salient or relevant to the consumer;
- Is noticed and elicits an emotional response;
- Carries with it relevant mental associations;
- Refreshes and builds memory structures;
- Reaches out to consumers;
- Has a continuous presence, pervasively affecting people's awareness.

Consumers of any product – whether it is detergent or a weekend vacation destination – are often busy and make relatively speedy decisions that are often driven by their previous experiences and/or exposure to advertising. The challenge, therefore, is to put your town, your city or your region in front of potential visitors or investors as often as possible and in ways that will both attract their attention and be remembered.

Marketing researchers also challenge economic development practitioners to rethink their priorities when it comes to identifying what is special with respect to their town, city or region. Whereas earlier generations of marketing research, and contemporary practice in place branding, emphasizes the need to make the product unique, innovative or in some other way special, Sharp (2010) shows that it is the marketing elements that need to be distinctive if a brand or product is to grow. This includes the brand name, but may also include a color, a logo, a tagline or association with a celebrity. These 'distinctive assets' help build awareness of the product across consumers as a whole and help make the brand easier to find. It is these distinctive assets that can be built upon, promoted and ultimately used to drive greater market penetration.

There are two key features of a distinctive asset – uniqueness and prevalence – which Sharp and Romaniuk (2010) argue needs to be 'taught' to potential consumers over a long period and across a range of media. Wine branding is a good example; when asked to consider a wine from the US most non-Americans (and many Americans) would think of California, despite the fact that wine is produced in many other states.

The mainstream marketing literature offers some important lessons for how economic developers go about branding or marketing their region, city or town in order to drive growth. These implications include the following:

- Advertising is an important part of place branding, and strategies that emphasize the development of physical assets or facilities while neglecting advertising and promotional efforts are unlikely to achieve their potential;
- Individuals only consume products they can gain access to – mentally and physically. Strategies that raise awareness of a city or town, and steps to improve access to it, are those most likely to be effective;
- Places should develop distinctive 'marketing elements' and use them consistently to keep them 'front of mind' amongst potential customers and investors;
- Brand awareness should be multidimensional. In the current era that means that advertising needs to be digital as well as making use of conventional media. But it also calls for all goods and services that come from a place to use those elements to help build awareness of the variety of experiences and goods it offers;
- Cities and towns can overcome the problem we identified in our discussion of China's 'speciality towns' of having too many potential competitors with comparable assets, if they focus on creating distinctive assets, rather than differentiating their product. This conclusion challenges conventional wisdom in economic development.

It is, however, possible to overextend the parallels between places as brands, and consumer products as brands. Fan (2005) pointed out two fundamental, and far-reaching, differences between the two: first, products can be relaunched, altered, replaced or taken off the market, whereas cities, regions and communities cannot; and second, products have a single owner, whereas place brands are frequently available to any enterprise seeking to associate with it (Baker and Cameron 2008).

More broadly, Kavaratzis and Ashworth (2008) addressed the administrative challenges associated with successfully implementing a place branding or marketing campaign and they paid particular attention to the role of community involvement as a driver of success. They suggested there was a need to:

- First ensure that there is a shared understanding of the need for place marketing, and this should be a discussion involving a wide range of stakeholders and participants in order to develop a common sense of what can be achieved and how various parties can contribute to that effort;

- Second, establish arrangements for coordinating activities and ensuring all tasks are allocated appropriately;
- Third, adopt a long-term and structured approach to place marketing that conforms with standard practice for marketing campaigns;
- Fourth, expand the place marketing agenda beyond the attraction of tourists to include potential new residents, investors and future markets for products;
- Fifth, include local communities in the development and delivery of the branding strategy. Residents can become vehicles for the delivery of marketing messages as well as being a key audience;
- Sixth, examine the ways in which place branding can form the basis for collaboration with other cities or communities. Strategies that see cities work together to promote a region as a whole or seek to establish reciprocal arrangements with distant urban centers may have an advantage in the long term;
- Seventh, monitor and evaluate the progress of marketing efforts;
- Additionally, effective place marketing calls for a strong Internet presence, providing customers with up-to-date and effective information. To be effective, the websites need a comprehensive set of features that meet the expectations of potential customers and are easily navigated. Websites also need to be promoted broadly in order to be effective, including strategies that optimize their discoverability in web-searches, as well as conventional awareness campaigns in print, digital and other media. Finally, they need to be supported by the effective use of customer relationship management (CRM) systems that maintain contact with visitors to the site, provide data for e-mail marketing campaigns and provide a foundation for an ongoing dialogue (Wang and Fesenmaier 2006).

Festivals and other events can be an important tool in enhancing the perceived amenity and 'brand' of a region, community or city. Festivals raise awareness, attract media attention, provide a focus for civic activities and generate additional tourism and retail revenues. Commonly they seek to build upon the unique economic structure or history of a place, such as the Lighting Festival held by the Danish city of Frederikshavn (Freire-Gibb and Lorentzen 2011). Importantly, festivals and other events 'activate' public spaces, restaurants and shopping centers, while creating a 'buzz' that adds to vibrancy and raises awareness.

The conduct for festivals or events and the hosting of major sporting fixtures can be an important part of the marketing of a region, community or city. However, it can be dangerous to overstate the value created through these channels. Researchers have found the economic impacts vary greatly, and in sport, for example, these impacts are dependent on the type of sport, the level of the competition – senior versus junior competitors, the number and origin and of nonlocal participants and supporters, and the duration of the event and resultant visitation by participants (Mondello and Rishe 2004). Importantly, not all events are equal when it comes to drawing in economic activity, and some relatively low-profile events can be very impactful. Similarly, the value of hosting major sports stadia is likely to depend on where they are located, with CBD locations generating longer visitor stays, greater levels of ancillary spending and business-to-business interactions than those located in the outer suburbs (Nelson 2001).

 ## 7.5 Conclusion

In the modern economy, every city, region and community needs its place in the sun. The marketing of places and the managing of their brand has become a critical activity for economic development practitioners and city managers alike. As shown in this chapter, the benefits extend from the attraction of a skilled labor force that in turn attracts investment, through to the generation of additional demand from tourism, conventions and securing external markets. We have argued that economic development professionals might have been able to learn from the experience of marketers working in other fields, and in the future place a greater emphasis on advertising their city or region as a destination of choice, while also continuing to enhance their physical assets.

## Key messages

- Places should look to offer a high quality of amenity in order to boost tourism revenue, attract new businesses and bring in highly qualified individuals who will, in turn, either attract additional businesses or start new enterprises;
- Urban regeneration strategies can redevelop run-down urban areas but may not achieve the very broad goals often associated with their implementation;
- Main Street programs provide a well-documented set of strategies that support conventional retailing and add to the appeal of many communities;
- Place marketing has the potential to deliver multiple benefits and reach a number of different targets, including tourists, incoming residents, export markets and businesses seeking to relocate;
- Place marketing is a complex process that extends far beyond simple advertising campaigns:
  - Community and stakeholder buy-in is essential to success;
  - Festivals, sporting and other events can be an important part of the place marketing strategy and can deliver a variety of benefits.
- Lessons taken from the conventional marketing literature suggest that the promotion of places needs to be multichannel, frequent and evolve over time to reflect changing circumstances, but seek to transmit an enduring theme.

## Discussion questions

As a group, think about the ways in which places are 'branded' and marketed. Draw up a list of ten things that are unique about that ways a place (town, city, region, state) are marketed compared to consumer products (laundry powder, cars, et cetera). Also, create a list of similarities in place marketing and consumer products marketing. What can be learned about economic development strategies from comparing these lists?

Identify six key components you would seek to include in a place branding strategy for these four types of community:

- An attractive rural community in the mountains a three-hour drive from the nearest major city;
- A manufacturing city that has experienced an economic downturn and is seeking to find a new future;
- A commuter community on the outskirts of a major metropolitan center that has little employment and few facilities;
- An inner-city neighborhood that has suffered from urban blight and is looking to rebuild itself.

## Note

1 Washington's Community Renewal Law allowed cities to use eminent domain to acquire distressed properties, which has created some controversy (Peterson 2009).

## References

Baker, M. and Cameron, E. 2008 Critical factors in destination marketing, *Tourism and Hospitality Research*, 8:2, pp 79–97.

Bloomfield, J. 2010 Birmingham's Frankfurt Christmas market, *Local Economy*, 25:1, pp 74–80.

Bradley, A., Hall, T. and Harrison, M. 2002 Promoting new images for meetings tourism, *Cities*, 19:1, pp 61–70.

Bramwell, B. and Rawding, L. 1996 Tourism marketing images of industrial cities, *Annals of Tourism Research*, 23:1, pp 201–221.

Davies, L. 2008 Sport and the local economy, *Local Economy*, 23:1, pp 31–46.

Fan, Y. 2005 Branding the nation, *Journal of Vacation Marketing*, 12:1, pp 63–70.

Florida, R. 2002 *The Rise of the Creative Class*, Basic Books, New York.

Florida, R. 2005 *The Flight of the Creative Class*, Basic Books, New York.

Florida, R., Adler, P. and Mellander, C. 2017 The city as innovation machine, *Regional Studies*, 51:1, pp 86–96.

Florida, R., Mellander, C. and Stolarick, K. 2011 Beautiful places: the role of perceived aesthetic beauty in community satisfaction, *Regional Studies*, 45:1, pp 33–48.

Freire-Gibb, L. and Lorentzen, A. 2011 A platform for local entrepreneurship: the case of the Lighting Festival of Fredrikshavn, *Local Economy*, 26:3, pp 157–169.

Fromm, J. 2017 How brands can win with millennials in the experience economy. Forbes, July 21. Available at https://www.forbes.com/sites/jefffromm/2017/07/27/why-experience-innovation-matters-when-marketing-to-millennials/#1d40a9ec7682.

Gibson, C. and Davidson, D. 2004 Tamworth, Australia's 'country music capital': place marketing, rurality, and resident reactions, *Journal of Rural Studies*, 20, pp 387–404.

Grindlay, D. 2016 Chinese tourists flood isolated grain town, *ABC News Rural*, https://www.abc.net.au/news/rural/2016-03-24/sea-lake-chinese-tourism-drought-grain-rural-environment-water/7272248.

Haider, D. 1992 Place wars: new realities of the 1990s, *Economic Development Quarterly*, 6:2, pp 127–134.

Harris, J. 2015 Keeping up with the Joneses: hosting megaevents as a regenerative strategy, *Local Economy*, 30:8, pp 961–974.

Hospers, G. 2004 Place marketing in Europe: the branding of the Oresund region, *Intereconomics*, September/October.

Jacobs, J. 1961 *The Death and Life of Great American Cities*, Random House, New York.

Jarmon, C., Vanderleeuw, J., Pennington, M. and Sowers, T. 2012 The role of economic development corporations in local development: evidence from Texas cities, *Economic Development Quarterly*, 26:2, pp 124–137.

Kavaratzis, M. and Ashworth, G. 2008 Place marketing: how did we get here and where are we going? *Journal of Place Management Development*, 1:2, pp 150–165.

Lee, N. 2014 The creative industries and urban economic growth in the UK, *Environment and Planning A: Economy and Space*, 46:2, pp 455–470.

Loukaitou-Sideris, A. 2000 Revisiting inner-city strips: a framework for community and economic development, *Economic Development Quarterly*, 14:2, pp 165–181.

Luque-Martinez, T., Barrio-Garcia, S., Ibanez-Zapata, J. and Molina, M. 2007 Modeling a city's image: the case of Granada, *Cities*, 24:5, pp 335–352.

Markusen, A. 2006 Urban development and the politics of a creative class: evidence from a study of artists, *Environment and Planning A*, 38, pp 1921–1940.

Mcgranahan, D. and Wojan, D. 2007 Recasting the creative class to examine growth processes in rural and urban counties, *Regional Studies*, 41:2, pp 197–216.

Mitchell, J. 2001 Business improvement districts and the 'new' revitalization of downtown, *Economic Development Quarterly*, 15:2, pp 115–123.

Mondello, M. and Rishe, P. 2004 Comparative economic impact analyses: differences across cities, events and demographics, *Economic Development Quarterly*, 18:4, pp 331–342.

Mooney, G., McCall, V. and Paton, K. 2015 Exploring the use of large sporting events in the post-crash, post welfare city, *Local Economy*, 30:8, pp 910–924.

National Main Street Center (NMSC) 2019 Available at https://www.mainstreet. org/home, accessed January 4, 2019.

Nel, E. and Binns, T. 2002 Place marketing, tourism promotion, and community-based local economic development in post-apartheid South Africa: the case of Still Bay – the 'Bay of Sleeping Beauty,' *Urban Affairs Review*, 38:2, pp 184–208.

Nelson, A. 2001 Prosperity or blight? A question of Major League stadia locations, *Economic Development Quarterly*, 15:3, pp 255–265.

Neumann, U., Schmidt, C. and Trettin, L. 2011 Fostering local economic development in urban neighbourhoods: results of an empirical assessment, *Local Economy*, 26:1, pp 18–29.

Nichols Clark, T. 2003 3. Urban amenities: lakes, opera, and juice bars: do they drive development? In Nichols Clark. T. (ed.) *The City as an Entertainment Machine (Research in Urban Policy, Volume 9)*, Emerald Group Publishing Limited, pp 103–140.

OECD 2005 *Building Competitive Regions: Strategies and Governance*, OECD, Paris.

Page, S. and Hardyman, R. 1996 Place marketing and town centre management: a new tool for urban revitalization, *Cities*, 13:3, pp 153–164.

Peck, J. 2005 Struggling with the creative class, *International Journal of Urban and Regional Research*, 29:4, pp 740–770.

Peterson, J. 2009 *The Use and Abuse of Washington's Community Renewal Law.* Washington Policy Center Policy Brief. Available at https://www.washington policy.org/library/docLib/Nov._2009_CRL.pdf.

Rainisto, S. 2004 Success factors of place marketing, Unpublished PhD thesis, Helsinki University of Technology, Helsinki.

Rainnie, A. 2005 Hurricane Florida: the false allure of the creative class, *Sustaining Regions*, 4:3, pp 3–10.

Reich, R. 1991 *The Work of Nations*, AA Knopf, New York.

Renew Adelaide 2015 Available at https://renewadelaide.com.au/, accessed January 18, 2019.

Robertson, K. 2004 The Main Street approach to downtown development: an examination of the four-point program, *Journal of Architectural and Planning Research*, 21:1, pp 55–73.

Rogerson, C. 1999 Place marketing for local economic development in South Africa, *South African Geographical Journal*, 81:1, pp 32–43.

Sharp, B. 2010 *How Brands Grow*, Oxford University Press, South Melbourne.

Sharp, B. and Romaniuk, J. 2010 Differentiation versus distinctiveness. In *How Brands Grow*, Oxford University Press, South Melbourne, pp 89–111.

Singhal, S., Berry, J. and McGreel, S. 2009 A framework for assessing regeneration, business strategies and urban competitiveness, *Local Economy*, 24:2, pp 111–124.

The Economist. 2017 China pushes towns to brand themselves, and then regrets it, www.economist.com/news/china/21732826-officials-beijing-fret-local-boosterism, accessed January 11, 2018.

Tually, S. 2006 Streets ahead? The limits to Main Street programs as an economic development strategy, unpublished PhD thesis, Flinders University, Adelaide.

Wang, Y. and Fesenmaier, D. 2006 Identifying the success factors of Web-based marketing strategy, *Journal of Travel Research*, 44, pp 239–249.

Zenker, S. 2009 Who's your target? The creative class as a target group for place branding, *Journal of Place Management and Development*, 2:1, pp 23–32.

Zukin, S. 1995 *The Cultures of Cities*, Oxford University Press, Oxford.

# 8 Assessing the region and data-driven strategic economic development planning

This chapter:

▶ Presents data sources and analytic techniques used to understand the challenges and opportunities confronting the region, community or city;

▶ Provides the foundation for developing data-driven economic development strategies including traditional industry-based analyses, modern workforce assessments and the use of supply chain analysis to build viable strategies for business development and recruitment;

▶ Expands traditional economic development research practices into critical areas of quality of life measures;

▶ Introduces students to techniques used to value the growth of industry in a region or locality.

ECONOMIC DEVELOPMENT PLANNING is increasingly a local exercise representing bottom-up approaches that engage and empower local actors and agencies. As noted in Chapter 1, in a globalized economy localities become more, not less, important. Development depends on the provision of sophisticated infrastructure, high-quality resources, specialty supply chain networks and an appropriately skilled workforce. Successful economic development planning requires data and information on *what is*, and the changes that must be made to achieve the *what could be*.

When manufacturing dominated economic activity and development meant plant expansions and attracting new firms that often produced nearly identical products as existing firms, economic development planning could be based on a *past as prologue* approach and the gut reactions (judgment) of economic development practitioners. This is not an indictment of economic development practices and practitioners in past decades. With an absence of data on local/regional economic performance and limited theoretical perspectives being translated into practice, local economic development was often analogous to flying by the seat of your pants. Fortunately, both of these circumstances have improved and the professionalism of local economic development practitioners is greater than ever. This is not to say that one cannot find local economic development plans that are based on little more than a wish and a prayer, but successful economic development strategic planning is a data-driven exercise.

# ■ 8.1 Data-driven economic development planning

Data-driven planning can also be described as evidence-based decision making (Bresciani 2010). In the practice of local and regional economic development, data are used to assess current economic strengths (weaknesses), identify gaps and opportunities for targeted growth, and provide measures for program monitoring. There are three distinct advantages of using a data-driven approach in creating an economic development strategic plan:

1. Avoid mistakes created by anecdotal misperceptions. This can take the form of local actors assuming they possess a competitive advantage when in fact their perceptions are based on out-of-date assumptions. These misperceptions can also include assuming that an industry cannot succeed in the local economy simply because it has not done so in the past;
2. Identify unexpected opportunities. Using the data techniques described in this chapter, it is not unusual to uncover industries/occupations for which there is current unmet demand that are not readily apparent to local leaders. These opportunities can be based on emerging industries/technologies that have not previously existed or represent economic growth based on import substitution;
3. Support plan stability. *All politics are local and all economic development is local* (Clower 2005). The corollary to this statement is that there is a distinct political element to economic development planning and practice. The outcomes of economic development planning do not happen overnight, and often are years in the making, which requires patience among local leaders. However, patience is a luxury that is sometimes hard to afford under relatively short political terms. If economic development success is not immediate, or if an unusual damaging event occurs, knee-jerk responses to immediate political/economic challenges can derail a solid economic development plan. Having a plan based on data offers economic development leaders, including politicians, a basis for staying with a plan, or making thoughtful revisions if circumstances require.

The advantages described above may suggest the exclusive use of empirical data. Qualitative data and information, particularly when gathered through a community consultative process, is equally valuable in creating and sustaining a successful economic development plan. Empirical market data may clearly show unmet demand for particular goods or services, but the representative industry can be a poor match for the community. For example, a technology-dominant local economy will include residents who consume beef as a part of their diets; that does not mean that it makes economic development sense to open a local feedlot/abattoir to meet local demand. Critical considerations for economic development planning include community mores, social goals, self-image and quality of life features, none of which will appear as a data element in a secondary source.

'Data-driven' is likely too strong a description for the reality of economic development planning. Data, quantitative and qualitative, are the basis for analyses that provide information to local and regional economic development leaders. However, the phrase does convey a necessary condition for developing successful economic development strategies based on evidence.

In the remainder of this chapter, you will be introduced to data and analytic techniques most commonly used in economic development strategic planning. The data organization schemes and sources presented focus on the United States. Supplemental materials describing the data and data sources in other nations (Australia, Canada, UK) can be found on the textbook website (www.gpaled.com). The website also includes descriptions of other data tasks, such as responding to requests for information (RFIs), that are related to the economic development process.

## ■ 8.2 Data for economic development planning

In general, data-driven economic development planning begins with demographics, measures of economic performance, the business environment and local/regional quality of life indicators. Key demographic data for economic developers include population size and growth, age, race/ethnicity, migration patterns (net domestic immigration, international immigration), educational attainment, and the structure of local and regional political boundaries.

Economic performance can be divided into economic and labor market categories. The economic measures could include changes in gross regional product (the local equivalent to gross domestic product), total sales of firms (or procurement spending in the case of government agencies), personal income, and related

**FIGURE 8.1**   Data elements in a regional profile
*Source*: Tveidt and Clower 2015.

| Economy | Business climate |
|---|---|
| Major industries<br>Economic output<br>Major employers<br>Per capita income<br>New business starts | Taxation<br>Sites and buildings<br>Major highways<br>Airports/ports<br>Utility rates |

| Population | Quality of life |
|---|---|
| Size and growth<br>Age/ethnicity/race<br>Migration patterns<br>Educational attainment | School quality<br>Climate<br>Housing costs<br>Cost-of-living<br>Crime rates |

per-capita measures of each of these metrics. Labor market information includes jobs by industry, jobs by occupation, and total or average labor income (salaries, wages, benefits), hours worked and other measures. Jobs can be measured as headcount (number of jobs without distinction between part-time and full-time employment) or a full-time equivalent job (generally calculated by dividing the total number of hours worked by 2080 (40 hours/week × 52 weeks per year). Hours worked is paid hours and includes paid holidays and earned vacation time. Labor market data is usually the most readily available data and is reported much more frequently than other data categories. For some rural communities, population counts serve as a measure of economic performance. In many farming communities, slowing or stopping long-term population decline would be a strong indicator of success in local economic development planning.

It is important to note that economic growth is a necessary, but not sufficient condition for economic development. Total income, and even per-capita income, can be rising, but if that income growth is realized by only a small segment of the population (such as the top 1 percent of earners), then the economy may not be developing. Economic development includes:

- Improving living standards;
- Lowering the incidence of poverty;
- Having opportunities for individuals and families to improve their economic prospects across the spectrum of local households.

The business environment includes real estate market conditions (the availability of suitable commercial or industrial properties), taxation, regulatory regimes, availability and costs of utilities, and the quality and capacity of key infrastructure including roads, ports, airports and broadband network capacity. Regulatory characteristics cover a wide range of issues from local permitting and licensing to development restrictions based on environmental issues. For example, in the US, it is difficult for industrial plants that emit air pollutants to locate in cities that are designated as non-attainment air quality areas by the US Environmental Protection Agency.

Over the past several years, quality of life features have emerged as critical local characteristics that exert an impact on economic development success. Given that businesses increasingly include a locality's ability to attract and retain skilled workers in their site selection criteria, the economic developer must be able to speak equally about local labor costs, tax rates, and quality of life features such as the quality of public schools, housing costs, other cost of living measures, availability and quality of public transportation, climate, crime rates, and recreational and entertainment amenities. For some communities, strategies of amenities-based economic development, as discussed in the previous chapter, may offer the best opportunities for attracting and retaining workers.

## 8.2.1 The geography of economic development data

The geography used in economic development data gathering and analysis depends on: a) the research question being addressed; and b) the availability of data. As will be discussed later in this chapter, analyzing local economic performance is often contextualized to national characteristics and trends. For subnational areas, political boundaries provide the basis for most economic and demographic measures including states,[1] metropolitan statistical areas, counties,[2] cities/places and census tracts. It is relatively rare for economic development analyses to focus on individual census tracts, but areas of a city may be the focus of specific plans that represent agglomerations of census tracts. The most widely used geography of regional economic analysis is the metropolitan statistical area.

Designated by the White House Office of Management and Budget (OMB), metropolitan areas are made up of one or more counties for use by federal agencies in collecting, analyzing and reporting a wide range of data. Table 8.1 provides a brief description of metropolitan areas. There are 382 metropolitan statistical areas and 551 micropolitan statistical areas in the United States, representing about 94 percent of the population. In performing data analyses, comparisons may be made between statistical areas (metropolitan and micropolitan areas), but not between a statistical area and a statistical division.

Economic data often focuses on metropolitan areas and counties in order to better assess economic and labor markets. For assessing economic development assets and characteristics, the relevant geography is a city, or 'place,' using census terminology. Examining neighborhood performance often requires sub-city/county-level data, which can be found at the census tract level. Census tracts represent a given range of population count, which means their geographic size varies dramatically based on area population density. A suburban census tract usually covers a larger area than tracts in the urban core. Similarly, rural census tracts can be quite large.

**TABLE 8.1**    Metropolitan statistical areas

| Area | Description |
| --- | --- |
| Metropolitan statistical area/ New England city and town area* | One or more counties. Includes urban core of 50,000 population. Includes areas adjacent to urban core with social and economic connections based on worker commuting patterns. |
| Micropolitan statistical area/ New England city and town area | One or more counties. Includes an urban core of at least 10,000, but less than 50,000 population. Includes adjacent areas with social and economic connections based on worker commuting patterns. |
| Combined statistical area | A combination of multiple statistical areas (metro and/or micro areas) with social and economic connections, but at a lower level than within the individual metro or micro areas. |
| Metropolitan statistical division | A core area of a metropolitan statistical area with a population of at least 2.5 million. A metropolitan statistical area may have one or more divisions. |
| Census place | City or town with its own governance structure. |
| Census tract | Smaller area of a county with a population between 2,500 and 8,000. Where practical, the boundaries for census tracts follow recognizable features such as roads, rivers or other features. |

*Specific to New England states (ME, VT, NH, MA, RI, CT). Same criteria as metropolitan or micropolitan areas.

For any of these geographies, the analyst must be aware of changing defini-tions over time. Counties can be added to, or dropped from, metropolitan areas. Cities/places can annex additional territory. Census tract geographies can change over time, especially in areas with substantial population change.

Selecting the appropriate geographic area of study for an economic develop-ment project needs to consider several factors. Figure 8.2 offers a representation of key factors in choosing a study area. Defining the effective labor shed, the geogra-phy from which an employer can reasonably expect to draw workers, may be the single most important characteristic in a postindustrial economy. Employers prefer to have most workers living close enough to commute to work in 30 minutes or less. It is generally regarded that longer commutes lead to employee frustration and increased labor turnover, both of which negatively impact worker productiv-ity. However, the expected commute time must take into account local conditions, road infrastructure, and the presence of artificial or natural barriers, such as limited access highways or rivers. In Los Angeles rush hour traffic, 30 minutes does not get you very far. Other key factors include travel corridors (longer distance commutes and intercity freight movement) and market factors, such as the location of supply chain suppliers, support services providers and proximity to markets.

## 8.2.2 Categorizing industries and occupations

In providing information on the structure of an economy, data agencies in the United States, Canada and Mexico classify industries by product or service sim-ilarities using the North American Industry Classification System (NAICS). The

**FIGURE 8.2**　Key factors in the selection of a study area
*Source*: Poole 2015.

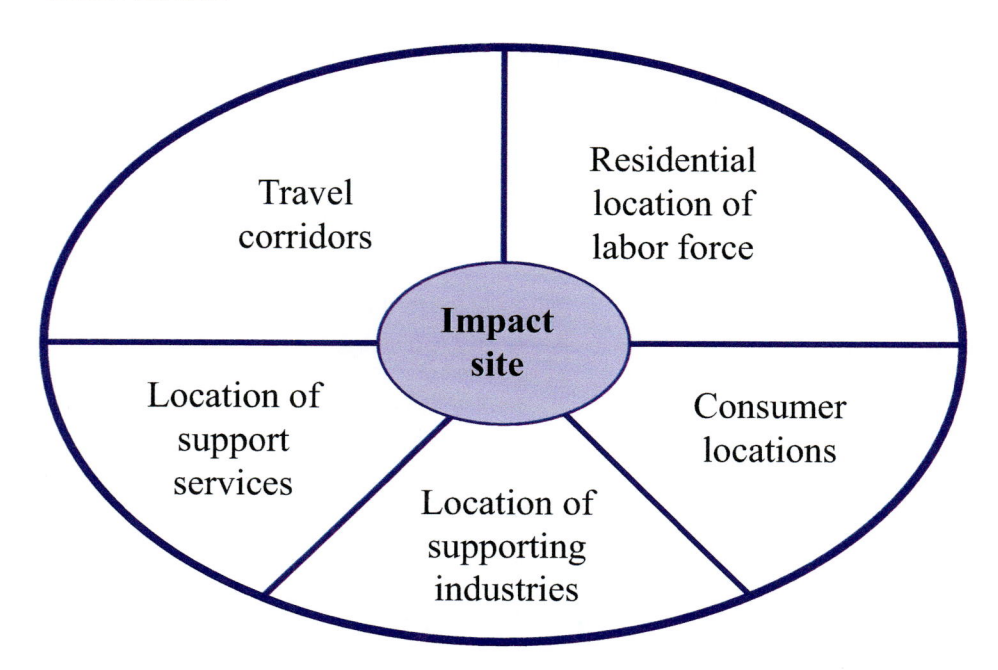

NAICS coding scheme replaced the Standard Industrial Classification (SIC) system in 1997 and represented major changes in line with new technologies (particularly electronic communications equipment and services). The current version of NAICS was last revised in 2012. Care must be taken when comparing data across different versions of the NAICS system, though there are crosswalk tables available to help researchers make appropriate comparisons over time. The NAICS manual is available through an online search tool at www.census.gov/eos/www/naics/. The structure of the NAICS code runs from two digits to as many as six digits. The greater the number of digits, the more detailed the industry description. Table 8.2 and Table 8.3 show the sectoring scheme for NAICS codes.

Similar to industry classifications, the Standard Occupational Classification (SOC) system managed by the US Department of Labor classifies all occupations in the economy, including private and public sector employers, as well as the military. There are 23 major groups of job classifications as shown in Table 8.4. Importantly, the Bureau of Labor Statistics (www.bls.gov) offers a database that provides occupation data by industry, which allows the analyst to examine the labor force needs of particular industries to answer important research questions such as: 1) Does the local labor force have the skills required by a desired industry? 2) What industries would match well with the existing labor force? Table 8.5 shows an example of a detailed occupation classification using the SOC structure.

**TABLE 8.2**    Major (two-digit) sectors, North American Industry Classification System

| 11 – Agriculture, fishing, forestry | 42 – Wholesale trade | 53 – Real estate | 62 – Health care and social assistance |
|---|---|---|---|
| 21 – Mining and extraction | 44–45 – Retail trade | 54 – Professional, scientific, technical services | 71 – Arts, entertainment and recreation |
| 22 – Utilities | 48–49 – Transportation and warehousing | 55 – Management of companies | 72 – Accommodation and food |
| 23 – Construction | 51 – Information | 56 – Administration, waste and remediation | 81 – Other services |
| 31–33 – Manufacturing | 52 – Finance and insurance | 61 – Education | 92 – Government |

**TABLE 8.3**    Examples of sector detail, North American Industry Classification System

| NAICS Code | Description |
|---|---|
| **31** | Manufacturing |
| **311** | Food manufacturing |
| **3113** | Sugar and confectionary product manufacturing |
| **31131** | Sugar manufacturing |
| **311311** | Sugar cane mills |
| **311312** | Cane sugar refining |
| **311313** | Beet sugar manufacturing |

**TABLE 8.4**    Standard Occupational Classification, major groups

| Code | Title | Code | Title | Code | Title |
|---|---|---|---|---|---|
| 11 | Management | 27 | Arts, design, sports, entertainment and media | 43 | Office and administrative support |
| 13 | Business and financial operations | 29 | Healthcare practitioners and technicians | 45 | Farming, fishing, forestry |
| 15 | Computer and mathematical | 31 | Healthcare support | 47 | Construction and extraction |
| 17 | Architecture and engineering | 33 | Protective service | 49 | Installation, maintenance and repair |
| 19 | Life, physical and social sciences | 35 | Food preparation and serving | 51 | Production |
| 21 | Community and social service | 37 | Building and grounds maintenance | 53 | Transportation and material moving |
| 23 | Legal | 39 | Personal care and service | 55 | Military |
| 25 | Education, training and library | 41 | Sales and related | | |

**TABLE 8.5**    Examples of occupation detail, Standard Occupational Classification

| NAICS Code | Description |
|---|---|
| **17–0000** | Architecture and engineering occupations |
| **17–2000** | Engineers |
| **17–2070** | Electrical and electronic engineers |
| **17–2071** | Electrical engineers |
| **17–2072** | Electronic engineers, except computer |

Table 8.6 offers an overview of some key public sources of data used in research for economic development planning in the United States. The textbook website provides a wider list of government and private sector data sources used for economic development planning and performance monitoring.

Under United States law, public entities cannot publish data that would reveal, or allow to be easily deduced, data on individuals and firms that would be considered trade secrets or competitively sensitive. For smaller (population) areas or areas with relatively few employers, this means that detailed data are masked. Masking data can be accomplished by simply leaving blanks, or the data can be presented as a range. For example, a county with only two or three employers in the medical equipment manufacturing sector may report employment as being in the 250–499 range. In percentage terms, that is a wide variance, but masking protects one employer from being able to deduce the number of jobs employed by competing firms. There are a number of ways to address data presented in a range. The analyst can take either the high or low point, use the midpoint, or calculate an estimate using other available data. The choice of approach for addressing data masking should be made in the context of the analysis.

## BOX 8.1  SITE CERTIFICATION AND MAXIMIZING ECONOMIC DEVELOPMENT OPPORTUNITIES

### Site certification

During the recovery from the Great Recession, several US Government economic stimulus programs provided funding for 'shovel ready' projects for constructing infrastructure and industrial building. This drew attention to a growing demand by companies for site locations that possessed little or no risk of development impediments. Though there is no standard definition of a 'Certified Site,' the following represent common characteristics of sites that are build-ready:

- Land title free and clear;
- Proper zoning in place;
- No environmental issues (contamination);
- No archeological/historic preservation issues;
- Basic utilities in place;
- Road infrastructure in place;
- No site drainage/flood plain issues;
- No unidentified easements.

An increasingly important data source for economic development practitioners, as well as professionals engaged in workforce development, is the O*Net database available at www.onetonline.org. This database allows planners and workers to examine a wide range of information regarding tools and technology used, education requirements, skills and specific tasks associated with a given occupation.

**TABLE 8.6**  United States public data sources

| Counting people | Counting money | Counting businesses and jobs |
|---|---|---|
| Census Bureau **www.census.gov** | Bureau of Economic Analysis www.bea.gov | Census Bureau www.census.gov |
| Decennial Census | National economic accounts | Economic Census (five years) |
| Population | Gross domestic product | Establishments by industry |
| Age | Personal income and | Jobs and payroll by |
| Race/ethnicity | outlays | industry |
| Household composition | Corporate profits | Sales, revenue, investment |
| Home owner/renter | Fixed assets | By state, metro area, cities, zip codes |
| American Community Survey | International accounts | County business patterns |
| Demographics | International transactions | Annual (week of March 12) |
| Education | Trade in goods and | Jobs by industry |
| Household income | services | Establishments by industry |
| Occupation/industry | International services | Payroll |
| Commuting | Imports/exports of | Zip code business patterns |
| Housing characteristics | services | |
| | Sales through affiliates | |
| | Direct investment (FDI, US) | |

(*continued*)

**TABLE 8.6**   (continued)

| Counting people | Counting money | Counting businesses and jobs |
| --- | --- | --- |
| Population estimates and projections<br>  Annual estimate of population<br>  Components of change<br>    Births, deaths, migration | Regional accounts<br>  GDP by state and metro area<br>  State personal income<br>  Local area personal income<br>  Regional input–output models | |
| Current Population Survey<br>  Joint program with BLS<br>  Employment/unemployment<br>  Earnings<br>  Hours of work<br>  Demographics | Industry economic accounts<br>  GDP by industry<br>  Benchmark input–output | Bureau of Labor Statistics<br>www.bls.gov Jobs by occupation and industry earnings |

#  8.3 Methods of data analysis

In this section of the chapter, we introduce readers to some of the most widely used data analytic techniques in the practice of economic development. Our focus is on methods that can be used with readily available public data and that require little or no advanced technical training. These methods include location quotients, shift-share analysis and cluster analysis. We also provide an overview of more advanced methods of regional economic analysis that are sometimes employed by well-staffed economic development organizations, but are more likely to be performed by outside consultants on behalf of these organizations, including measures of economic specialization, trade flow analysis, economic impact analysis and fiscal impact analysis. To begin, we start with a technique that is no longer commonly used but provides a basis for understanding the structure of a local economy.

## 8.3.1 Economic base analysis

As covered throughout this textbook, long-term economic success requires a robust trade economy with imports and exports. Exports, whether they are goods or services, bring new money into a region. Economic geographers use the terms 'basic' and 'nonbasic' industries. **Basic industries** are those that produce goods and services that are sold to consumers outside the region. **Nonbasic industries** sell exclusively to local consumers, but keep in mind that some of those local business consumers will be basic/exporting industries. Thus, when a business earns revenue from an export sale, some of that money winds up in the hands of other local businesses that provide goods and services to the exporting business. As noted by Meek (2003): 'A region's export [basic] industries are its economic foundation, all other industries thrive by servicing the export industries and one another.' If a basic industry increases its sales, there will be a concomitant increase in total nonbasic industry sales. Unfortunately, the converse also holds true, which is why the closure of a firm in the basic sector of a regional economy can potentially devastate

**FIGURE 8.3**  Economic base model

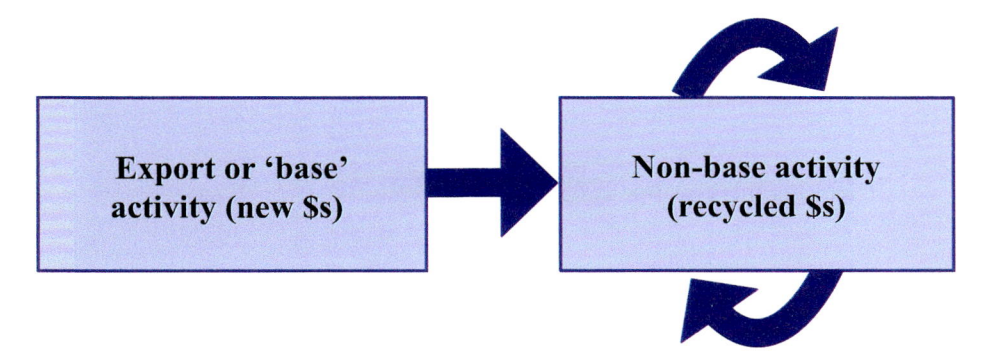

Examples:
- Manufacturing
- Tourism
- Some hospitals
- Regional shopping malls
- Social security

Examples:
- Auto repair services
- Small convenience retail
- Outpatient medical
- Personal services
- Print and copy shops

a wide range of local businesses. Figure 8.3 provides a graphical representation of the economic base model with examples of basic and nonbasic industries.

In the examples shown in Figure 8.3, you will note that the economic base model is focused on the money trail more than classifications of business activity. Tourism is a basic industry because it is about attracting spending by consumers who do not live in the local area. Hospitals become basic industries when they attract patients, and related patient-family spending, from outside the local market, such as the Mayo Clinic in Rochester, Minnesota or the MD Anderson Cancer Institute in Houston, Texas. Social security is not a business, but it is a source of 'external' money received by local residents, which is also true for other transfer payments such as private retirement payments.

The economic base model, which was developed in the late 1920s, was an early effort to understand regional economic structures using relatively simple metrics. It begins with a simple equation:

$$E^T = E^B + E^L \tag{1}$$

where $E^T$ is total employment, $E^B$ is basic (export) employment and $E^L$ is local (nonbasic) employment.

Defining r as the ratio of local employment to total employment:

$$r = E^L/E^T \tag{2}$$

which can be re-expressed as:

$$E^L = r\, E^T \tag{3}$$

Substituting (3) into (1) we get:

$E^T = E^B + r\ E^T$

Collecting the $E^T$ terms on the left side of the equation:

$E^T - r\ E^T = E^B$

Factoring this equation results in:

$(1 - r)\ E^T = E^B$

Which yields the equation:

$$E^T = \frac{1}{[1 - r]}\ E^B$$

Expressed in words, total employment in the region is equal to basic employment *multiplied* by a factor.

$$\frac{1}{[1 - r]}$$

By definition $0 \leq r \leq 1$; therefore $\dfrac{1}{[1-r]}$ must be greater than 1.0.[3]

Basic industries also sell to local residents and businesses. A manufacturer of candy bars undoubtedly sells some of their products to local residents. Locals also visit tourism destination sites. The challenge with economic base modeling is determining which portion of employment is attributable to exports. The analyst needs to be able to determine, or at least estimate, the jobs exclusively supported by export sales within basic industry firms. Two of the early methods to provide this estimate were the judgment method and business surveys. The judgment method gathered a group of individuals with knowledge of the local economy who made an educated guess regarding the size of the exporting sector. The analyst could also survey local businesses and ask them to provide specific information on sales patterns (exports versus local), but this approach raises two significant problems. First, such a survey would be laborious and very expensive in anything larger than the smallest of communities. Second, it is unlikely that enough businesses would share such important competitive information. Therefore, researchers turned to a technique known as location quotients to estimate the export share of total regional employment.

Here we draw a close on our discussion of economic base modeling. You can access the textbook website to find an example of an economic base calculation using the formulae described above. The representation of a local economy provided by economic base analysis is, in many ways, oversimplified, and therefore it is rarely, if ever, used by modern economic development practitioners. Still, it provides an excellent way for students and decision makers to conceptualize important structures in a regional economy.

## 8.3.2 Location quotients

Location quotients compare the relative concentration of employment in a given industry for a study area to the concentration of employment in that same industry for a reference area. The reference area used is often total national employment, though the reference area could be a state or a substate region. The formula for a location quotient (LQ) is:

$$\frac{e_{ir}\Big/\sum e_{ir}}{E_i\Big/\sum E_i}$$

where:

- $e_{ir}$ = Employment in some industry (i) in some region (r)
- $\sum e_{ir}$ = Total employment in the region
- $E_i$ = Reference area employment in some industry (i)
- $\sum E_i$ = Total reference area employment

An LQ equal to 1.0 indicates that the proportion of a given industry in the local economy is the same as the reference area. Location quotients less than 1.0 means the industry is relatively underrepresented, while a location quotient greater than 1.0 indicates overrepresentation. From an economic base analysis perspective, our interpretations of location quotients are:

LQ = 1.0: Local production just meets local demand.
LQ < 1.0: Local production does not meet local demand; the difference must be imported.
LQ > 1.0: Local production exceeds local demand; the difference is exported.

Basic employment is represented by the proportion of the LQ above 1.0. Modern economic development practitioners focus on a slightly different interpretation. If the LQ is meaningfully larger than 1.0, then the local region may have a competitive advantage for attracting and developing business in that industry sector. Industries with LQs less than 1.0 could be examined for development potential since a portion of local demand must be met by imports. The question for the economic development practitioner is, can industries with apparent comparative weaknesses be developed or attracted to the local economy? See Box 8.2 for an example of location quotient analysis.

Location quotient analysis is a good general technique for an initial assessment of local/regional economic competitiveness. However, there are several major assumptions in the location quotient analysis that limit the degree to which economic development practitioners should use an LQ as a sole performance indicator. These assumptions include:

- Patterns of consumption do not vary geographically. In our Missouri example, we are implicitly assuming that average beer consumption is the same across the US. It is quite likely this is not true. Residents in Tennessee or Kentucky may exhibit preferences for spirits, on average;
- Labor productivity is also assumed to be constant between the study area and reference area;
- Each firm in an industry produces identical products. For example, NAICS does not differentiate between 'regular' yogurt and Greek yogurt, but there are substitutions in consumption patterns as consumer demand shifts between these two products;

- Location quotients do not account for cross-hauling, which is the simultaneous import and export of goods. Residents of Missouri do, on occasion, drink Coors or other beers not produced in Missouri;
- Location quotient analysis does not pick up international trade patterns, which can distort the LQ calculation.

Even with these limitations, a location quotient analysis is relatively easy to perform and easy to explain to a nontechnical audience. The technique can be applied to several types of data beyond employment by industry, such as employment by occupation, income measures and industry output. It is a useful way of estimating basic employment in a region and can serve as one metric in an analysis to target industries for local and regional economic development.

## BOX 8.2  LOCATION QUOTIENT FOR MISSOURI'S BREWING INDUSTRY

### Raise your glasses. A toast to the Missouri economy!

Study Area: State of Missouri
Reference area: United States
Sector: 31212 Breweries
Data source: US Census Bureau, County Business Patterns 2014

|  | Industry | Total |  | Industry | Total |
|---|---|---|---|---|---|
| Missouri | 1,447 | 2,404,701 | US | 37,973 | 121,079,879 |

$$\frac{\frac{1,447}{2,404,701}}{\frac{37,973}{121,079,879}} = \frac{0.000602}{0.000314} = 1.92 = LQ$$

Interpretation: the Missouri economy, which is home to Budweiser and other national brands, has almost twice the concentration of employment in the brewing industry as the US as a whole. There are clear competitive advantages for industries associated with the brewing of malt beverages.

   Base Economic Analysis: $(0.000602–0.000314) \times 2,404,701 = 693$. The difference in the proportion of total jobs at brewers in Missouri versus the proportion of total jobs at brewers in the US multiplied by the total jobs in Missouri indicates that of the 1,447 total brewery jobs in the state, about 693 are related to exports.

A variation of a location quotient analysis is the dynamic location quotient (DLQ). Dynamic location quotient analysis looks at how the LQ changes over time. For example, an industry with an LQ of 1.8 could be considered a highly competitive sector for the regional economy. But, what if the LQ had been 2.3 a few years earlier? Does this mean that the region is losing its competitive edge? Not necessarily. An LQ can change because other local sectors of the economy are growing faster than the subject industry. A constant, strong LQ over time could be an indicator of maintaining competitiveness, but the number would not change if there was simultaneous change in study area and reference area industry employment – such as an overall drop in employment across the US in certain industries. Therefore, it becomes important for the economic development analyst to understand broad influences on regional industries. The most common methodology used for this type of analysis is called a shift-share.

### 8.3.3 Shift-share analysis

Shift-share analysis is a standard method of regional economic analysis that attempts to separate regional job growth into its component causes. The three main causes identified are the 'national growth effect,' which is regional growth that can be attributed to the overall growth of the entire US economy; the 'industrial mix effect,' which is regional growth that can be attributed to trends in the specific industry or occupation at a national level; and the 'regional competitiveness effect' or 'regional shift,' which is growth that cannot be explained by either overall or industry-specific trends. The underlying assumption is that industry performance not linked to overall economic trends or specific industry trends at the national level is the result of locally driven market dynamics affecting regional competitiveness. Academic researchers sometimes use the regional competitiveness effect as a proxy for endogenous (from within) growth factors in modeling economic performance.

A positive value for the regional shift/competitive effect indicates that an industry has a competitive advantage compared to the nation. Positive shift-share values do not explain why an industry has a competitive advantage, only that there are potential factors that contribute to the industry's ability to outperform the national average rate of growth/decline. Shift-share analysis can be calculated for any time period, but practically it is best to have at least five years between the two data points.

Shift-share is a step up in analytical sophistication from a location quotient analysis. Some of the weaknesses of the LQ apply to shift-share, especially regarding productivity, not accounting for product differentiation among brands, cross-hauling and international trade. Still, it is a relatively easy measure to employ and provides a reasonably valid measure of regional economic competitiveness (the regional shift). In conducting target industry studies, we often use an additional measure derived from the shift-share analysis. Expected change is the sum of the national share and industrial mix components of the shift-share. Expected change can offer an assessment of the magnitude of opportunity for growth in the region based on national trends, similar to calculating the jobs equivalent of unmet demand using location quotients.

**FIGURE 8.4**  The shift-share model

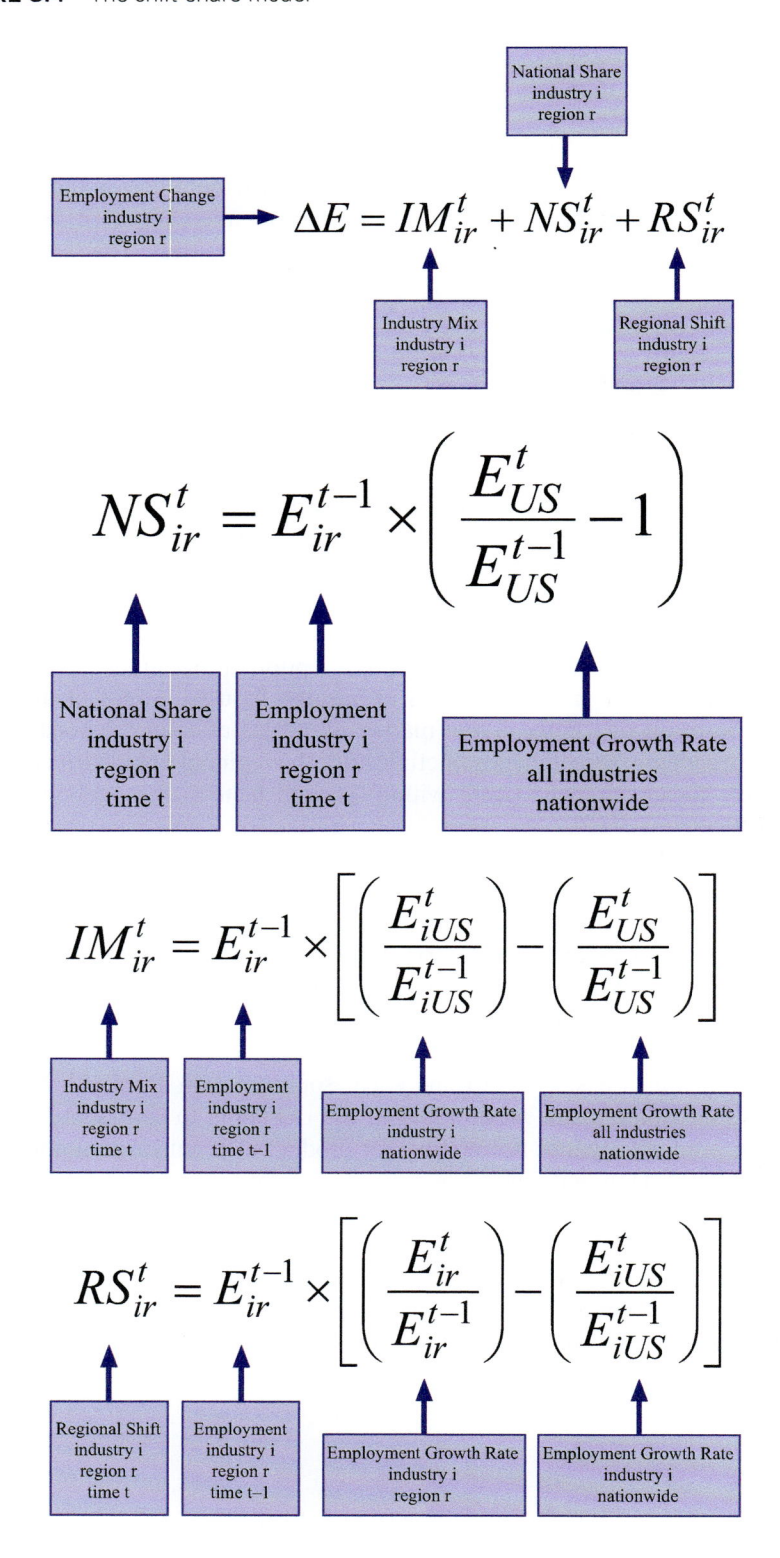

## BOX 8.3  SHIFT-SHARE ANALYSIS OF VIRGINIA WINE MAKING

### Fruit of the Vine

Study Area: State of Virginia
Reference area: USA
Sector: 31213 Wineries

Data source: US Census Bureau, County Business Patterns 2006, 2014

|      |          | Industry | Total     |    | Industry | Total       |
|------|----------|----------|-----------|----|----------|-------------|
| 2006 | Virginia | 371      | 3,174,363 | US | 29,926   | 119,917,165 |
| 2014 |          | 1,119    | 3,160,539 |    | 44,369   | 121,079,879 |

Note: numbers in the calculations below may not add up precisely due to rounding.

$$NS = 371 \times \left[\frac{121,079,879}{119,917,165} - 1\right] = 371 \times 0.009696 = 4$$

Based on the growth rate of employment for all industries in the United States, we would expect the growth of employment for Sector 31213 wineries in the Commonwealth of Virginia to be 4 jobs.

$$IS = 371 \times \left[\frac{44,369}{29,926} - \frac{121,079,879}{119,917,165}\right] = 371 \times [1.4826 - 1.009656]$$
$$= 371 \times [0.4729] = 175$$

Overall, the wine industry in the US grew, creating (44,369–29,926) 14,443 new jobs between 2006 and 2014. If the wine industry in Virginia grew at the same pace as the industry across the US, we would expect the state to gain 175 new jobs in wineries.

$$RS = 371 \times \left[\frac{1,119}{371} - \frac{44,369}{29,926}\right] = 371 \times [3.0162 - 1.4826]$$
$$= 371 \times [1.5335] = 569$$

Even when accounting for overall national economic growth and national level industry trends, the wine industry in Virginia grew impressively between 2006 and 2014. Of the [1,119–371] 748 jobs gained in Virginia's wine industry, 569 of these jobs can be potentially attributed to competitive factors associated with the state.

### 8.3.4  Other methods

There are several other methods used in economic development research whose technical requirements or data skills are beyond the scope of this text. Nonetheless, we offer an overview of several of these methods and encourage you to review materials on the textbook website as well as sources referenced below.

### 8.3.4.1 Economic impact analysis (input–output)

Economic impact analyses estimate how spending associated with a particular event, project, industry or firm flows through a regional economy. Input–output models are based on concepts developed by Wassily Leontief in the mid-20th century and are an extension of economic base modeling that provide a mathematical formulation for explaining the interdependencies among sectors of the economy. Firms purchase raw materials, equipment and goods (inputs) that are then transformed into products for consumption (outputs) by other producers, households or government. The goods that are specifically produced for use in other products are called *intermediate* goods. (Please note that services can also be intermediate goods, but illustrations are easier with manufactured products.) The gears that are sold to a fine watchmaker are intermediate goods. When a product is sold as a finished good to households or government, we call that **final demand**. Table 8.7 shows a stylized input–output table.

Notice that the input–output table looks similar to a double entry accounting ledger. In general, the columns in the interindustry transactions represent the purchases that a given industry must make to produce their products. The agriculture sector of the economy buys 21 'dollars' worth of other agricultural products,[4] a small amount (1) from the mining sector, some manufactured products (3), a lot of transportation (31) and other (10) services for a total of 66. Continuing down the column, we then see that the agriculture sector 'consumes' value added and imports. Value added represents the industry's purchase of labor services (employees), business profits and dividends, income from property, and purchases of government services (taxes).

Going across the rows we see that the agriculture sector sells to itself, does not sell to mining, provides 9 'dollars' worth of goods to manufacturers and has sales to the transportation sector for a total of 33 interindustry sales. Final demand for agriculture products includes sales to households (30), government (15) and export sales (22), which sums to 67. Add the interindustry sales (33) to final demand sales (67) for total sales of 100.

The data that are used to build an input–output table in the United States come from the National Income and Products Accounts (NIPA) produced by the Bureau of Economic Analysis in the US Department of Commerce. These data come largely from the quinquennial (five yearly) economic census conducted by the US Census Bureau augmented by price and labor market data from the Department of Labor, as well as special data gathering programs for retailers, manufacturers, miners and other industry sectors. Other nations have similar data programs. These data are used to build tables of transactions that describe the interindustry purchases. The NIPA program data allow the distinction between commodities and industries that describe the materials, equipment and products 'used' by a given industry, and the products that industry 'make.' Make and use tables can be used in target industry studies as described later in this chapter.

An economic input–output model uses transaction data from the NIPA tables to build a set of multipliers similar to what is described in an economic base analysis, but provides industry-specific detail. Detailing the construction and mathematics of an input–output model is beyond the scope of this text, but students are encouraged to examine any number of excellent textbooks and primers on

**TABLE 8.7**  Conceptual input–output table

| Sector | | Interindustry transactions | | | | | Final demand | | | Total final demand | Total sales |
| | | | | | | | Households | Government | Exports | | |
| | | 1 | 2 | 3 | 4 | 5 | 6 | 7 | 8 | 9 | 10 |
|---|---|---|---|---|---|---|---|---|---|---|---|
| 1 | Agriculture | 21 | 0 | 9 | 3 | 0 | 30 | 15 | 22 | 67 | 100 |
| 2 | Mining | 1 | 8 | 7 | 29 | 0 | 25 | 7 | 23 | 55 | 100 |
| 3 | Manufacturing | 3 | 20 | 0 | 50 | 7 | 5 | 9 | 6 | 20 | 100 |
| 4 | Transportation | 31 | 2 | 38 | 0 | 3 | 12 | 13 | 1 | 26 | 100 |
| 5 | Services | 10 | 25 | 26 | 1 | 4 | 9 | 19 | 6 | 34 | 100 |
| 6 | Total intermediate | 66 | 55 | 80 | 83 | 14 | 81 | 63 | | | |
| 7 | Value added | 20 | 40 | 10 | 17 | 40 | 2 | 62 | | | |
| 8 | Imports | 14 | 5 | 10 | 0 | 46 | 77 | 55 | | | |
| 9 | TOTAL INPUTS | 100 | 100 | 100 | 100 | 100 | 160 | 180 | | | |

*Source*: Council for Community and Economic Research 2014.

input–output analysis.[5] However, we can offer a qualitative description of what input–output models provide for the economic development analyst.

Spending by an organization creates direct, indirect and induced impacts. Using a firm that manufactures tortillas and other flatbreads for institutional (school districts, government entities, et cetera) and consumer markets as an example, direct impacts relate to the value of the bakery spending money for facilities, equipment, flour, seasoning, packaging, transportation and other business services. Indirect impacts capture associated upstream spending such as the vendor that provides the plastic bags used to package tortillas, who needs to purchase plastic as well as ink for printing labels on the bags. They also purchase equipment and hire an accounting firm to do bookkeeping and maintain financial records. Indirect impacts also include subsequent rounds of spending such as the accounting service purchasing office supplies, renting office space and hiring a janitorial service business, which in turn purchases cleaning supplies. Induced impacts capture the effects of employees of all of these firms spending a portion of their earnings in the regional economy for goods and services.

At each round of impacts, the model adjusts for spending that leaves the region. For example, if our subject firm is located in Boston, we know that the fuel used

## BOX 8.4  ECONOMIC IMPACTS OF ATTRACTING A NEW FIRM TO A REGION

### Tina's Terrific Tortillas

Industry: Tortillas Manufacturing
NAICS: 311830
IMPLAN Code: 98
Study area: Washington, DC Metropolitan Statistical Area
Model: IMPLAN Economic Input-Output Model

Study description: Due to the rapid growth in the popularity of Hispanic cuisines, Tina's Terrific Tortillas has contacted a regional economic development agency to express an interest in locating a new plant in the DC region that will serve the Mid-Atlantic market. The analysis is to examine the economic impacts of this new firm arriving in town.

Anticipated annual company sales: $35 million (producer prices).

| Impact type | Output | Value added | Labor income | Jobs |
| --- | --- | --- | --- | --- |
| Direct | $35,000,000 | $11,534,284 | $6,083,810 | 164 |
| Indirect | $9,938,621 | $5,776,110 | $3,813,725 | 40 |
| Induced | $6,955,471 | $4,236,927 | $2,464,215 | 45 |
| Total | $61,894,092 | $21,547,321 | $12,361,750 | 249 |

Summary: attracting Tina's Tortillas to the Washington, DC area would increase total area output (business activity) by $61.9 million per year, increasing total value added (gross regional product) by $21.5 million, and support 249 total jobs paying $12.3 million in salaries, wages and benefits.

by the trucks to deliver tortillas to local stores is not refined in the local economy; therefore, only a relatively small portion of the price of the fuel is counted in the impacts on the Boston economy. There is some local impact associated with selling and distribution expenses. As you may suspect, the definition of the study geography is very important in economic impact analysis. Even when the spending is adjusted to capture only local impacts, the sum of the direct, indirect and induced effects are more than the original spending by the tortilla maker – hence the term 'multiplier effect.' Input–output models provide estimates of economic activity, labor income and employment. Economic activity, sometimes referred to as 'output,' is essentially a measure of the value of transactions (spending) that you would see in the input–output table. Labor income includes salaries, wages and benefits paid to employees plus proprietors' income. Employment is the number of jobs created by the spending. Though there are continual efforts to improve input–output modeling, the analyst must always be aware that the results of an input–output modeling exercise are estimates. Additional information on the development and use of economic input–output modes can be found on the textbook website. See Box 8.4 for an example of an economic impact analysis using a commercially available input–output model.

## 8.3.4.2 Fiscal impact analysis

Fiscal impact analysis assesses the impact of a firm, industry, project or land use on government finances. In the simplest model, the economic development researcher estimates the likely tax revenues that will accrue to relevant jurisdictions (federal, state, local) related to a given firm, industry, project or event. The industry standard for techniques in performing a fiscal impact analysis is Burchell's *The Fiscal Impact Handbook* (1978). Burchell defined the cost and revenue parameters of a fiscal impact analysis as having three characteristics: direct, current and public. His use of the term 'direct' is not exactly the same as described in economic input–output analysis, though there are similarities. If a new manufacturing firm comes to town, the company will pay property taxes, license and permit fees, and possibly other taxes to the host taxing jurisdiction. The city/county will provide and maintain infrastructure (roads, sewers, water) that serve the facility and provide services (fire, police, administration). These are direct revenues and costs and are paid to/ by the public entity. The 'current' characteristic addresses the timing of cost. For example, if supplying the new manufacturing facility with water utilities requires the city to lay new service pipelines, it is likely that the expense of building the line would be financed through capital bond issuances; therefore, the current cost of that new pipeline would be the annual cost of debt service, not the total cost summed across a number of years.

Ancillary costs and revenues are not included in most fiscal impact analyses. Continuing with our example of a new manufacturing firm locating in a city, the new company employs workers who may go to a local restaurant for lunch, thereby generating sales that are taxed by the local jurisdiction. However, these sales taxes are typically treated as indirect revenues in fiscal impact analysis, and thus are not counted in determining the net fiscal benefit of the new manufacturing firm. This is where economic and fiscal impact analyses often diverge. Economic impact analyses of new sports venues often tout ancillary spending at local restaurants and

## BOX 8.5  ASSESSING THE FISCAL IMPACTS OF CONSERVED LAND ON VIRGINIA'S EASTERN SHORE

A recent study examined the net fiscal impacts of conserved lands in two counties of Virginia. The two counties are located on a peninsula with the Chesapeake Bay on one side and the Atlantic Ocean on the other. In sum, the two counties have about one-third or their total land area in conserved status, which means the property cannot be developed. This includes federally owned property (government facilities, protected wilderness and seashore areas), state parks and private land that has been placed under voluntary deed restrictions – usually with an attendant reduction in taxable property value. This region has struggled to attract industries to their somewhat remote location to offset long run declines in the agriculture sector, placing great strain on the counties' ability to provide public services. The analysis, performed by Dr. Dean Bellas of Urban Analytics, found that even though having land in conserved status reduces total government revenues, this is more than offset by also reducing public services required to support the land. The analysis revealed that for every dollar spent on providing local government resources to properties in conserved status, Accomack County saw $2.38 in property tax revenues. The analysis found a smaller net impact for Northampton County, but overall, conversed lands are net generators of fiscal revenue for both local jurisdictions (Clower and Bellas 2017).

shops during the sporting season. The tax revenues associated with marginal sales away from the ballpark attributed to sports fans attending games would not usually be counted in a traditional fiscal impact analysis.

Some commercially available input–output models estimate government revenues including income taxes, property taxes, sales taxes and other sources of government revenue for direct, indirect and induced effects. This can create confusion among decision makers and our only suggestion is that the authors of analyses used in assessing the fiscal, or economic, impacts associated with a company coming to town should state their methodologies clearly. It is also important that any fiscal impact analyses only count revenues that are net of any incentives offered to the firm.

Harrison and French (no date) offer a succinct but clear review of Burchell's methods of fiscal impact analysis, including: per-capita multiplier method, case study method, service standard method, comparable city method, proportional evaluation method and employment anticipation method. Each of these methods can be labeled as belonging to a broader scope of fiscal impact assessment called an 'average cost model.'

In the average cost model, the cost of providing services to a business, or residence for that matter, is based on some per-capita estimation. This could include estimating, based on current budgets, the average cost of providing roads, utilities and protective services to developments by type of land use. A calculation would be made assigning a portion of government costs to industrial properties, commercial (office/retail) properties, residential properties and other land uses. Then an average cost would be determined as average costs per square foot of building space, cost per employee/resident, cost per acre of land occupied, or other.

The other important concept in average cost modeling is that the expense of adding new infrastructure, unless it is designated as exclusive to a new development, is spread across all similar taxpayers. Conversely, a marginal cost model would assign the full cost of new infrastructure to the project that created the demand, even if the infrastructure would be available for use by future users not associated with the arriving firm.

Fiscal impact analyses can be complicated by practices in how local and state governments treat certain costs in a fiscal impact analysis. It is standard practice that the costs of providing public education are treated as an expense related to residential properties – an intuitively satisfying approach given that households generate the children that consume public education. However, a widely recognized expert in fiscal impact analysis, Dr. Dean Bellas, observes that since businesses do not want to locate in an area where the available labor force is uneducated, it would be appropriate to assign at least some of the costs of public education to business land uses (Bellas 2017). The assignment of public education costs to residential land uses is frequently touted as a reason to deny planning and permitting authority for new housing developments, especially affordable housing that generates relatively less property tax revenues to state and local jurisdictions. Helping leaders appropriately value the fiscal impacts of various land uses is, perhaps, the best reason for regional researchers, planners and practitioners to build the necessary skills and knowledge about fiscal impact analysis.

It is worth repeating that the most important thing in preparing or reviewing a fiscal impact analysis is to have a clear understanding of the methods and assumptions used. There are many examples of government costs, especially the value of incentives, being compared to economic output or fiscal impacts (not net) as if it were a return-on-investment analysis, which is incorrect.

### 8.3.4.3 Cluster analysis

Economic development plans based on a cluster strategy take into account inter-industry activities, intra-industry activities, shared markets and commonalities among factors of production. Interindustry activities typically refer to supply chain business-to-business purchases on goods and services. Intra-industry activities take on many forms and can include trade association connections, joint marketing strategies and collaborations on research or product development. Commonalities among factors of production include shared labor pools, key infrastructure (roads, ports, communications networks, utilities), the presence of research universities and other factors. The data analysis method used for a cluster analysis would depend on the basis for the cluster formation.

Given data analytic techniques developed for big-data exercises, one could take the approach of throwing a large volume of data into an analysis and look for patterns to emerge. However, the more common approach is to narrow the scope of the data analysis by screening data to identify key regional industries that either represent an existing cluster or present the best opportunity for cluster development. Using location quotients and/or shift-share analysis, combined with other data elements, the analyst can identify key industries for a more detailed analysis.

There are two general approaches when examining industry clusters based on supply chain transactions. The first is to use existing cluster definitions from previous studies. One such effort is the Cluster Mapping project led by Michael Porter at Harvard University, which can be found at www.clustermapping.us. Resources available on this website show interindustry structures for more than 100 clusters providing economic development practitioners with ready-made cluster maps. The second approach is to develop cluster definitions based on an analysis of 'make' and 'use' tables. Make and use tables are available from the US Bureau of Economic Analysis from the national product accounts and treat industries as commodities. Make tables show the flow of products from the manufacturer to other industries, which are called intermediate goods, essentially answering the question, which industries use the product being made by a given industry?

Use tables look in the other direction. If you are the manufacturer, what goods and services do you 'use' as inputs for your production processes? The make and use tables allow the analyst to identify the markets, upstream and downstream, that are connected with leading local industries. Some of these connected industries may already exist in the local economy, others may be targets of opportunity for business recruitment or development.

Clusters based on shared labor pools can be identified using occupation data and the occupations-by-industry data available from the US Bureau of Labor Statistics. For example, if a region has a concentration of aerospace engineers, which could be supplemented by graduates of nearby university programs, then a cluster of industries could be identified that require that skill set.

Identifying clusters based on trade associations, collaborations on research and product development, or joint marketing efforts could be accomplished through data searches. However, interactions with a set of key informants representing these industries, whether through formal interviews or more casual community meetings, can provide the information needed for identifying the dynamics of these types of industry cluster activities.

 ## 8.4 Target industry analysis

In economic development planning, the target industry analysis component is where a strategic decision is made on which industries or types of businesses will receive attention and resources. Even for well-funded economic development organizations, it is not practical to target every industry that may appear to have some level of opportunity for local development. The target industry uses the data gathered from one or more of the methods described above, reduces it to a form that facilitates strategic decision making, and applies inputs from a range on community stakeholders. The table below offers some general guidelines on using the analytical output from the methods described above in targeting industries for local economic development.

## 8.5 Program evaluation

This chapter has focused on measures of local and regional economic performance and metrics associated with given industries or land uses. Program evaluation shifts this focus to the economic development organization. Whether the economic development organization is a public or private sector entity, it is important that the organization has a clearly defined program of performance evaluation. An ongoing

**TABLE 8.8**  Using data for a target industry analysis

| Data | Use |
|---|---|
| **Location quotient** | Strong location quotient (LQ > 1.4). Possible local advantage. Weak location quotient (0.5 < LQ < 0.8). Possible opportunity. If LQ < 0.5 there may be some structural mismatch. |
| **Shift-share** | |
| **Regional shift** | Relatively strong regional shift, in absolute or percentage terms, generally indicates an existing competitive advantage. |
| **Expected change** | The sum of the national and industry shifts. Provides an indication of broad industry trends. Even if there is a local competitive advantage for a given industry, if the overall industry trend is declining it may not represent a viable industry target. |
| **Input–output** | |
| **Output multipliers** | The output multipliers derived from an input–output table can help identify firms that have deeper local supply chains. Attracting or expanding firms with comparatively large multipliers provides more economic bang for the level of investment (buck). The level of multiplier depends, in part, on the size of the local/regional economy, but in general an output multiplier greater than 1.5 is a reasonable initial criterion. |
| **Employment (jobs) multipliers** | Similar to output multipliers, industries that are likely to generate more upstream and downstream jobs make better economic development targets, though the analyst should consider the nature of the jobs. Look for jobs multipliers greater than 2.0 for larger economies. |
| **Earnings per job** | Average direct earnings per job in the industries being considered as targets of opportunity are often used to qualify companies for incentive packages. It is not unusual to see expectations of expected earnings of $17–$24 per hour, depending on local cost-of-living conditions. |
| **Projected job change** | The US Bureau of Labor Statistics offers an annual publication called 'Industry Outlook.' While no forecast is perfect, the idea is to identify industries that are expected to grow over the next several years at the national level. Look for industries with projected job growth rates greater than the overall expected rate of growth for all industries. |
| **Cluster analysis** | The findings of a cluster analysis identifies a set of connected industries that help focus economic development strategies. An important output of a cluster study is to identify industries that provide goods and services to more than one cluster. These 'boundary spanner' industries are excellent targets for economic development. |

system of performance evaluation provides important feedback on operations and strategies, as well as offering data to assure citizens that the resources being devoted to economic development are well managed and are meeting community goals for economic and community development. In measuring performance, it is important to distinguish between output and outcome measures.

Output measures describe things that are done. For example, an organization that is working to attract new firms to the region will probably keep track of the number of prospective firms (prospects) that are contacted or the number of RFI requests that are fulfilled. Many organizations track the number of jobs that are attracted or retained through economic development-related activities. However, a new job is certainly an output, but outcomes also consider if the result is going to meet broader economic development goals. For example, having a large mall located in a community will create jobs, but those jobs are likely to be relatively low paying. On the other hand, if the desired outcome is to boost local tax revenues, a mall that generates both property and sales taxes may be a desired outcome.

---

## BOX 8.6 COMMON PERFORMANCE METRICS FOR ECONOMIC DEVELOPMENT ORGANIZATIONS

- Inquiries/responses to prospects;
- Jobs created at median wage;
- Number of businesses opened;
- Population;
- New business investment attracted;
- Building permits (commercial/industrial);
- Unemployment rate;
- Business closures;
- Third-party rankings (best place for business).

---

Developing a set of relevant and effective performance measures for a state or local economic development agency must be highly contextual and flexible. The measures need to reflect the organization's mission and resources. If, for example, the mission of an economic development agency is to promote tourism businesses, it is hardly appropriate to judge program success on the creation of permanent, full-time jobs that pay more than $20 per hour. Alternatively, the creation of these kinds of jobs would be appropriate if the economic development goal is to diversify away from dependence on the local hospitality sector. Performance metrics also need to change as circumstances and strategic goals remain the same. The authors have seen examples of economic development agencies that have measured their performance the same way for close to two decades. Few communities have specific, actionable economic development goals that are functionally relevant for that long.

There is a remaining issue for most economic development agencies in reporting their performance. Since the majority of these agencies are public sector entities, there are performance evaluation measures that must be monitored as a part of the public compact. As a public agency in the United States, economic development organizations often must operate differently than their private sector clients. Even a successful agency can run into serious trouble if they forget their internal metrics, and procedures must adhere to public agency standards and withstand public scrutiny. These can include employee performance records, detailed program agreements that can withstand public audits, and increasingly the need to balance transparency with the secretive nature of business site selection processes. We refer you to the textbook website for more on evaluating economic development agency performance.

# ■ 8.6 Conclusion

The development of a good business plan requires data, analysis, and insight if there is to be success. The same is true in economic development planning and practice. Whether the focus is on new business startups, growing existing firms in the region or attracting new firms to relocate to a given community, using data to focus on the best industry development opportunities and understanding how economic growth will impact the regional economy, state and local governments, and the community are essential for long-term success. This chapter has provided a primer on some of the most common data analysis tools and techniques used in the practice of economic development.

A key point to remember is to always understand the data you use, the sources of that data and the degree to which the data are valid for the analysis you wish to undertake. In addition, each of the analytic techniques presented offers its own strengths and weaknesses, which should influence how you interpret the findings of any analysis. It never hurts to step back a little and take a wider view on what your analysis is telling you and how you will communicate your findings to decision makers, and potentially the public. However, with these cautions in mind, the tools and techniques presented in this chapter can provide planners, practitioners and decision makers with data-driven evidence that will support successful economic development planning.

You will find more resources on these and other analytic techniques, as well as informative case studies, on the textbook website.

## *Key messages*

- Data-driven economic development planning offers key advantages over anecdotal-based plans, but data analysis needs to be augmented with community input;
- Choosing the correct geography is critical to economic development research, but is often limited by the availability of data;
- Location quotients and shift-share analyses are excellent starting points for understanding the structure of a local economy and identifying potential target industries;
- Supply chain analysis provides insights into intra-regional economic interactions, as well as identifying industries for attraction or development;
- Economic and fiscal impact analyses are important tools for decision makers, but analysts and decision makers need a conceptual understanding of the strengths and weaknesses inherent in these techniques;

- In developing a list of target industries for focusing economic development efforts, multiple quantitative and qualitative techniques should be employed in the selection process;
- Quantitative performance measures are increasingly required for economic development agencies to facilitate program evaluation and increase public confidence in economic development investments.

## Discussion questions

One of the important themes in Chapter 8 has been the spatial scale of data reflecting that often the generation of strong economic development strategies is held back by the absence of good data at an appropriate spatial scale. Using online, publicly available resources only, investigate the availability of economic data for planning purposes at the following scales:

- Washington, DC;
- Washington–Arlington–Alexandria, DC–VA–MD–WV Metropolitan Statistical Area;
- City of Fairfax, VA.

What conclusions can be drawn about the adequacy of data at smaller spatial scales, and are there ways existing limitations could be overcome?

## Notes

1 For our discussions, states also include state-like jurisdictions in the US including the District of Columbia, Puerto Rico and US island areas.
2 County equivalent entities include boroughs (AK), parishes (LA), municipios (PR) and independent cities (MD, MO, NV, VA).
3 For those paying close attention to the formula, it is *theoretically* possible that $r = 0$ and thus the multiplier is 1.0, but it does not work that way in practice. No region is absolutely self-sufficient in the long run. Even the earliest human societies were either hunter-gatherers, who moved from region to region for resources, or agrarian societies, who traded for materials and foods they could not grow.
4 An example would be a cattle ranch purchasing hay and corn for animal feed.
5 One such reference text is Miller, R. and Blair, P. 2009 *Input-Output Analysis: Foundations and Extensions*. 2nd edition. Cambridge University Press, New York.

## References

Bellas, D. 2017 Private conversation on June 30, 2017.
Bresciani, M. 2010 Data driven planning: using assessment in strategic planning. In *New Directions for Student Services,* 132, Winter. DOI: 10.1002/ss.374, http://www.utsa.edu/Students/sanews/2014/issue05/files/Bresciani2010SAStrPlanAsmnt.pdf.

Burchell, R. 1978 *The Fiscal Impact Handbook*, Center for Urban Policy Research, Brunswick, NJ.

Clower, T. 2005 Economic applications in disaster research, mitigation, and planning. In McEntire, D. (ed.) *Disciplines, Disasters and Emergency Management: The Convergence and Divergence of Concepts, Issues and Trends in the Research Literature*, Federal Emergency Management Agency, Washington, DC.

Clower, T. and Bellas, D. 2017 *Socio-Economic Impacts of Conserved Land on Virginia's Eastern Shore.* Center for Regional Analysis, George Mason University, Arlington, VA.

Council for Community and Economic Research 2014 *Basic Economic Research Course.* Available at www.c2er.org.

Harrison, T. and French, C. (no date) *An Introduction to Fiscal Impact Analysis*, University of New Hampshire Cooperative Extension. Available at https://extension.unh.edu/resource/introduction-fiscal-impact-analysis.

Meek, A. 2003 *Economic Development Research.* Training materials from the Council for Community and Economic Research. Available at www.c2er.org.

Poole, K. 2015 *Basic Regional Economic Course.* Unpublished training materials, Council for Community and Economic Research.

Tveidt, T. and Clower, T. 2015 *Foundations of Applied Economic Development Research.* Unpublished training materials, Council for Community and Economic Research.

# 9 Planning and coordinating economic development

This chapter:

▶ Builds upon the discussion of analytical techniques and maps out how to create an economic development strategy;

▶ Examines the process of strategic planning and its translation into a set of action plans;

▶ Looks at the outcomes of economic strategy formation and their relationship with other public sector and business agencies;

▶ Examines differences in planning for economic development in urban and rural settings;

▶ Discusses public sector coordination and the strategies that can be employed to achieve better outcomes;

▶ Considers the experience of practitioners in implementing economic development plans;

▶ Discusses the use of community reference groups and leadership groups to mobilize community resources to achieve development goals.

STRATEGIC PLANNING IS one of the fundamental tools of economic development: it informs land use planning, shapes the expenditures and decisions of local or state government agencies, provides both the context and rationale for economic development actions, and provides a point of engagement with external stakeholders. In many respects, strategic planning is one of the most generic tools used by economic development professionals. The strategic planning processes used by economic development professionals are similar to those used by major corporations and large institutions, except that they also need to embrace community input. The context and content of strategic plans for economic development are also distinctive as communities planning their future have little capacity to shape either their external environment or their inventory of natural assets to better meet their priorities. A large corporation, for example, can restructure relatively quickly in response to changing markets, but regions and cities cannot readily change their fundamental conditions – the skills of the workforce, their access to core infrastructure or how they are perceived at the national or global scale. Often the capacity to plan at the local, regional or community scale far exceeds the ability to deliver outcomes. This inevitably creates both challenges and tensions in the work of economic development planners and practitioners. Understanding how government programs work, and how to gain access to public funding, can determine whether a strategic plan is successful or not, and this chapter also considers the ways communities can tap into government resources.

## ◼ 9.1  Strategic planning

Strategic planning has its origins in the military, where it was developed to provide a more flexible and effective approach to realizing objectives.

Strategic planning for economic development centers on the identification of a community's goals, and the mapping out of pathways to achieve those ends. Action plans then set out the detailed steps to put strategies into action. Importantly, strategic plans must:

- Set out how best to use the available resources to achieve the specified goals;
- Drive actions – ruling some activities out while giving priority to others;
- Be used to determine the allocation of resources (McLean and Voytek 1992).

An economic development strategy can be defined as a plan for the development of a region, a city or a community that sets out its economic goals, the strategies and activities it will use to achieve them, an understanding of the processes affecting the economy, and a set of priorities for action. Successful strategies focus on the businesses, networks and institutions most likely to deliver growth, while also balancing environmental, social and economic aspirations. They need to be achievable and give attention to a community's economic fundamentals – including how it pays its way in the world. They are dynamic, inform the work of relevant professionals and agencies, and provide a mechanism for updating as necessary. Strategic plans need to serve as the 'shop front' for economic development efforts and as a point of engagement with both external stakeholders and the broader community.

Economic development strategies are usually developed through a consultative process that ensures that those charged with the responsibility of delivering growth – whether it is a city planning department, regional development agency or other government entity – receive the views of relevant stakeholders. Various bodies, such as the World Bank (2006), and McKinsey and Co. (1994), recommend the establishment of a steering group to guide the process and comment upon the final outcomes.

Strategic plans set out to answer the following questions:

- Where is the region or city now economically – what are its current prospects, strengths and constraints?

- Where would the community or city like to be – what is the future sought by the community?
- How does this locality get to where it would like to be – what actions need to be put in place to deliver development, and who will take responsibility for those tasks?

Various authors have discussed how best to prepare an economic strategy; the following approach is based on the work of McLean and Voytek (1992 pp 2–3). They recommended an approach to local strategic planning that includes a number of analytical and decision-making steps:

1. *Audit the local economy and local resources:* evaluate the structure and performance of the existing local economy; analyze local industries and the characteristics of the business base. Benchmark the economy against both comparator communities and places that the region or city would wish to emulate. Assess labor and nonlabor resources; identify assets and liabilities in terms of industry competitive advantage and prospects for business investment;
2. *Formulate a mission statement:* identify critical issues and articulate broad goals. Consider how the mission statement can connect the community's past with its future, and how it makes a statement to investors, consumers and existing businesses;
3. *Develop strategies:* acknowledge the characteristics of the region or community and relate those characteristics to current and emerging trends – economic, demographic, social and political. Strategies need to identify potential economic opportunities or threats and ways to take advantage of opportunities while minimizing the impacts of threats;
4. *Implement action plans:* develop and pursue detailed plans for securing funding, managing programs, monitoring performance and communicating outcomes;
5. *Evaluate results:* monitor, update and adjust the plan in response to ongoing change in the economic environment;
6. *Communicate the process and communicate the outcomes:* ensure you reach out to all interested individuals and organizations, and make the outputs publicly available on the Internet.

## 9.1.1 Auditing the economy

Local economic audits set the scene for strategy formation and the development of plans. They need to be both sufficiently broad-ranging to provide an accurate snapshot of the community and its infrastructure, while also examining issues in sufficient depth to generate fresh insights into the city or region's economy. Local economic audits may use one or more of the methods described in the previous two chapters, with economic profiling, SWOT (strengths, weaknesses, opportunities and threats) analysis and industry projections commonly used.

Typically, the results of a local economic audit are made available to participants in the planning process and as a report to both internal and external stakeholders.

## 9.1.2 A mission and vision for the future

There is a need to articulate a vision for the future development of the region, which addresses input from key stakeholders and individuals, including political leaders, businesses, community groups, major institutions and other government agencies.

The establishment of a written 'vision statement' is an important part of planning for a region's economic future. While such statements are dismissed by some as lacking meaning, communities need to agree their aspirations if they are to progress.

A good vision statement within an economic development strategy needs to be:

- **Short**. It should be a succinct statement that summarizes both the community's position now, and where it would like to be in the future;
- **Authentic**. The vision statement needs to be relevant to that place, mindful of its history and informed by the possibilities for its future;
- **Unique**. Vision statements too similar to those in comparable communities suggest an inability to appropriately analyze local economic conditions and identify a distinctive trajectory;
- **Realistic**. Cities, regions and communities need to have grounded goals. Small rural communities or midsized cities shouldn't plan to emerge as the next major financial center, but they can be aspirational;
- **Informed**. Vision statements should reflect both strong empirical analysis of the city or region's economy and the perceptions of its communities;
- **Accepted**. The statement needs to be acknowledged by the community as reflecting their hopes for the future.

Box 9.1 provides examples of vision statements taken from economic development strategies around the globe. Some better reflect the assessment criteria outlined above, with Singapore's statement clearly future focused, but also grounded in the city-state's history of planned development and economic leadership.

Economic development strategies often include a statement of values and ethics alongside the mission statement. Such statements make clear the principles the organization or agency stands for, and the judgments they will make as they develop into the future.

Mission statements often emerge over an extended period of time, as key individuals and organizations assess, debate and modify their goals for the future. Commonly, mission statements find their first expression in a meeting, often undertaken in conjunction with a SWOT analysis and the discussion of the local economic profile. That initial output is then discussed with a broader audience, and revised as a range of perspectives are considered. Occasionally agencies mistake vision for mission, and being precise is less important than clearly articulating principles, ambitions and actions.

## BOX 9.1 EXAMPLE VISION STATEMENTS

### Strathcona County, Alberta, Canada, 2015

Strathcona County, located in the heart of Alberta, is an energetic and thriving community. A leader in North America's petroleum industry and a champion for advancing diverse agricultural business, we use our energy to power our new tomorrow (https://www.strathcona.ca/council-county/plans-and-reports/strategic-plan/).

### Nuu-chah-nulth Economic Development Corporation (NEDC), Canada

To continue to develop and grow to be the best Aboriginal Corporation dealing with financial, banking and business development services. NEDC will play a major role in helping Aboriginals and First Nation communities on Vancouver Island become healthy, wealthy and socio-economically independent by seizing all existing and emerging business opportunities and building on the new economy (https://www.nedc.info/about-nedc-2/).

### City of Ferris, Texas

Preserving the historic downtown area, Ferris will be a sound economic competitor, providing opportunities for new commercial, industrial, and residential development which does not appreciably alter the historic nature of the community (http://ferristx.org/forms/econdev/VISION_-_MISSION_STATEMENT_Joint_adoption_Sept_2012.pdf).

### Economic Development Board, Singapore, 2015

A Global Leader; A Great City; A Home in Asia; For Business, Innovation and Talent (https://www.edb.gov.sg/en/about-edb/who-we-are.html).

### 9.1.3 Developing strategies

Having set a mission statement, practitioners need to develop targeted goals and objectives that can be used to logically identify the programs and actions to be taken. As the World Bank noted (Swinburn et al. 2006), this assists decision making and helps communicate both the broad intent and detail of the strategy.

It is necessary to identify a series of goals that reflect the outcomes the community wants. These development goals are both more descriptive and concrete than the vision statement, and reflect the outcomes of the economic audit. The broadscale development goals form the framework within which more specific objectives are presented. Examples could be one of the following:

- Improving the quality of the workforce in our city;
- Taking better advantage of the natural beauty of our region.

Under the World Bank (2006) schema, development goals are followed by development objectives and these are very specific statements on how the community should develop. Ideally, each development objective will have a defined time horizon, and the capacity to be measured – so as to assess progress. The objectives will address the issues identified in the economic audit, and set out pathways for leveraging existing strengths, deal with weaknesses, take advantage of opportunities and reduce threats.

If we consider the two example goals set out above, the development objective of 'improving the quality of the workforce in our city' can be matched to a number of objectives:

- Increasing high school completion rates by 20 percent over five years;
- Growth of 30 percent over ten years in persons with post-high school qualifications;
- The addition of ten new vocational courses in priority areas within three years;
- A 20 percent increase in the number of technical studies students graduating with a cybersecurity certification.

The development goals of 'taking better advantage of the natural beauty of our region' could be matched with the following goals:

- 5 percent increase in tourist numbers for each of the next five years;
- Attracting investment in a major hotel and conference center within three years;
- A more active campaign of tourism marketing resulting in a 20 percent growth in visitors to our website for each of the next three years;
- Diversifying the range of social media used to advertise the region, with five new technologies to be employed over the next three years.

As the World Bank (2006) notes, many places are confronted by a multitude of challenges and potentially a very substantial set of opportunities. This leads to the tendency to try to address all issues at once. This is evident in terms of the number of development goals identified, as well as the nomination of specific development objectives. It is tempting to add to the list of priorities as planning process becomes more detailed. The challenge is to only identify the highest priority topics in order to concentrate resources and effort on those areas likely to generate the greatest returns. The World Bank (2006) also recommends that actions that have a clear champion – a local leader willing and able to advocate and work for their fulfillment – should be given priority.

### 9.1.4 Implementing action plans

Action plans provide the detail of which economic development tasks are to be undertaken, and by whom. They specify the time frame for action and allow for the monitoring of performance. Action plans relate to activities on the ground in at least two ways: first, the World Bank (2006) suggests all activities should be organized as programs. These programs potentially address more than one development objective. For example, a city marketing campaign could contribute to both the attraction of new businesses and rise in the tourism industry. A second approach is to organize all activities under a single development objective, with all workforce actions, for example, grouped under that theme, while place marketing projects would sit with community awareness objective. Both approaches have their merits, and whether a planning strategy is organized one way or another reflects personal preferences and the circumstances of the community.

The World Bank (2006) has provided a template for action plans, setting out clearly how they should be considered and implemented (Box 9.2).

## BOX 9.2 THE KEY COMPONENTS OF AN ACTION PLAN FOR ECONOMIC DEVELOPMENT PLANNING

**Project objectives**: each project should have clear objectives that meet program goals.

**Project inputs**: what are the capital and revenue costs? Which staff will work on each project, and does the organization already host the requisite skills? Will additional staff be required? Are other inputs required, such as land or access to facilities?

**Project outputs**: what are the direct outputs from the project? What will be delivered, by whom and in what time frame?

**Project outcomes**: what are the broad scale outcomes of this initiative? That is, how does this project contribute to reshaping the local economy and achieving the vision for the future?

**Project impacts**: what are the long-term impacts on the local economy? For example, does the project contribute to raising productivity, or making that city a more attractive place to do business?

**Project management**: who takes responsibility for this project? Sponsors could be internal or external to the organization, but it is important that clear lines of accountability are established.

Source: Modified from Swinburn et al. 2006 p 43.

Completion of this template assists in the selection of activities and helps bring development strategies to life. Projects that require too many resources, or require skills that do not exist within the agency – or cannot be acquired – will not be supported.

## 9.1.5 Evaluate the results

The development of an economic development plan or strategy makes little sense if the outcomes are not evaluated. Many economic development plans are developed and placed on shelves, never to be consulted again. The failure to review and evaluate the outcomes of an economic strategy may reflect a sense that the plan has been overtaken by events, such as the closure of a major manufacturing plant or a shift in the national economy. Changes in key personnel working in economic development – especially the chief executive – may produce the same result. Competing priorities may also make it difficult to find the time to review progress. Economic development and planning is a hectic field, and it can be difficult to prioritize reflecting on what has been achieved.

While there are many reasons why economic development plans may not be evaluated, there can be no doubt that the failure to review a strategy limits an organization's capacity to learn. Without such learning it cannot improve, ultimately reducing its value to the community.

The World Bank (2006) suggests that part of the process of establishing an economic development strategy should include the formulation of a monitoring and evaluation framework that commences soon after the plan is finalized. Monitoring and evaluation should take place as a series of meetings, with a timetable specifying which program elements should be reviewed when, and how outcomes should be reported.

Economic development plans need to be modified over their life to recognize successes, changes in market conditions or when plan elements do not perform as expected. This process does not necessarily require the redevelopment of the mission statement, or even the plan's goals, but rather a fine-tuning of objectives and actions. Such fine-tuning is best practice in economic development rather than an admission of failure.

### 9.1.6 Communicating economic development plans

Economic development plans must be developed in consultation with key stakeholders, including those within and outside the organization. Without consultation and debate the economic development plan is unlikely to secure widespread support, and therefore meet stated goals and objectives.

The economic development plan needs to be communicated during its development, once finalized and adopted, and as it goes through periodic review. It should be published and made available in a range of formats. Fortunately, Web-based publishing and social media make this task straightforward and inexpensive. Critically, however, a communications plan must be part of the economic development strategy, and some of the necessary elements include:

- 'Town hall' discussions where members of the local community have the opportunity to both contribute to the plan and comment on its final form;
- Consultations with stakeholders in the public and private sectors, as well as the not-for-profit sector and community groups. Where appropriate, indigenous groups should be consulted;
- Hard copy distribution of the economic development plan, as well as Web publication;
- The development of a plain-language summary published in hard copy and electronically;
- Development of a dedicated Facebook page, Instagram account and Twitter feed, as well as other social media;
- A formal media strategy, including engagement with the electronic, print and local broadcast media.

## ■ 9.2 Working with government agencies

Many accounts of planning for local economic development either focus solely on the techniques used internally to formulate strategy, or discuss the private sector alone. While the private sector is the dominant driver of growth locally and nationally, the public sector is also influential and can be the largest component of a local economy. We need only think of Washington, DC or a community that hosts a large military facility to visualize how important the public sector can be.

Across the OECD national public sector outlays as a percentage of GDP vary, with the US at the lower end of the spectrum at 26 percent of GDP, the UK hovering at 35 percent and some Scandinavian countries recording rates as high as 42 percent (Figure 9.1). In all instances, the public sector is large and represents a significant stock of resources to assist local economies. With the exception of Scandinavia, nations within the OECD tend to converge towards a relatively narrow range of government outlays as a percentage of GDP, which suggests there is both a level of public sector expenditure necessary for the efficient functioning of the economy, and a level above which diminishing returns become evident. For many nations, public sector expenditures as a percentage of the economy tends to be stable over time, which suggests that while the detail of government programs changes, total outlays remain constant.

The fact that governments are the most significant investor – and in some instances monopoly provider – of infrastructure and facilities is a second reason those planning for development should consider the public sector. The decisions of these agencies have a pivotal impact on a city or community's growth. Major infrastructure provided by national governments – such as major highways – can determine the growth of a city or community for decades to come.

Public sector agencies have important regulatory roles that may impede or facilitate development locally, and this is a third reason local economic development planners need to focus on government processes as part of their strategy formation.

**FIGURE 9.1**   Public sector outlays as a percentage of gross domestic product (GDP), selected nations, 1965–2016

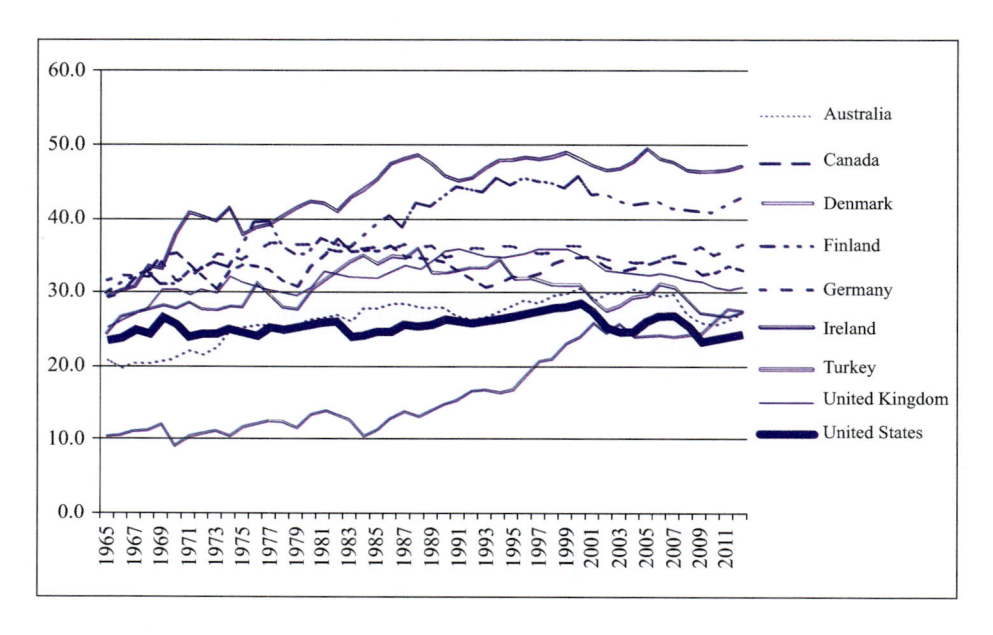

## 9.2.1 Coordinating government programs

In many parts of the world the development of places is put into question by the decisions and actions of government agencies, with different agencies sometimes appearing to behave in ways that conflict with the direction taken by other government bodies. One agency may promote the development of irrigated agriculture in a rural community even as a second government body is reducing the capacity of farmers to draw down on water resources. Similar problems can be found in the delivery of government services: one agency can endeavor to extend the range of services provided to vulnerable groups in urban or rural settings, while another introduces policies that cut back on resources and support for exactly the same groups. These difficulties may be more obvious when two or more tiers of government are involved. Federal systems (for example, the US, Canada, Brazil and Australia) may be more likely to experience these challenges, but the same issues arise in unitary systems of government – such as the UK and New Zealand.

Government agencies often have specific mandates or objectives – the preservation of a river system, the reduction of air pollution, the delivery of the most efficient transport system possible – that they focus on in isolation, and which are not part of an integrated development plan. These agencies may be exempt from local planning processes. Often the outcome of fragmentation in the delivery of government services at the local level overlaps in some areas of need, and public sector inattention to others. The singular focus of much government action is commonly referred to as a 'policy silo,' with individual agencies standing alongside of, but not integrated with, broader engagement with the community or region.

In many nations attempts to break down these 'policy silos' have failed, but the need to address this challenge remains. Sweden examined how to do this (Niklasson 2007), while the OECD (2010) considered how governments can break out of 'policy silos' to deliver integrated services. The OECD (2009, 2010, 2012a and b) argued that encouraging growth is a multifaceted task that isn't simply a responsibility of town planners or economic development practitioners alone. For the OECD (2010), success is dependent upon the capacity to span the boundaries that exist between government agencies, as well as those that sit between government and private sector organizations.

The Swedish agency Statskontoret (Niklasson 2007) noted that there is a global challenge to implement 'joined-up' development in regions, while the OECD (Froy and Giguere 2010) acknowledged the negative impacts of policy silos for development and well-being within regions. Froy and Giguere (2010) found some nations had developed strategies and tactics to encourage cross-portfolio working. In a report for the Swedish Government, Niklasson (2007) drew a number of conclusions about the delivery of services and policy to the regions:

- Policy integration at the regional, local or community scale is a challenge in all nations, and this is expressed differently in different places depending on the system of government, history, cultural traditions, scale and geography;
- The joining up of policies and programs is challenged both vertically – between different tiers of government – and horizontally – across portfolios within a single tier of government;

- Unitary and federal systems of government are both confronted by the challenges of integration and neither system necessarily performs better than the other;
- Governments can encourage integration for the delivery of services and policies from either the 'top down' or from the 'bottom up';
- Westminster systems of government are more prone to politicize regional decision making and support, with consequent greater challenges for integration;
- The political and administrative systems of Anglo-Saxon nations (US, UK, New Zealand, Australia and Canada), it has been argued, are dominated by a focus on the control of single organizations. That is, each agency of government is held to be answerable to the minister, and ultimately the legislative authority, with little scope to accommodate broader accountabilities. This set of arrangements makes policy and service integration difficult.

Five broad strategies for the regional coordination of policies were identified by Niklasson (2007):

- Centralize control of the public sector: effectively internalizing conflict in the expectation that a single agency will address these challenges effectively;
- Launch centrally designed and funded integration projects where agencies are expected to behave in a particular way:
  o   Such approaches are variously described as 'joined-up government' or 'horizontal management.'
- Devolve power to elected officials at the local scale;
- Delegate decision making to central government public servants based in the regions;
- Encourage networking by subordinate agencies.

Niklasson (2007) concluded that none of the identified solutions guaranteed success. The pathway to integration, he argued, was to identify and implement the most appropriate solution for each nation. Strategies and actions likely to be effective in one could be expected to have minimal or negative impacts elsewhere. He observed that for Sweden greater coordination within the cabinet was likely to be the most effective solution, but such mechanisms would have no place in the US or Australia (Beer 2000).

Froy and Giguere (2010) argued that governments can break out of 'policy silos' to provide better integrated and more effective government for regions while achieving their own goals and that

> in most cases policy integration at the local level was *ad hoc* and could not be judged as 'business as usual'. *Where policy integration was effective, however, it had the effect of capitalising on local opportunities and effectively diffusing local threats.*
>
> (Froy and Giguere 2010 p 14)

The message from these authors is clear: integrated approaches to regional development generate substantial benefits for regions, the communities they encompass and the nation as a whole. Policy and service integration, they argued, help governments:

- Effectively deal with complexity at the local level;
- Increase efficiency in the provision of services at the regional scale, reduce duplication and minimize service gaps;
- Achieve critical mass in dealing with problems. Local issues often require considerable resources and an integrated approach adds to the quantum of funding available;
- Build trust between individuals and institutions, which helps find local solutions in the longer term.

Most importantly, the OECD research concluded, giving local officials flexibility in the interpretation of national policies was the most important pathway to integration at the local level (Froy and Giguere 2010).

## 9.2.2 Local coordination of public policy: leadership, networks and influence

The policies and programs of central governments are often poorly coordinated, and this outcome is often inevitable. It is clear that while central government authorities can do more to integrate their programs to better meet the needs of cities and communities, there is little evidence of sustained success. What then can local communities do in order to deliver better integrated public services and secure the infrastructure and facilities they need to secure growth? Many economic development practitioners and planners spend considerable time focusing on ways to influence both public debate and the decisions of governments. This reality can be seen worldwide (Beer et al. 2003), though it is a topic often passed over.

In many ways, getting the best outcomes for communities and their development is a question of relationship building and the generation of new capacities in both central government and at the city, regional or local level. It is also dependent on being able to implement a focus on outcomes.

### 9.2.2.1 Networks

One of the most basic strategies available to communities seeking to grow and coordinate the efforts of public sector agencies is to create both formal and informal networks of cooperation and collaboration. The eminent Finnish scholar Markku Sotarauta has written at some length about the important working relationships between economic development planners, practitioners, politicians and central government officials and how they have brought about positive change.

The establishment of formal networking opportunities results in:

- The exchange of information:
  - o   As a starting point, the publication of a local economic development plan informs others of the goals and priorities of the region. It represents an important starting point for discussions.

- The building of trust – social capital – between individuals working locally;
- Opportunities to provide ideas and other advice to central government plans and policies;
- An increased stock of knowledge about developments in the region, and one less vulnerable to shocks if one or more key staff leave;
- The creation of a shared institutional memory on the development strategies and plans used in the past, and their success or otherwise in seeking growth.

The creation of networks should be part of the economic development planning for a city, community or region.

## 9.2.2.2 Work in partnership with other agencies and governments

Many development needs within communities remain unfulfilled because the resources they require – capital investment, staff time to manage projects, et cetera – are substantial. These needs are often far beyond the capacities of individual communities.

Sometimes places can achieve their development objectives by developing 'cocktails' of funding from a number of sources – national governments, state/provincial governments, philanthropic organizations, community groups and industries – to support initiatives. Such composite funding is common in Europe, with European Union funding for territorial development – the development of places – commonly dependent upon co-investment by partners. For example, the Berlin and Brandenburg regions of Germany jointly formed innovation clusters, with the European Union providing €15.7 million of the total budget of €33.7 million, with the remainder coming from national or more local sources (EU 2015). Other examples include a new financial mechanism for delivering energy in upper Austria, investment in sewerage in Hungary and encouraging business ecosystems in Galicia, Spain.

Communities, cities and regions should plan for the leveraging of their own funds. They need an economic development plan in order to identify which projects they will, or will not, partner with others, as well as to establish a priority ranking. Their planning needs to include dealing with the issue of risk – how much they are willing to accept, under what circumstances and from whom. Importantly, the co-funding of projects inevitably builds closer working relationships between individuals and organizations, and can be a point of departure for future collaborations between public agencies.

To be effective, local development communities need to structure their budgets in order to make leveraging arrangements possible, including managing funds left over in any year. How to do so will vary from locality to locality, and will depend upon the authority ceded to localities. For example, in the US the authority of local jurisdictions to engage in actions related to economic development varies across states and their use of local governance regimes including home rule, Dillon rule and general law cities.

## 9.2.2.3 Communicate successes and needs

The revolution in information and communication technology (ICT) that has swept the world since the 1980s provides regions, cities and communities with

## BOX 9.3  LOCAL GOVERNMENT AUTONOMY IN THE UNITED STATES

### Home rule versus Dillon rule

An important principle of federalism, as it is practiced in the United States, is the degree of authority granted to states versus other levels of government. The founding fathers wrote the US Constitution with an eye to keeping central government in check. In general terms, the powers of the federal government are limited to national defense, international relations, citizenship, currency, interstate commerce and other issues enumerated in Article 1, Section 8 of the Constitution, including procuring the means to enact these activities through taxation and the issuance of debt. All other powers are held by states or citizens. The states 'lend' powers to the federal government – in principal. Constitutional law, after all, can be messy. States may also grant powers to local government authorities according to their own constitutions. The degree to which local governments have been granted independent authority varies across the US. Two approaches to local government independence emerged during the 19th century: Dillon rule and home rule.

Dillon rule: named after Iowa Supreme Court Justice John Dillon and based on a legal case in the 1870s, municipalities in Dillon rule states, in oversimplified terms, can only exercise those powers that are expressly granted to them (or implied) by state government, or powers *essential* for accomplishing the stated purpose of the local authority.

Home rule: in home rule states, local governments can effectively enact laws, procedures and activities unless they are expressly prohibited from doing so by state law. This is not unlimited authority but offers substantial flexibility for local leaders that can be used to engage in competitive differentiation with other cities in economic development.

In practice, there are few states that align strictly with either governing principle. The majority of states employ some combination of approaches to local government autonomy. For example, many home rule states only apply this principle to larger communities. In Texas a municipality must have more than 5,000 residents before it can apply to the state for home rule status. Smaller communities, or those that choose not to seek home rule status, are called general law cities and are effectively governed under Dillon rule limitations.

See Russell and Bostrom (2016) for a more detailed review of home rule and Dillon rule principles.

many more ways to exert influence, at relatively low cost. Communicating the real needs of a region or city offers an opportunity to shape public debates – including government decisions – on how places should develop, and at what rate. These messages are even more powerful if accompanied by evidence of stakeholder support – for example, co-badging of campaigns, joint events, the sharing of logos or other branding, co-signatories on submissions for funding or access to facilities.

Communicating a message is not simply a matter of directing attention upwards to key local decision makers or the most significant agencies in central governments. Public support is an important asset in economic planning and development, as it underpins both the legitimacy of economic development agencies and provides additional avenues for achieving priorities (as discussed below). Earlier research has observed that economic development planners and agencies may be seen to lack legitimacy (Maude and Beer 2000) because they are disengaged from their communities. Communication overcomes this hurdle.

Some strategies for communication include:

- Newsletters;
- Hosting conferences, symposia or other high-profile professional events;
- Participating in conferences and other professional events, both within the region and outside the region;
- Developing a suite of 'media collateral':
  - o Social media, including Facebook, Twitter, Instagram, et cetera;
  - o Developing and maintaining a high-visibility website:
    - Seeking professional advice on how to maintain visibility within search engines.
  - o Advertising in the formal media;
  - o The provision of news items to the formal media.
- Community forums where the public has an opportunity to hear of proposed developments, offer new ideas and comment on existing plans;
- Sponsoring local events – including community fairs, sporting events and related activities;
- Publishing an annual report.

### 9.2.2.4 Lobby

Lobbying is simply one form of communication but it is targeted at specific audiences of decision makers, either elected or appointed. Many working in economic development invest a great deal of time and energy in lobbying governments, and this reflects a number of factors, including:

- Acknowledgment that only central governments have the power or resources to deliver certain desired outcomes, such as building a major highway, constructing a dam, granting access to natural resources, for example a forest;
- The potential high return for effort from lobbying, with the potential for a relatively speedy economic and political outcome;
- An expectation among some stakeholders – including those who are lobbied – that this is an integral part of the economic development planning process;
- The desire to influence public sector processes to achieve the best possible outcomes for the community.

Not all places are equally successful at lobbying. Some have the benefit of political circumstances that appear to be at odds with their objective importance to the national economy. Most cities and communities do not benefit from being a focus of national political attention. Some places may achieve temporary significance for the broader political process, while others remain forever in the shadows. Regardless of political prominence there are a number of steps communities and regions can take:

- Engage with local political representatives by inviting them onto committees, as well as providing information updates;
- Where there is more than one elected representative in the community, create a subcommittee on economic development planning to which they can provide input;
- Participate in broader national/state policy forums in order to better understand current political agendas;
- Find time to travel to the local legislature to meet politicians and their staff;
- Establish awards for local political figures acknowledging their contributions to the community.

## 9.2.2.5 Contract with central government

Some nations use contracts between central governments and cities or regions to achieve their goals of integrated development, the coordination of public sector activity and high standards of service provision. The OECD (2007) considered this strategy and concluded that it is potentially a productive approach to economic development. It observed there are two types of contract for regional development:

1. The first type of contract is *transactional* and may be thought of as a relatively simple agreement where both parties identify their respective commitments before signing, and then deliver against those undertakings over the period specified.
2. The second type of agreement is a *relational* contract where both parties commit to cooperate into the future after specifying a governance mechanism for that purpose (OECD 2007 p 11). The latter type of contract tends to rely upon cooperation and bilateral enforcement of the spirit of the agreement.

Theoretically, contracts between regions and central governments can be used to:

- Guarantee a level of service provision in a region (a transactional contract); or,
- Bind national governments to an ongoing process of engagement with a prescribed set of issues in a region (a relational contract).

Importantly, contracts between tiers of government relate to wider issues of multilevel governance, that is, the sharing of powers and responsibilities across agencies and jurisdictions. The OECD (2007) concluded that creation and delivery of regional contracts was most effective when used to deliver ongoing engagement between central governments and the regions.

The OECD (2007) noted several examples of contracts between regions and central governments, including regional planning in France, regional policy in Italy, the use of contracts and 'joint tasks' in Germany, and the establishment of the Vancouver Urban Development Agreement in Canada (Box 9.4).

## BOX 9.4 THE VANCOUVER URBAN DEVELOPMENT AGREEMENT, 2000–2010

Downtown Eastside (DTES) was Vancouver's first settlement and was once a vibrant section of the city with head offices, banks, theaters, hotels, department stores, a library and housing for people of low and moderate incomes. The gradual loss of low-income housing in other parts of the city and the deinstitutionalization of thousands of psychiatric patients drove more people to the DTES for affordable housing. In the early 1990s, greater numbers of people with addictions entered the community, making it a center for drug dealing and related crimes. This affected the entire community with a significant impact on local businesses.

In 1998, the City of Vancouver approved A Program of Strategic Actions for the Downtown Eastside to address crime, safety, poverty, substance abuse, homelessness, health and economic revitalization. A five-year comprehensive DTES Revitalisation Program was launched, with the goal to 'create a safe and healthy community.'

The Vancouver Agreement (VA) was signed in 2000 as one of the mechanisms to implement the City's *Program of Strategic Actions for the Downtown Eastside* and address public health issues.

The strategic initiatives for actions to achieve this vision were:

- Economic revitalization;
- Safety and security;
- Housing;
- Health and quality of life.

During the VA's first years, activities were intensely focused on bringing together all relevant parties to address particular issues. Task teams composed of government agencies worked together to identify and implement community-based actions such as a Four Pillars Drug Strategy, Enhanced Enforcement and the Homelessness Action Plan. Although coordinated by the VA, these areas remained the responsibility of the respective government agency.

With an infusion of federal and provincial funding in 2003, the VA assumed the additional role of providing grants to community agencies to support action on the four strategic initiatives. Most of these grants complemented funding provided by governments, foundations and nonprofit organizations. During the VA's lifespan, more than 70 projects were funded through almost 50 different organizations. In 2009/10, the final year of the VA, many of the activities were integrated into other government programs.

Source: Adapted from Vancouver Agreement (no date).

Contracts for regional development have the potential to achieve positive ends for communities, but they do not have a track record of success under strong central governments. Since the 1990s, UK Governments have introduced measures to encourage joined-up solutions to local problems, though it is difficult to conclude that these policies have been an unquestioned success (Box 9.5). In part this initiative has not met expectations because central government failed to provide resources commensurate with the challenges at hand.

## BOX 9.5  POLICY INNOVATION IN THE UK: THE CAMERON GOVERNMENT'S CITY DEALS AND COMMUNITY BUDGETS

The Cameron Coalition Government elected in 2010 made a commitment to driving the growth of the major English cities – the eight largest urban centers outside London. City Deals were developed as a customized approach to the needs and potential of each of the nominated urban areas, in the expectation that they would: give cities the tools and powers they need to drive local economic growth; unlock the projects or initiatives that will boost their economies; and strengthen the governance of each city (Her Majesty's Government 2012).

The City Deals emerged in the context of highly centralized power within England. While England has some of the largest local governments in Western Europe, 90 percent of their funding comes from direct payments from the national government. Only 10 percent of revenues are raised and spent locally. While each City Deal is unique, some of the key features include the 'Earn Back' system of taxation, whereby cities that invest in growth receive a greater share of national taxation revenues, the use of tax increment financing for critical infrastructure and the pooling of funding streams into a single investment fund to leverage private sector capital and invest in local priorities.

The City Deals represent a continuation of policy initiatives in this area since the early 1990s (Sandford 2012). These initiatives all seek to combine funding streams and give local communities greater control of resources as a mechanism to reduce policy silos. Community budgets focus on meeting the needs of troubled families, focusing on households involved in crime and antisocial behavior; who have children not in school; have an adult on out-of-work benefits and cause high costs to the public purse. Community budgets were piloted in October 2010 with 16 local government areas participating. The selected areas ranged in size from inner London boroughs to all of Birmingham.

Given this discussion the key question is, what does this mean at the local level? How can economic planners and developers working at the local level bring these concepts to life?

There are a number of pathways:

- Contracts for development are essential bilateral or multilateral arrangements and do not necessarily imply that one tier of government is more significant than another. Communities could initiate a contract with the state/provincial government, or formalize their working relationship with a particular agency or portfolio;
- Communities can seek to establish transactional contracts for specified objectives – for example the delivery of services or roads expenditure. They could propose relational contracts with government agencies as a way of solidifying working relationships and providing a platform for ongoing discussions.
- Cities, regions and communities could integrate the monitoring of contracts for development into their economic development planning process, especially the evaluation of development plan outcomes.

## 9.3 Mobilizing community resources

Agencies and groups responsible for developing and implementing regional plans are – at best – facilitators of development (Beer et al. 2003; Sotarauta and Beer 2016), controlling limited resources relative to the size of the local economy. Economic development planners are therefore challenged to develop ways of recruiting others – individuals, businesses and government agencies – to help achieve their goals for that community.

### 9.3.1 Leadership groups

One of the fundamental ways of mobilizing community members to contribute to local economic development planning and action is through the creation of a board or other agency. Around the globe specialist local economic development boards or agencies have been created within a wide variety of contexts: as a subcommittee of city councils; as incorporated entities; as unincorporated joint ventures; and as a unit of government. Board members are recruited in a number of ways, through direct election, through identification by existing board members and recruitment, as an appointment of government or as a representative of another organization, such as a local government representative on a regional board. Board membership is one important way to engage with local leaders.

The organization of the economic development efforts of the City of Weatherford, Texas typifies arrangements in many parts of the world. Weatherford is part of the Dallas–Fort Worth metroplex – a conurbation of 6 million people – with Weatherford on the northwest edge of the metropolitan region. Historically it has been an important primary industry center, has seen growth and decline cycles related to natural gas production and is the focus of the cutting horse industry in the US. It has some manufacturing and over recent years commuting from Weatherford to the downtown regions of Dallas and Fort Worth has increased substantially.

The City of Weatherford has an economic development board created under its local government. The board's membership includes a president drawn from the city council, the CEO of the major hospital in the region, the president of the local chamber of commerce, representatives of the utility – electricity, water and gas – sectors as well as individuals from the higher education sector. The board supervises the work of the Weatherford Economic Development Authority (WEDA), an independent not-for-profit corporation. The WEDA has a chief executive officer – an economic development professional – who also supports the work of the board.

The City of Weatherford's Economic Development Authority engages in a range of activities, including advising the City council, strategic planning, providing information to businesses seeking to relocate and/or plant relocation agencies. Direct action includes marketing the city as a place to do business, real estate development and the provision of subsidies to attract or retain businesses. Importantly the board acknowledges the importance of community resources and leadership, and this is reflected in the creation of two committees – a Business Retention and Expansion Committee (in conjunction with the local chamber of commerce) and a Business Leadership Committee. The members of the latter committee are local proprietors and senior managers, active in the community's economy and able to provide advice on development opportunities and potential threats.

As a second example, The Polaris Centre is the economic development agency that serves the City of Salisbury and the adjacent City of Playford, residential and industrial hubs in outer Adelaide, South Australia. The Polaris Centre runs a number of development programs, including Northern Economic Leaders (NEL), an invitation-only business leaders network that supports growth in the region. Northern Economic Leaders is an ongoing forum for leaders to share their knowledge of opportunities and challenges in the region. It is promoted as an opportunity to exchange ideas, provide input into government policy and address mutual concerns. It focuses on four areas:

1. Bringing local businesses together to showcase success;
2. Advising on economic issues that are important for the region and its community;
3. Improving industry development in the region and business performance;
4. Building the region's global competitiveness by promoting innovation, leadership development and best practice.

The City of Weatherford and the Polaris Centre provide two examples of local community resources to drive economic growth. Both approaches acknowledge the skills and experiences of individuals within the region, and develop ways to draw out that knowledge to fuel further growth. Other examples abound, highlighting the significance of this approach.

### 9.3.2 Business angels, philanthropic organizations and the not-for-profits

This section considers business angels, philanthropic organizations and not-for-profit bodies and the potential contribution they make to the growth of communities, cities and regions. Each is potentially an important driver of growth, but often overlooked in conventional analysis of local development and planning.

### 9.3.2.1 Business angels

Business angels are a potentially important source of economic growth. The term is given to wealthy individuals who invest in a small firm – often a startup – providing the capital needed to enable growth in exchange for a share of the business while also sharing their own business expertise with the founding entrepreneur. Business angels may enter a firm as an individual investor, or as a consortium of investors. Business angels are important, filling a significant gap in the demand for capital by small, relatively insecure firms.

Business angels can have a substantial impact, with Ramadani (2009) observing that several iconic US companies, including Bell Telephone, Ford Motor Corporation, Apple Computers, Body Shop and Amazon, received business funding in their early development. Typically business angels are middle-aged entrepreneurs with experience running their company. They typically invest in between two and five companies and hold a minority share in the companies (Mazzarol 2012). The decision to invest is often a personal one, with the business angel taking a considerable risk. They often invest close to where they live (Mazzarol 2012) and make their decisions based on the personality of the entrepreneur – especially their level of passion for the venture, their age and creativity (Mitteness et al. 2012). Maxwell et al. (2011) suggested business angels invest according to eight broad criteria:

1.  The willingness of the market to adopt;
2.  How far along the development stream the product sits;
3.  Protection for the intellectual property;
4.  The probability that customers will engage with the product;
5.  How the product will find a route to market;
6.  The potential for market growth;
7.  The experience of the management team;
8.  The soundness of the finance model.

Von Bargen et al. (2003) noted business angels play an increasingly important role in America's innovation system and in the growth trajectories of new firm startups. They are an important part of the venture capital market, especially for smaller projects (OECD 2011) as venture capital is unwilling to invest in projects of less than US$3 million (Von Bargen et al. 2003). Business angels and the reinvestment of early profits appear to be the major mechanisms for overcoming this hurdle, with the former important for firms whose early profits are modest or who take longer to generate a surplus. Smilor et al. (2007) found the growth of business angel activity – alongside venture capital – was pivotal to the success of the Research Triangle Park in North Carolina, while Bates (2002 p 55) noted that angel investors were attractive for many startups because

> Angels will indeed invest several hundred thousand dollars in early-stage ventures that show great growth promise. Most of these deals will yield little in the way of payoff. Some will discontinue operations entirely, and others will generate little growth. But the angel investor is the ultimate provider of patient capital, willing to wait years while a few early stage investments mature into high-value firms. The payoff comes when such firms either become attractive acquisition targets or go public via an initial public offering (IPO).

Economic development practitioners can maximize the impact of business angels by:

*   Acknowledging that business angels live locally. They are part of the community and there is value in becoming aware of their activities and creating networks between angels and entrepreneurs. Angels should be publicly recognized for their contribution;
*   Developing linkages within the formal networks of angels that exist in all nations, either as online entities or as formal meetings. The region and its entrepreneurs can be promoted to these venture investors;
*   Providing training and education for those who would seek angel investment, as Mazzarol (2012 p 4) noted, most failed attempts to secure angel investment can be attributed to 'the lack of well-considered business models by those entrepreneurs seeking funding';

- Encouraging business angels to either emerge within the region, or migrate to the region. The emergence of business angels can be facilitated by peer-on-peer mentoring, or through the promotion of investment opportunities. Such activities can also contribute to the community's entrepreneurial culture. Many business angels move between cities and communities, and it is important to identify new angels in the region to link them to business opportunities.

A special case of business angels is the growing use of 'Shark Tank' and other 'pitch events' where early-stage entrepreneurs present their ideas and companies to a panel of potential investors.

## 9.3.2.2 Not-for-profit organizations and philanthropic organizations

Not-for-profit organizations are essentially entities that operate to deliver a public good or service. While they differ in important ways from conventional for-profit businesses, they are often substantial entities in their own right, potentially employing hundreds – if not thousands – of staff. They also control substantial assets. A 2012 study found that more than 10.7 million workers were employed in the not-for-profit sector in the US, the third largest workforce behind retail and manufacturing (Salamon et al. 2012). There are more than 1.5 million not-for-profits registered with the Internal Revenue Service in the US, 900,000 in the UK, 170,000 in Canada, 97,000 in New Zealand and 600,000 in Australia (ACPNS 2019). In total the not-for-profit sector accounts for a substantial percentage of the total economy in developed nations, ranging from 7.1 percent of GDP in Canada, to 5.5 percent in the US, 3.2 percent in Australia and 2.8 percent in New Zealand.

The not-for-profit sector is active in aged care, health services, employment assistance, social welfare, consumer lending and retailing. Not-for-profit enterprises can hold significant assets that drive local growth, and their investment decisions are important for the functioning of the economy.

Philanthropic organizations can be considered a subset of the wider pool of not-for-profit organizations and they are important in their own right. As of 2011, there were more than 76,000 grant-making foundations in the US, with total outlays in excess of US$46 billion, from an asset base of just under US$650 billion. In the UK, some 12,400 charities controlled £30 billion in assets and made grants to the value of £5 billion in 2011. Other nations have comparable levels of philanthropic activity, which underlines the importance of this sector and its potential to contribute to cities and communities.

The not-for-profit sector is important:

- As a not-for-profit entity they are more likely to be grounded in a particular community or region, and their business decisions will have a substantial impact on the wellbeing of the economy, especially with respect to employment;
- Many not-for-profits are active in sectors that are growing and likely to expand in the future. Aged care is one area where not-for-profits are significant;

- Measures taken to assist the growth of not-for-profits can have substantial benefits for the local economy;
- As substantial asset holders, it is important their resources are used for the maximum benefit of the economy.

For these reasons it is important to include not-for-profits in economic development planning. Particular attention needs to be paid to the philanthropic sector, as they can be a source of grants for:

- Funding economic development initiatives that would extend the ambition and reach of existing programs and may achieve outcomes beyond the capacity of existing resources;
- Funding education or training assistance for disadvantaged individuals. In addition to assisting the recipient, such programs add to the human capital of the community, city or region;
- Investment in key infrastructure or resources that would not otherwise be available. For example, a capital subsidy for a child-care center could enable working mothers to return to work, boosting their income and freeing up an additional pool of labor.
- Local and regional not-for-profit groups are often led or guided by leaders who should be involved in economic development planning and action. Engagement with these entities provides access to these leaders.

### 9.3.3 The business community: chambers of commerce, tourism associations

### 9.3.3.1 Place entrepreneurs

Research has long recognized that existing business often generate a powerful dynamic propelling the further growth and development of their city or community (Stone 1989). While capital is fluid, many forms of investment are not, and the owners of businesses – including shops, tourism venues and other commercial property – have a strong interest in encouraging the growth of their locality. This is a powerful dynamic and one that can fuel local growth. Chambers of commerce and tourism associations – or other industry forums – can be an important partner on projects.

One body of literature suggests that business associations and other forms of 'collective capitalism' have helped businesses in some nations become more competitive than those elsewhere, as these institutions have assisted innovation and the development of new products (Piore and Sabel 1984). These associations have performed an important role in identifying workforce needs for the local region, contributing to skills formation, promoting new business startups and assisting cluster formation. These organizations are significant, with McCormick et al. (2008) arguing they take two types of role:

1. Transaction-cost savings, which are relatively static and help businesses reduce the costs of operating within their current economic model;

2.   Adaptive-cost savings, which help member firms transform their enterprise through the introduction of new technologies, entry into new markets or changing labor management relationships.

McCormick et al.'s (2008) study found that American business associations undertook a wide array of activities, including political lobbying, the provision of advice to members, information provision on upcoming legislation, providing economic information and marketing assistance, as well as technical assistance, such as the development and refinement of standards. They were involved in workforce development and the authors concluded that 'American business associations are more proactive economic development and workforce development actors than previously thought.' (McCormick et al. 2008, p 223)

Economic development planners can integrate these associations into their programs. For example, Lowe (2012) examined the development of the highly successful life sciences precinct in North Carolina. This industry cluster was partly built through the provision of incentives with a number of high-profile corporations brought into the region. The local chamber of commerce and its members were integrated into this process of firm recruitment, with events organized by the chamber for existing businesses to meet incoming firms in order to create networks and business-to-business opportunities.

Steps for integrating business associations into economic development efforts include:

•   The participation of business associations in economic development boards and the formation of plans;
•   Co-hosting of events and major economic development projects such as cluster formation or workforce planning;
•   The development of industry-focused sector plans for key industry in the city or region;
•   Integrating business associations into firm recruitment efforts, as well as building links between them and other elements of the local institutional infrastructure such as universities or research institutes.

# ■ 9.4 Conclusion

Planning and coordination of economic development activities are fundamental to the success of a city, community or region. Places that can map out their future and then achieve their targets are more likely to grow, and are also less vulnerable to economic shocks or changes in national economic conditions.

The coordination of government investment, services, infrastructure and regulation is critical for the growth of local economies as each of these publicly provided services serves as either a precondition for growth or a barrier to development (Von Bargen et al. 2003). Conventionally the literature on local economic development and planning has paid considerable attention to the 'nuts and bolts' of strategy formation and review, with much less consideration given to the influence of governments. Government and governance have been left to those studying politics or public administration, and as a result the practical, local level implications have not been examined. Communities and local governments naturally engage in many of the activities discussed above, but it is important they build on best practice and develop more effective strategies.

Finally, it is worth acknowledging that there is a great deal that can be achieved to better prepare for the development of any locality – regardless of its size or location. The planning and coordination mechanisms discussed in this chapter are robust, and have been demonstrated to be successful. The challenge for students, practitioners and communities is to implement them effectively.

## Key messages

This chapter has shown that:

- Economic development at the local, community or regional scale is most likely to proceed where it is well planned, and where the community has identified its priorities and made a commitment to concentrate its efforts in those activities seen to offer the most locally;
- Economic development plans by themselves are of little value; they need to be supported by action plans and a strong commitment to action. The plans need to be evaluated periodically and progress against goals measured;
- The government sector is a large part of any community's economy and should not be overlooked. Planners and economic development practitioners need to consider the strategies they use to bring about greater government sector integration at the regional scale;
- The resources and capacities embedded within the community are fundamental for delivering growth. Economic development planning and practice should include strategies for mobilizing local leadership and the not-for-profit sector.

## Discussion questions

Find out if your current state of residence uses Dillon rule or home rule principles for determining local government autonomy. How might an economic development strategy be different in a Dillon rule versus home rule-governed community? (You can limit your discussion to one type of economic development activity, such as business recruitment.)

In this chapter we have looked at the processes used to develop and implement strategic plans and the strategies that can be used to get better outcomes from working with governments. As a class, consider how you would develop a strategic plan for an inner-city area in need of refurbishment and new investment. In developing this plan consider:

- The economic structure of that neighborhood and how to improve its employment prospects;
- The quality of the physical assets;

- The needs of the community;
- The consultation and dissemination processes to be used in preparing the plan;
- How best to implement the plan;
- The integration of other government agencies, community groups and not-for-profits in realizing the plan's ambitions.

## References

Australian Centre for Philanthropy and Nonprofit Studies (ACPNS) 2019 Available at https://www.qut.edu.au/business/about/schools/school-of-accountancy/research/australian-centre-for-philanthropy-and-nonprofit-studies.

Bates, T. 2002 Government as venture capital catalyst: pitfalls and promising approaches, *Economic Development Quarterly*, 16:1, pp 49–59.

Beer, A. 2000 Listening, talking and acting: a new approach to regional policy and practice in Australia? *Australian Planner*, pp 24–32.

Beer, A., Maude, A. and Haughton, G. 2003 *Developing Locally*, Policy Press, Bristol.

European Union (EU) 2015 Available at http://ec.europa.eu/regional_policy/en/projects/germany/berlin-and-brandenburg-join-forces-for-innovation-clusters, accessed April 15, 2015.

Froy, F. and Giguere, S. 2010 *Breaking Out of Policy Silos: Doing More with Less*, OECD, Paris.

Her Majesty's Government 2012 *Unlocking Growth in Cities: City Deals – Wave 1*, London.

Lowe, N. 2012 Beyond the deal: using industrial recruitment as a strategic tool for manufacturing development, *Economic Development Quarterly*, 28:4, pp 287–299.

Maude, A. and Beer, A. 2000 Regional development agencies in Australia: a comparative evaluation of institutional strengths and weaknesses, *Town Planning Review*, 71:1, pp 1–24.

Maxwell, A., Jeffrey, S. and Levesque, M. 2011 Business angel early stage decision making, *Journal of Business Venturing*, 26, pp 212–225.

Mazzarol, T. 2012 Business angels: what are they and why are they important? *The Conversation.* Available at http://theconversation.com/business-angels-what-are-they-and-why-are-they-important-8794.

McCormick, L., Hawley, J. and Melendez, E. 2008 The economic and workforce development activities of American business associations, *Economic Development Quarterly*, 22:3, pp 213–227.

McKinsey and Co 1994 *Lead Local, Compete Global*, McKinsey and Co, Boston, MA.

McLean, M. and Voytek, K. 1992 *Understanding Your Economy: Using Analysis to Guide Local Strategic Planning*, Planners Press, Chicago, IL.

Mitteness, C., Sudek, R. and Cardon, M. 2012 Angel investor characteristics that determine whether perceived passion leads to higher evaluations of funding potential, *Journal of Business Venturing*, 27, pp 592–606.

Niklasson, L. 2007 *Joining Up for Regional Development*, Statskontoret, Stockholm.

OECD 2007 *Linking Regions and Central Governments: Contracts for Regional Development*, OECD, Paris.

OECD 2009 *How Regions Grow: Trends and Analysis*, OECD, Paris.

OECD 2010 *Regions Matter*, OECD, Paris.

OECD 2011 *Regional Outlook 2011*, OECD, Paris.

OECD 2012a *Promoting Growth in All Regions*, OECD, Paris.

OECD 2012b *Growth in All Regions*, OECD, Paris.

Piore, M. and Sabel, C. 1984 *The Second Industrial Divide: Possibilities for Prosperity*, Basic Books, New York.

Ramadani, V. 2009 Business angels: who they really are, *Strategic Change*, 18:2, pp 249–258.

Russell, J. and Bostrom, A. 2016 January. Federalism, Dillon rule and home rule. *White Paper.* American City County Exchange. Available at https://www.alec.org/app/uploads/2016/01/2016-ACCE-White-Paper-Dillon-House-Rule-Final.pdf.

Salamon, L., Sokolowski, S. and Geller, S. 2012 Holding the fort: nonprofit employment during a decade of turmoil, *Nonprofit Employment Bulletin*, 39, Johns Hopkins University, Center for Civil Society Studies.

Sandford, M. 2012 Community budgets and city deals, House of Commons, library, Parliament and Constitution Centre, SN/PC/0595.

Smilor, R., O'Donnell, N. and Welborn, G. 2007 The research university and the development of high-technology centers in the United States, *Economic Development Quarterly*, 21:3, August, pp 203–222.

Sotarauta, M. and Beer, A. 2016 Governance, agency and place leadership: lessons from a cross-national analysis, *Regional Studies*. DOI: 10.1080/00343404.2015.1119265.

Stone, C. 1989 *Regime Politics: Governing Atlanta, 1946–1988*, University of Kansas Press, Lawrence, KS.

Swinburn, G., Goga, S. and Murphy, F. 2006 *Local Economic Development: A Primer Developing and Implementing Local Economic Development Strategies and Action Plans*, The World Bank, Washington, DC.

Vancouver Agreement (no date) Available at http://www.vancouveragreement.ca/history/.

Von Bargen, P., Freedman, D. and Pages, E. 2003 The rise of the entrepreneurial society, *Economic Development Quarterly*, 17:4, pp 315–324.

World Bank 2006 *Investment Promotion Agency Performance Review 2006, Providing Information to Investors: A Report of Global IPA Performance Results,* Multilateral Investment Guarantee Agency, World Bank, Washington, DC, pp 15–16.

# 10 Land use planning and economic development

This chapter:

▶ Offers a brief review of the history of land use planning;

▶ Reviews traditional and emerging land use regulatory mechanisms and their existing and potential relationships with economic development;

▶ Considers new approaches to urban planning from an economic development perspective;

▶ Reviews the tools used to promote (economic) development in special needs areas.

L AND USE PLANNING is collectively the processes used to research, evaluate, determine and regulate the use of land to meet societal goals. Notwithstanding recent events in the South China Sea and the history of the Netherlands, land is a precious commodity because 'we are not making any more of it' – as the saying goes. Balancing the allocation of land to economic uses, of all types, and the growing imperative to preserve natural environs is challenging, especially in a world where accelerating growth has pushed the global population to more than 7.4 billion. While many call for the protection of pristine environments, land use, in one way or another, forms the basis of almost all economic activity. The built environment represents 85 percent of the total capital stock in OECD nations (Krawchenko and Schumann 2017).

There is a general view, at least in the United States and in other nations such as the UK, New Zealand and Australia, that land use planning is focused on reducing the negative spillover effects of economic activity, correcting for unregulated market forces, while also addressing sociopolitical issues (Kim 2011; Sayce and McIntosh 2002). It is not seen to prioritize supporting economic development and wealth creation. However, some nations including France, Ireland, Germany, among others, use economic planning as the main means for regulating land use including architectural features, urban design and other controls on the built environment (Silva and Acheampong 2015).

In the United States, land use planning and regulation has evolved into a complex mix of rules and regulations administered, in sometimes contradictory fashion, among all levels of government (local, state, federal). The regulations are most often a mix of relatively inflexible rules and a complex maze of incentives to achieve desired goals. However, the planning and economic literature, and popular press, are increasingly reporting the failures of traditional land use planning tools in the United States that have led to an overreliance on auto-based travel, skyrocketing housing prices in many communities, increased pollution, jobs–housing imbalances, and other issues (Kim 2011; Krawchenko and Schumann 2017). It is not clear if the blame for these problems lies with the planning tools or with the resulting decisions of leaders. Nonetheless, land use planning influences much about the way we live and our ability to generate sustainable economic opportunity (Krawchenko and Schumann 2017). Given the rapid changes underway in the nature and form of economic activity in the 21st century, a careful re-examination of the connections between land use planning and economic development is a current and likely ongoing challenge.

The purpose of this chapter is to provide students who are not studying in planning programs an overview of the history and major approaches to land use planning, and to offer an assessment of current and emerging land use planning and regulatory approaches that should be integrated with economic development planning and practices. Our focus will be on the United States, but students are encouraged to visit the book's website where we will address land use planning issues unique to Australia and other nations.

## ■ 10.1 Historical perspective

Land use planning, and the subdiscipline of urban planning, are not constructs of the industrial age. Historical records show that ancient Mesopotamian societies engaged in early forms of land use planning in their cities, though not necessarily in a function or form that would be readily apparent in a modern city. Early forms of planning were largely based on military defense premises, but as the size of towns grew in population and geography, planning elements more frequently emerged in the spatial organization of land uses, particularly after a disaster, such as the Fire of London in 1666. Of course, the theory of the economic organization of agricultural land uses saw its beginnings with the writings of Johann Heinrich von Thünen.[1]

A relatively early example of urban planning using modern precepts was the redesign of Paris in the mid-19th century. Emperor Napoleon III wanted to 'rebuild Paris as a modern capital that was worthy of France.' (Alvarado 2017) The emperor and his designer, Georges-Eugene Haussmann, undertook a project that created wide transportation thoroughfares connected by an integrated road network, the development of infrastructure (sewers, street lights), creation of recreation spaces and the changing of facades. Of course, being emperor greatly facilitated Napoleon's ability to acquire/seize and demolish existing structures required in this reimagining of Paris's urban form – an approach not possible in modern democracies with well-established property rights. The plan addressed the need to support rapid population growth with demands on housing, transportation and social needs; the need to enhance public health through improved sanitation; and the desire to create a sense of place that would be 'exquisite and French.' As the role of manufacturing in urban economies grew throughout the 19th century, a new set of reasons for regulating land uses became increasingly important – protecting urban residents from the negative spillover effects of industrial pollution.

If you are a regular watcher of Netflix, you may have seen the show *Peaky Blinders*, which is set initially in 1920s Birmingham, England. The images portray dense, squalid, worker housing in proximity to the workplace, with smoke and grime that renders the entire color scheme one of muted greys and ear-splitting noise coming from the furnaces and machinery of the city's manufacturers. This setting is not an exaggeration for dramatic effect. Industrial pollution and its toxicity became synonymous with most major cities. Early 20th century factory workers did not own cars and transit systems were still in their infancy; therefore, worker housing was placed close to factories, with the cheapest housing located where prevailing winds and downstream water flows took the worst of the pollution. Cities sought a way to separate increasingly incompatible adjacent land uses through regulatory mechanisms to better organize the urban environment, though there is debate if planning and zoning was meant to protect workers from negative environmental spillovers of industry, or to protect industrialists from the complaints of nearby residents (Wilkins et al. 2006).

## ◾ 10.2 The mechanisms of land use regulation

In the United States, land use regulation that restricts land uses to specified types of activity, such as housing, commercial and industrial uses, is often called Euclidean zoning. In 1926, a developer sued the town of Euclid, Ohio claiming that the city's zoning regulations limiting the height of structures and land use were an unconstitutional infringement on his property rights that reduced the value of his property.[2] In 1926, the US Supreme Court ruled in favor of Euclid and solidified the authority for local governments to regulate land use within their jurisdictions. After this ruling, the use of Euclidean-type zoning became the dominant approach to land use regulation in the US. With each local jurisdiction creating its own zoning codes, it was inevitable that land use regulations would become highly variable and complex. One jurisdiction in northern Virginia has more than 70 separate land use zoning categories. As suggested above, by keeping industrial and commercial activities separate from residential uses, public welfare is enhanced by limiting the spillover effects of population, heavy traffic and noise from intruding on neighborhoods (Kim 2011). However, the spread of the urban footprint that attended the democratization of automobile ownership, and the regulatory and financial support that encouraged home ownership in the post-World War II era, changed the nature of planning and pulled many more regulatory bodies (city level planning boards) into the regulatory fray as exurban farming communities became suburban enclaves of the middle class.

As the US economy moved into the postindustrial era, it became increasingly clear that 19th century based land use regulatory approaches were failing planners as demand shifted from industrial to nonindustrial commercial uses, or in addressing the effects of urban sprawl. In some cases, the form of regulation became the designation of growth boundaries that restricted spread/sprawl effects, while many cities chose annexation as a key regional planning tool.

To be clear, land use regulation is not land use planning (Kim 2011). Land use regulations are the tools used by planners to achieve planning goals. For the purposes of this discussion, we modify Silva and Acheampong's (2015) typology of development management instruments into:

- Regulatory instruments;
- Incentive-based instruments;
- Fiscal instruments.

In some instances, this typology is somewhat arbitrary due to overlaps in the practical application of these instruments.

## 10.2.1 Regulatory instruments

Regulatory instruments can include temporarily stopping development (moratoria), greenbelts, rate of growth controls, urban growth boundaries, agricultural preservation zones, building codes and zoning policies. Effectively, a development moratorium is when the regulating body (usually a locality) *temporarily* halts new development to allow for infrastructure to catch up with new demand. For example, the addition of 5,000 new housing units will require new roads, water lines and sewer lines, but the marginal increase in demand may also require the addition of a new water pumping station at the local reservoir or the creation of a new wastewater treatment plant that is not proximate to the new housing development. In growing suburban and exurban communities, growth may be halted while the new facilities are put into place. Another oft-cited reason for imposing development moratoria, particularly with respect to the development of new housing, is the impact of rapid population growth on local school systems. If a new family-oriented housing development adds several hundred school-age children in a short period of time, the school district must accommodate this new demand with facilities, faculty and support personnel. It is important to keep in mind that the perception of school quality, services and facilities is a key determinant in attracting highly skilled workers with families, and thus impacts local competitiveness.

Like moratoria, rate-of-growth controls help communities to keep up with growing demand for infrastructure and public services by slowing, but not stopping, new development. Rate-of-growth controls, though most often employed against housing development, can also be used to promote economic diversification. If a community achieves a reputation for being a great locale for a particular economic activity, such as warehousing and logistics, they can experience a high volume of speculative construction from industrial property developers. This could result in the local economy becoming too reliant on one industry sector. Rate-of-growth controls applied to specific land uses can be an effective way to achieve balanced economic development. Of course, this requires a deft touch by local regulators in applying these controls in a manner that doesn't simply drive economic opportunity elsewhere.

The designation of greenbelts prohibits the development of buildings in designated areas. Often, these lands have reasons why they are not ideal for buildings, such as being in flood-prone areas or environmentally sensitive habitats. However, greenbelts can contribute to local economic development goals by being used for recreational amenities (hiking/biking trails, parks, sports fields) that contribute to the local quality of life or provide infrastructure for sporting events.

Urban growth boundaries are drastic approaches to reducing city sprawl. A set line is established that separates physical spaces between those allowed to develop and those that are not. They are an extreme case of what Hopkins (2001) identified as the enforceable reassignment of property rights. Properties outside the boundary may be used for economic purposes but are limited to low-impact uses such as agricultural production. The City of Portland, Oregon is the most well-known example of a community that chose to establish an urban growth boundary. In terms of economic development, urban growth boundaries can be used to support economic development strategies by encouraging service sector industry growth over land use–intensive manufacturing. If a city continues to grow after the imposition of an urban growth boundary, supply and demand forces will dictate property values and rents will increase. These higher costs can be offset for companies by the comparative ready availability of skilled labor from communities who like the 'vibe' of a dense urban environment. For bounded urban areas to succeed, there must be high-quality multimodal passenger transportation networks and carefully planned urban spaces. See more about Portland's approach to regulating physical space on the textbook website (www.gpaled.com).

Euclidean zoning that regulates the allowed uses of land and restricts the characteristics of the urban form, such as building height, is the dominant regulatory approach to the organization of the built environment in the United States. While we won't go into the variety of land use categorizations that appear among cities, counties and other local jurisdictions, we will make two observations. First, with most communities using highly customized land use categories, there is a substantial loss of economic efficiency as developers must almost continuously adapt their development programs and designs to meet highly localized requirements. Second, institutional inertia has meant land use categories are often out of date with market demand and development trends. In many communities, we virtually lock in inefficient designs that impede development and/or drive up prices. (See building height restrictions in the District of Columbia as an example.)

Building codes are the regulatory mechanisms that address building and human safety issues. Most of these focus on structural issues related to architectural design and building engineering, construction materials, and systems qualities. Building codes address issues including maximum building occupancy that can affect revenue potential in commercial and residential buildings. Building codes can affect facility operating costs and efficiency. For example, general building codes specifying the number of parking spaces required for a given building size could require the developer of a 60,000 square foot commercial data center to provide 150 parking spaces to accommodate 20 employees. Requirements for parking spaces and loading docks can have a notable impact on the potential return-on-investment analysis of commercial and industrial properties that, in turn, affect site location decisions.

## 10.2.2 Incentive-based instruments

As the name implies, incentive-based land use management instruments are designed to encourage specific economic behavior among developers, investors and/or businesses – usually to overcome an obstacle to development or achieve a desired social goal. In this overview, we cover several of the most commonly used incentive-based instruments in the US. Many of these instruments have no operational basis in other nations, usually due to the degree to which property taxes are emphasized at the local level in the US. In the following paragraphs, we provide information on development-focused tax credits, tax increment financing, special economic zones, conservation easements, brownfield redevelopment programs, and transfer of rights development. While this is not an exhaustive list of incentive-based instruments, it is generally representative of the most common approaches for this type of land use regulation in the US. See this book's website for other examples.

Development-focused tax credits incentivize development in a way that influences land uses for which the market may not provide sufficient justification to achieve. These are not the same as economic development incentives targeted to business activities. One of the most widely recognized examples of development-focused tax credits is the Low-Income Housing Tax Credit (LIHTC) program. Essentially, a developer gets a credit against their federal income tax liability for offering a portion of the units in a given development at rates deemed affordable for households earning less than 60 percent (or 50 percent depending on the proportion of total units) of area median household income. Because these units are not targeted to the lowest income level households in a community, this is often perceived as a *workforce* housing development program, which ties in with the need to match labor force supply to labor force demand. The LIHTC program has been in existence since 1986 and is the largest source of affordable housing unit development in the United States, with a current inventory of approximately two million units according to the National Housing Law Project.[3]

Though not exclusively used for property development or redevelopment, the New Markets Tax Credit program, managed by the US Department of the Treasury, can be used to preserve and rehabilitate commercial and industrial properties to attract business activity to underperforming areas. In late 2017, the US Congress enacted major tax reform legislation that reduced the top marginal corporate federal tax rate from 35 percent to 21 percent. It is not yet clear what impact this change in tax rates will have on real estate markets; however, lower corporate tax liabilities will reduce the demand for development-focused tax credits that may limit the effectiveness of this approach to land use management.

Tax increment financing (TIF) programs form the basis of public–private cost sharing that is meant to encourage specific types of real estate investments in a community. The easiest way to illustrate this land use regulation mechanism is through an example. Let's say you own three old, outdated commercial buildings in a downtown area that is targeted by the city for redevelopment. These properties have a total value of $8 million and generate $64,000 per year in city real estate taxes ($0.80/$100 value tax rate). The city creates a tax increment financing district that includes your property. You then spend $1 million updating the building facades and fixtures, which attracts new restaurants and retail outlets to your building. Because of tenant success, you charge higher rents and the value of your properties grows to $24 million. As the value of your property increases, the effective tax revenue grows, but instead of keeping the marginal increase in tax revenue (the tax increment), the city refunds the increment to you to pay back your $1 million investment.

Using the tax rate in our example, the revitalized property generates $192,000 per year in property taxes, $128,000 of which is the increment. Once you are repaid, the city will keep the new tax revenues. Through this incentive, the city encourages private investment that shapes the highest and best use for a given building/plot of land. This type of incentive is also used to support major shifts in land use. For example, the Trinity River Vision project in Fort Worth, Texas is using a multi-jurisdiction tax increment program to encourage the redevelopment of a largely abandoned industrial area into commercial and residential uses.

Special economic zone programs are exemplified by Enterprise Zones, which offer businesses various tax incentives, grants, or regulatory relief to encourage job creation in distressed communities. While many of these programs are tied explicitly to business activity, there are some programs that incentivize real estate investments that affect land use. For example, the Commonwealth of Virginia Enterprise Zone program includes grants for property redevelopment and new construction if the land use is industrial, commercial or mixed use.[4] In many jurisdictions, these programs are designed to enhance market demand to preserve land uses associated with job creation – meaning no commercial/industrial-to-residential conversions.

Conservation easements are lands where owners voluntarily surrender or sell their rights to develop or use for economic purposes to a government agency. Farmland that is placed in a conservation easement can often stay in agricultural production but cannot be otherwise developed. In many cases, by lowering the effective highest and best use of the land (from an economic perspective), the taxable value of the land is greatly reduced, especially in taxing jurisdictions that practice 'use-value' assessment methods. For example, property that may be zoned commercial or residential, but is used for agricultural purposes and is voluntarily placed into a conservation easement, is assessed as farmland regardless of zoning. This approach to land use management is popular in environmentally sensitive areas.

Brownfield development programs address environmentally contaminated sites. The Environmental Protection Agency (EPA) defines a brownfield as a property whose use or redevelopment is complicated, or blocked, by the presence or *potential* presence of contaminants.[5] Under US environmental laws, ownership of contaminated properties can be very risky – even if the owner did not cause the pollution. If your firm purchases contaminated property, even unknowingly, you could be held liable for the cost of pollution mitigation and remediation. The EPA estimates that there are more than 450,000 brownfield sites in the United States (EPA 2018). Even though these sites have very low market values, they do not attract investment because of the liability risks. These properties, which are often old industrial sites but could be former locations of gasoline stations, dry cleaning services and mechanic shops, are blighted and become deterrents to development and redevelopment.

The EPA, as well as several states, have programs designed to subsidize site assessment, planning and remediation of brownfield properties. Importantly, participation in these programs includes the granting of limitations to, or relief from, any future liability associated with known or unknown contamination. This reduces risk and makes redevelopment of these properties a much more attractive investment. Still, there is insufficient grant money, and the costs of mitigation can outweigh potential financial gains from investing in some brownfield properties. Thus the 'inventory' of these distressed properties has not materially declined and this remains a huge economic challenge for many older, formerly industrial, areas.

Transfer of rights development programs are used for preservation and to shape urban land uses. Effectively, the owner of a property sells or trades their right to develop their property to another property owner. From the donor/seller perspective, it is similar to a conservation easement. The receiving owner gains the ability to alter their development. This can include new development on vacant land or the transfer of 'air rights,' which is the transfer of unused development density. The transfer of air rights can lower the average cost of office space and make the local office market more attractive to potential business occupants. See Box 10.1 and 10.2 for examples of transfer of right development programs. Students can find additional information on incentive-based land use mechanisms from The Center for Land Use Education at the University of Wisconsin Stevens Point.[6] The transfer of air rights development has been used in New York City and elsewhere (World Bank 2018). In an important perspective from an economic development viewpoint, Karanja and Rama (2011) characterize the use of tradable development rights versus other traditional land use regulations as a movement from right-to-apply to right-to-build. We view this as an important shift that *encourages* versus *restricts* business investment.

## BOX 10.1 TRANSFER OF DEVELOPMENT RIGHTS – ZONING EXCHANGE

An urban property A is zoned for multifamily housing uses at a maximum density of 20 units per acre. The owner of this property pays a fee to a land owner B whose property is on the urban fringe, and who is using their land for agricultural purposes. Owner B agrees to designate 30 acres of their property for conservation (agricultural or open space) and receives a payment from owner A. Based on a formula determined by local authorities, this transfer of development rights allows owner A to increase their development density, which increases profitability and can encourage housing development near employment centers.

## BOX 10.2 TRANSFER OF DEVELOPMENT RIGHTS – AIR RIGHTS DEVELOPMENT

An office building is located in an area that is zoned to allow a floor-to-area ratio of 6:1. This means that the total floor area of a building can be six times the size of the land the building sits on. If the lot is one acre (43,560 square feet), then the building, by code, could be as large as 261,360 square feet ($43,560 \times 6 = 261,360$). Depending on set-back and parking space rules, this would be about an eight-story building. However, in this case, the building is only 170,000 square feet of floor area. The owner of this property could sell her unused development right, called 'air rights,' to another property owner who could then go higher than the density allowed by existing code. In our example, the receiving property owner could develop a building with a total of (261,360 + 170,000) 431,360 square feet of floor space on a one-acre lot.

## 10.2.3 Fiscal instruments for regulating land use

Fiscal instruments in land use regulation are taxes paid by developers in exchange for permission to build on land. Even in by-rights development states, the assessment of levies on developers can be structured to encourage or discourage land uses. These can include dedications, impact fees, tap and linkage fees, and other special assessments. Also included are facilities or other investments 'donated' by developers to the host community (Silva and Acheampong 2015). Dedications, such as infrastructure levies, are fees or taxes paid by developers, which then fund infrastructure or services in the host community. Dedications are widely used in developed nations. For example, the United Kingdom has a relatively new Community Infrastructure Levy scheme that can be used for roads, flood defenses, education facilities, hospitals, sports and recreation facilities, affordable housing, and for sponsoring open spaces (Faulkner 2016). In Australia, similar business-to-community arrangements are called Infrastructure Agreements. In the US, we typically group dedications with impact fees, tap fees and other development exactions.

Property developers are charged impact fees to fund the marginal cost of public infrastructure required for a new development, or significant redevelopment. The calculation of these fees is often complicated, especially when the approach used to quantify impact fees is more political than actuarial. The most clearly defined principle of impact fees is that the fees should pay for services directly connected to the proposed development. If you add a large housing development to a community, then the new infrastructure would be roads, wastewater and potable water systems, perhaps new fire or police stations, and new schools to be located in the new neighborhood – not elsewhere in the city. Tap fees are similar but are usually limited to the direct cost of tapping into existing infrastructure, such as adding a water meter for a new residential or commercial customer. For some communities, impact fees have become a negotiating tool for attracting development and new businesses. The impact fees can be reduced below actual costs or rebated through local taxes. For example, a new outlet mall in Texas required the addition of millions of dollars in new infrastructure to extend existing water and sewer lines to the shopping center site. However, the city agreed to refund the impact fee charged to the developer as an economic development incentive by rebating a portion of the local sales taxes generated at the mall until the impact fee was repaid.

A proffer is an offer of property, features, amenities or operating characteristics by a property developer to a local government in exchange for a favorable change in zoning or other land use regulation. For example, a residential developer donates land for a public school or park in exchange for being allowed to build more houses per acre of land. Proffers are not usually listed in academic articles as mechanisms of land use regulation, but for many communities they are a key strategy for addressing social goals through the property development process. Though there are variations, the proffer process typically begins with a request by a developer to change the zoning for a particular property. Perhaps the developer wants a different land use, such as converting commercial property to residential, or wants to increase the allowed density within a given use. The developer 'volunteers' to provide something for the community in exchange for the zoning change.

Proffers take many forms including donations of cash, land for open space or public services (fire stations, schools, et cetera), construction of public infrastructure (road interchanges, other), inclusion of units with below-market rents (affordable housing, low-cost office space for government or non-profit uses) and other features. Proponents of the proffer system call it a market-driven example of public–private sector cooperation. However, whatever proffer is offered must be built into the cost of the project and thus can be a deterrent to development or can lower the community's competitiveness when seeking to fill the developed space with tenants. There are also concerns about requesting proffers that are unrelated to the proposed development. In 2016, the Commonwealth of Virginia legislature felt that some communities were abusing the spirit of the proffer system, resulting in a law that required proffers to be 'specifically attributable' to a proposed development.[7] It is possible that the proffer system could be used to incentivize development, but most often it is viewed as an extra expense.

No discussion of land use regulation in the United States is complete without at least mentioning Houston, Texas, which is the largest city in the nation without formal land use zoning. In keeping with stereotype, Houston could be seen to be the 'wild west' of development that makes for some interesting mixes of land uses. It also provides ample material for bloggers, pundits and researchers trying to ascertain if the lack of zoning is a good thing or a bad thing.

Property development in the City of Houston and its extraterritorial jurisdiction is not governed by land use regulations but is subject to city codes that address issues such as adequacy of streets, access to sites, building lines/lot sizes, setbacks, parking, landscaping, residential buffers and a full slate of building design and safety codes. In addition, the business permitting process is used to effectively regulate the location and intensity of certain land uses, such as developments near airports, hotels/motels, locations where hazardous materials are handled or stored, junkyards, jails, manufactured housing, locations of cell phone towers and other activities. Therefore, even while avoiding zoning as a land use regulation tool, Houston still employs a variety of mechanisms to 'promote and protect the health, safety, and welfare of the public.' (City of Houston 2015 p 1)

Houston is one of the largest cities, both in population and land area, in the United States, with a diversified economy and many economic development successes to its credit. Yet we find no formal studies that conclude the lack of zoning gives the city a measurable advantage in attracting, retaining or growing businesses. This does not mean that there are no benefits, or detriments, from limiting the mechanisms of city regulation but to date the case one way or the other has not been proven.

## ■ 10.3 Impacts of land use regulation on economic development

The presence of land use regulations does not appear to greatly impact the overall ability of developers to create commercial and industrial properties in the US, though this may have more to do with biases promoting these developments in the taxing system (Kim 2011). But this same taxing system, especially at the local level, incentivizes cities and counties to use land use regulation to drive up property values, even at the expense of housing affordability (Krawchenko and Schumann 2017). Krawchenko and Schumann assert land use regulations, including building codes and environmental rules:

- Do not facilitate the emergence of community- or market-based drivers of land use change;
- Take too much time to navigate or change;
- Result in spiraling housing prices, mixed patterns of extreme growth or decline in specific areas of the community and overall induce sprawl over compact, efficient urban designs.

There is an argument that land use planning, even under relatively tight regulatory schemes, reduces risk and transaction costs for developers. Buitelaar (2004), building on the work of Alexander (2001), asserts that land use planning reduces the cost of information within total property transaction costs. In other words, by telling the developer what they can do, there is less risk of the developer making a wrong development choice. Kim (2011) observes that there is little empirical evidence to support Buitelaar's assertion, largely due to challenges of measuring the relevant effects. Our observation is that while some information costs are lowered, the net effect of land use regulations on developer success must account for the degree to which the development can respond to current and future market demand.

At the time this chapter was being written, the US economy was growing at a pace that was creating jobs, but not sparking excessive inflation. Before the end of 2018, the unemployment rate was expected to be at its lowest level since the late 1960s. Therefore, the mishmash of rigid, antiquated land use regulations that regulate business location do not appear to have tremendous negative effects at the macroeconomic scale. However, the indirect effects of land use regulations on economic activity through housing markets are notable.

Kim (2011 p 39) observes: 'residential land use regulations indirectly affect business location decisions and . . . distort the spatial structure of the region.' There has been a preference among suburban municipalities in the post-World War II era to encourage the building of single family homes. As late as the mid-1970s, the real estate literature found that preserving single family residential zones increased taxable property values (see, for example, Stull 1975). Interestingly, Lafferty and Frech (1978) observed that multifamily properties could be good for the tax base, if they are highly concentrated. However, as property values rise for low-density, single-family land use zones, they constrain overall housing supply and become economically exclusionary in nature, thereby creating housing–job imbalances (Kim 2011; Ihlanfeldt 2004; Lubell 2016). Land use planning approaches that restrict multifamily properties to specific residential submarkets exacerbate these exclusionary tendencies.

There is a clear relationship between employment growth and the supply of *local* labor, which is predominantly affected by the supply of [workforce] housing (Glaeser et al. 2006; Saks 2008; Vermeulen and Ommeren 2008). Or, as succinctly put by Glaeser (2006 p 2), 'no homes, no people, no jobs.' Moreover, Saks asserts that these negative effects on labor supply extend over time. But there is also evidence that the relationship between housing development and economic activity is more complicated if just viewed from the labor supply perspective. Ferm and

Jones (2016) have noted that policies in London (UK) that have fueled speculative investments in housing on sites previously occupied by businesses (think loft conversions) are supporting, rather than just responding to, deindustrialization.

Do land use regulations support or impede economic development? It's complicated. Because of the presumed lower cost per unit, however measured, for providing municipal services to commercial and industrial properties, many 'bedroom' suburban communities shift their bias from single family housing towards nonresidential development when they have reached a more mature stage of growth. This does not mean there won't be a dispute over approving zoning for a warehouse-sized retail outlet in the middle of a suburban neighborhood. To the extent they continue to approve new housing developments, many communities cling to mid-20th century preferences for large-lot suburban residential development – mostly due to the cost of providing education. But the world has changed. Industries are much 'cleaner,' there has been a shift to the services sectors, communications technologies have made remote work commonplace, and there are indications of a shift in work and housing preferences for the millennial generation. Moreover, there is widespread acceptance of the notion that suburban sprawl has created cost and livability problems for metropolitan regions. In the following section, we examine the economic development dimensions of Smart Growth and other anti-sprawl urban design choices.

## ■ 10.4  New urban designs and economic development

New urbanism, Smart Growth, transit-oriented development and knowledge-based urban development are approaches to land use planning, usually in large metropolitan areas, that have emerged over the past quarter century to address the perceived, and largely correct, environmental failings of traditional urban planning and to address the form of the built environment in a postindustrial economy. These approaches are largely overlapping or, in the case of transit-oriented development, reside wholly within the other approaches. The main symptom of earlier land use planning that the new urban designs seek to overcome is urban sprawl. Carruthers and Ulparason (2003) define sprawl as discontinuous, low-density suburban growth that is the result of uncoordinated and unplanned rapid growth. One can summarize much of the modern urban design literature as 'sprawl bad, density good.'

What is so bad about sprawl? In the space allocated here, it is not easy to list all the social, environmental and economic ills attributed to sprawl, but in summary they include but are not limited to:

- Lower efficiency/higher costs of providing public services due to a) distance and b) the delegation of municipal services across a larger number of smaller municipalities;
- Increased requirement for infrastructure, especially roads to connect far-flung residential communities to employment centers;
- Pollution effects of automobile and truck traffic;[8]
- Economic losses related to increased commute times;
- Decreased labor market efficiency;

- Promotion of de-urbanization that has created stark inequality in economic opportunity and the need for massive investments in urban regeneration (Sayce and McIntosh 2002).

Sprawl has some advantages. Decreasing density is clearly associated with lower land costs, which reduces the cost of doing business and the cost of housing. Urban sprawl can also contribute to the overall welfare of the residents of a region by providing a wide range of housing options. Some households want to live in a flat above a hotel and in easy walking distance of restaurants and retailers. Others prefer to live on larger lots with room for children to play on their property. Not everyone is attracted to the 'concrete jungle.' While it is currently out of fashion, in the late 1970s through 1980s the emergent form of business site was the large campus location (building surrounded by open space), which was meant to, among other things, enhance security and safety for companies and their employees.

Increasing urban density can presumably address each of the environmental, social and economic problems blamed on sprawl – some in obvious ways, others more indirectly. If roads, communications networks and public services can be delivered to a smaller geographic footprint, then the average cost of providing that service or infrastructure will decline. The nature and scale of the net fiscal benefits are unclear when infrastructure must be retrofitted for land that is being up-zoned (meaning a shift to increased density in existing urban areas). There is little reasonable doubt that the implications of climate change and depleting resources need to be addressed in land use and economic development planning (Wlodarczak 2012). Even for those who are climate change skeptics, can one argue that we shouldn't strive to have less of an impact on our planet if it is technologically and economically feasible? Having access to a wider and deeper pool of workers within a reasonable commute is highly desirable for employers. The Smart Growth movement, and new urban design in general, expands on the goal of higher density. Smart Growth America lists several goals that are shown in the accompanying box (Box 10.3).[9]

## BOX 10.3 SMART GROWTH AMERICA GOALS

- Strengthen and direct development towards existing communities;
- Preserve open space, farmland, natural beauty and critical environmental areas;
- Build compact communities;
- Building housing opportunities and choices;
- Build walkable communities;
- Mix land uses;
- Provide a variety of transportation choices [modes];
- Foster distinctive, attractive communities with a strong sense of place;
- Encourage citizen and stakeholder participation in development decisions;
- Make development decisions predictable, fair, and cost-effective (Smart Growth America).

It is important to note that Smart Growth principles go beyond urban design choices and specifically address policy issues and do so to a greater degree than some new urban planning approaches (Poticha 2000). It also attempts to draw in property developers by calling for predictable and fair land use decision making. But what are the connections between increasing density in the built environment, whichever design approach is used, and economic development?

Aside from issues of resource utilization and lower negative environmental effects of sprawl,[10] there are two primary, and related, streams of academic thought regarding new urban principles that increase density. The first takes in more than 100 years of economic agglomeration theory. Wlodarczak (2012) provides a succinct review of selected keynote theories of economic geography that advocates of new urbanism suggest will be the driving forces of enhanced economic growth in denser urban environments, which we augment for clarity.

Alfred Marshall (1920) described how firms in similar industries that are clustered together benefit from enhanced access to skilled labor (a wider and deeper pool of trade specialists), specialized suppliers (suggesting economies of scale for firms delivering specialized products or services) and knowledge spillovers among competing firms that enhance innovation. Jane Jacobs (1969) proposed that it is the flow of ideas and knowledge across *different* industries located nearby that leads to new 'work' and this is what defines a city.[11] Importantly, Jacobs included informal knowledge flows that arise from social interactions among individuals in her description of how urban economies function.

Van Geenhuizen and Nijkamp (2007) extended knowledge flows to include tacit knowledge,[12] and recognized that it is especially enhanced through face-to-face communication. Glaeser (1998) also noted that face-to-face communication supports information flows that enhance economic outcomes in cities. Porter (1990, 1998) included the presence of 'related firms' in his theory of national and regional economic competitiveness, which stepped beyond Marshall's supplier networks. As discussed in an earlier chapter, Porter's work on industrial clusters has come to dominate economic development strategic planning, even though some of his theoretical constructs have been challenged (Swords 2013). In sum, density enhances proximity, which enhances agglomeration benefits over those found in more dispersed urban-suburban settings. If being a little close is good, being very close is better.

The second theoretical construct used to suggest new urban designs will boost regional economic development relies on concepts we describe as amenities-based economic development, which some call place-based economic development. Live–work–play spaces with high-quality amenities, sensitivity to environmental goals and multimodal transportation options ranging from light-rail transit systems to bike trails are in high demand by young, highly skilled workers (Chapter 6). New urban designs, in theory, deliver on these desired traits. Portney (2013) and Wlodarczak (2012) draw connections between Smart Growth principles and the creative class theories of Richard Florida (2002). Florida's thesis holds that cities that can attract and retain highly skilled workers will succeed in the new economy. Malizia and Motoyama (2016) also discuss urban vibrancy, which is measured along many of the same characteristics as Smart Growth, to a city's ability to attract high-growth firms.

However, new urbanism, especially in forms that take a comparatively extreme stance that 'density is good,' attracts critics. Green Leigh and Hoezel

(2012) noted that Smart Growth has, at least historically, had a 'blind spot' for industrial redevelopment, especially in the urban core. These writers noted that converting comparatively inexpensive industrially zoned land to mixed-use commercial–residential may weaken the economic base, reduce the supply of jobs-producing land and result in industrial sprawl, a similar argument to that made by Ferm and Jones (2016). Moreover, Wygonik et al. (2015) observed that new urban design management does not adequately account for intra-urban goods movements, which in an age of Internet retail when almost any restaurant will deliver to your doorstep suggests a critical hole in planning.

Ciccone and Hall (1996) and Ciccone (2002) observed that the scale effects and agglomeration benefits of density cannot be fully realized if land use policies inhibit people and businesses from readily adapting to market shifts. Moreover, it is not clear how new urban designs are adapting their design principles to address the changing nature of work. The proportion of jobs that are not traditional employee–employer relationships has been rising for 20 years. More workers are treated as contractors and more individuals, by choice or force, are effectively self-employed. As jobs, or 'gigs,' become more temporary in nature, intra-regional mobility will become a key determinant of economic competitiveness. Live–work–play lifestyles become challenging if your work location changes frequently.

The benefits of new urban designs, in terms of public services, utilities and transportation efficiencies, are evident. It is also clear that new urbanism drives up land costs affecting housing affordability for workers and the competitiveness of business spaces. The balance of these forces in site location decisions by firms is not well established. The startup or small firm, because of limited financial resources, may gain the most from the effects of knowledge spillover and tacit knowledge resulting from proximity to other industry actors. But how does this help if the firm can't afford to rent space to run their business? The rapid growth of shared-space services addresses this challenge, but when firms grow too large for shared space, will they be forced to leave the area? While telecommuting will increasingly help firms address space affordability challenges, it is not a complete solution. And it is important to remember that tacit knowledge is best established and transferred face to face. Moreover, in high-density commercial districts large firms will have increasing challenges in finding sufficient contiguous space for their needs, which could hinder a city's ability to attract firm relocations.

A relatively new adaptation of new urban design offers intriguing possibilities for engaging in effective land use management as we enter the fourth industrial age. In general, form-based codes[13] regulate building aesthetics and design features with comparatively little concern over the actual use (economic function) of the space. This approach also emphasizes the look and feel of highly accessible public spaces. Proponents of form-based codes argue for creating centers of activity in walkable environments, preserving environmental spaces and, perhaps most dramatically, discarding traditional transportation designs that fragment street systems. This approach emphasizes community engagement in the design process. Its main advantage is flexibility. By not focusing on specific economic activities, areas managed with form-based codes can presumably adapt more readily to changes in market demand, which could stabilize property values and long-run economic performance.

New urban designs that are economically and environmentally more efficient, yet still support economic development competitiveness, will most likely be a combination of relatively dense urban cores surrounded by nodes of high-density mixed land uses (town centers). These will be connected through efficient public transportation and road networks, with less dense areas in between that allow for industrial or logistics uses. These urban forms maximize resident utility/welfare through a wide range of housing options, which include affordable, workforce-appropriate choices.

## ■ 10.5 Summarizing the impacts of land use regulation on economic development

When taken together, the approaches and mechanisms of land use regulation can impact economic practices, opportunities and outcomes in numerous ways, both positive and negative. The positive impacts include:

- Eliminating negative externalities, preserving public goods, promoting improvements to amenities;
- Encouraging more compact development with impacts on efficiency and agglomeration benefits;
- Improving transportation and increasing mobility;
- Decreasing uncertainty and transaction costs for land developers (knowing the rules).

It is important to recognize that these benefits accrue separately or collectively to individuals, businesses and communities, but require focus of purpose and fairness in implementation.

Conversely, if improperly implemented, land use regulations can impede, and even negate, the best economic development strategies by:

- Causing dispersed and/or mismatched development patterns (decreased efficiency);
- Decreasing site availability (limit opportunity for growth);
- Increasing land costs (reduce regional competitiveness);
- Preventing regions from adapting to new market demands in a timely manner (Kim 2011).

Achieving a highly integrated, effective combination of land use planning and economic development planning requires:

1. Zoning code quality (efficient, flexible, adaptable);
2. A zoning process that is transparent, fair and responsive;
3. Enforcement of codes that are consistent, well communicated and focused on compliance instead of penalties;
4. Integration of zoning with a well-conceived comprehensive plan including transportation planning;
5. Citizen support;
6. Local leadership that is predictable and transparent;
7. A well-executed economic development program (Wilkins et al. 2006).

# ■ 10.6 Conclusion

Land use policies and urban design principles have seen notable shifts in their goals over the past several decades. Land use planning was originally focused on protecting residents from the negative environmental spillovers of industrial activity and the organization of the built environment in areas of rapid population growth. It is now shifting its focus to broader environmental goals, such as regional air quality. This occurs amidst a realization that the best answer to growth challenges may not simply be 'build more roads.'

Policymaking in land use regulation in the United States is largely driven by local governments. As urban areas have become larger, it is more often the case that the number of municipalities across which land use planning must be actuated has expanded and become more complex. While regional metropolitan planning organizations (MPOs) take the lead in regional transportation planning, land use plans remain the purview of localities. Many observers, including Kim (2011), and Carruthers and Ulparason (2003) have called out the need for interjurisdictional cooperation on land use plans in urban areas, but the realpolitik of local control makes such cooperation problematic. Tiebout (1956), the father of regional science, suggested that the effects of the actions of individual communities can offset any benefits of local autonomy. Still, urban areas are systems of economic activity, and understanding the flow of those systems across a given urban complex can provide land use planning and management efficiencies that support economic success in a rapidly changing 21st century economy. For most companies, the most important site location criterion is labor availability. Labor sheds are not influenced by city/county boundary lines, and the imposition of boundaries hinders economic development.

Finally, we must join the voices of many in saying that improving land use planning to support regional and community economic development requires communication with stakeholders representing the broadest definition of our communities. While recognizing competing interests, key informants to this process must include regional and local transportation officials, planners, businesses, economic development practitioners, workforce development entities, housing providers and community leaders. Having the right leadership to bring all these interests together is a necessary condition of success.

## *Key terms used in this chapter*

### Regulatory instruments

- Moratoria – temporarily halting new development.
- Greenbelts – areas not open for development.
- Rate of growth control – limiting the number/size of developments within a specified time period.
- Urban growth boundary – limit of an area beyond which new development is not allowed, except to support low-intensity uses such as agricultural structures.

- Agricultural preservation zone – area reserved for agricultural or natural land uses.
- Building codes – enacted or adopted rules/regulations regarding building construction characteristics and/or sizes.
- Zoning codes – enacted or adopted rules that designate land uses and/or land use density.

## Incentive-based instruments

- Development-focused tax credits – incentivize property development through the issuance of tax credits.
- Tax increment financing – development incentive that captures the marginal tax revenues associated with a specified property to refund the cost of development and/or renovation.
- Special economic zone – designated area in which developers or businesses can receive incentives or regulatory relief, usually in areas in economic distress.
- Conservation easements – a voluntary restriction placed on developable land that restricts its future land use.
- Brownfield redevelopment programs – programs that incentivize development/ redevelopment on registered environmentally contaminated land.
- Transfer of rights development programs – exchanging the rights to development from one property to another, usually for a fee, that affects the location of development, but not the total amount of development in a given jurisdiction.
- Air rights development – a special type of transfer of rights development that allows a land owner to sell unused density rights on a property.

## Fiscal instruments for regulating land use

- Dedications – fees or taxes paid by developers to offset the cost of providing new public infrastructure or services associated with a proposed development.
- Proffer – an offer of property, features, amenities or operating characteristics by a property developer to a local government in exchange for a favorable change in zoning or other land use regulation.
- Impact fees – a type of dedication where a developer recompenses a public entity for the cost of providing new or significantly enhanced public utilities (water, sewer, roads) to a development.
- Tap and linkage fees – fees paid to a utility (public or private) for connecting to a service utility (water, electric, wastewater).

## *Key messages*

- Traditional approaches to land use planning and regulation are increasingly at odds with industrial shifts and worker housing needs in a postindustrial economy;

- Tax credit-driven incentive programs in land use regulation in the US have been the primary tool for addressing issues of affordable workforce housing that can impact site location decisions;
- Successful Smart Growth approaches to land use management will be characterized by dense inner-city developments with high-connected nodes of density in suburban communities with intervening areas of lower density development to support space-demanding industries and recreation spaces;
- Shifting from traditional land use regulations, such as Euclidean zoning, to form-based codes has several distinct advantages, the most important of which is to allow for flexibility in the actual economic use on any given plot of land to respond to changing market demand (residents) and industrial technology (fourth industrial age).

## Discussion questions

Recalling the discussion of fiscal impact analysis in a previous chapter, if a new office building is proposed, should the impact fee cover the average cost of providing treated water to the site based on the cost per square foot of all existing commercial buildings, or account for the fully allocated marginal cost if the new demand requires the water system to add a pumping station to the system, even if that pumping station will also serve future developments?

Comprehensive (land use) plans, transportation plans and economic development strategic plans are often developed by separate departments within local government and may engage different regional and state agencies within each of these planning processes. As a class discussion, consider the challenges and opportunities of aligning these three planning efforts.

## Notes

1 Von Thünen's *The Isolated State with Respect to Agriculture and Political Economy, Volume 1* was published in 1826 and posited a theory of the balance between land rent and transportation costs in the production of agricultural goods based on his observation of his own farm located in Germany.

2 Village of Euclid, Ohio v. Ambler Realty Co., 272 US 365 (1926).

3 See https://www.nhlp.org/resource-center/low-income-housing-tax-credits/.

4 Virginia defines mixed use as residential units in a building that also hosts industrial, office or other commercial uses. The residential floor space can be no more than 30 percent of the total building area. See other rules for the Virginia program at https://www.dhcd.virginia.gov/sites/default/files/Docx/vez/vez-code-of-virginia.pdf.

5 See https://www.epa.gov/brownfields/overview-epas-brownfields-program.

6 See https://www.uwsp.edu/cnr-ap/clue/Documents/PlanImplementation/Transfer_of_Development_Rights.pdf.

7 Labeled as Senate Bill 549 Conditional Zoning: Provisions Applicable to Certain Rezoning Proffers, the law added section 15.2–2303.4 to Chapter 322 of the state code. The text of this law is available at https://lis.virginia.gov/cgi-bin/legp604.exe?161+ful+CHAP0322.

8 Almost one-half of all United States residents live in areas that do not meet federal air quality standards, and cars and trucks are the largest source of air pollution. See Union of Concerned Scientists at https://www.ucsusa.org/clean-vehicles/vehicles-air-pollution-and-human-health#.WsZvNJch2Uk.

9 See https://smartgrowthamerica.org/our-vision/what-is-smart-growth/.

10 Alexander and Tomalty (2002) studied 26 municipalities in Canada and found that density is associated with efficiencies in infrastructure and reduced automobile dependence, with associated implications for economic and ecological impacts, but they also observed the previously noted negative impact on housing affordability.

11 See Welsh (2016) for his review of Jacobs' work which included the assertion that agricultural production does not advance without the innovation (our word) associated with cities and the explicit case of what happens when cities no longer engage in 'new' work, namely Detroit of the 1960s.

12 Tacit knowledge includes knowledge that comes from observation, participation and prolonged interactions among individuals (Wlodarczak 2012).

13 Descriptions of form-based codes and how they could affect economic activity can be found on the Form-Based Code Institute website at https://formbasedcodes.org/.

## References

Alexander, D. and Tomalty, R. 2002 Smart Growth and sustainable development: challenges, solutions and policy directions. *Local Environment*, 7:4, pp 397–409.

Alexander, E. 2001 A transaction cost theory of land use planning and development control: toward an institutional analysis of public planning. *Town Planning Review*, 72, pp 45–75.

Buitelaar, E. 2004 A transaction cost analysis of the land development process, *Urban Studies*, 41:13, pp 2539–2553.

Carruthers, J. and Ulparason, G. 2003 Fragmentation and sprawl: evidence from interregional analysis, *Growth and Change*, 33, pp 312–340.

Ciccone, A. 2002 Agglomeration effects in Europe, *European Economic Review*, 46, pp 213–227.

Ciccone, A. and Hall, R. 1996 Productivity and the density of economic activity, *American Economic Review*, 46, pp 213–227.

City of Houston 2015 Ordinance No. 2015–2639. Available at http://www.houstontx.gov/planning/DevelopRegs/docs_pdfs/Ord_2015-639.pdf.

Ferm, J. and Jones, E. 2016 Mixed-use 'regeneration' of employment land in the post-industrial city: challenges and realities in London, *European Planning Studies*, 24:10, pp 1913–1936.

Florida, R. 2002 *The Rise of the Creative Class*, Basic Books, New York.

Glaeser, E. 1998 Are cities dying? *Journal of Economic Perspectives*, 12:2, pp 139–160.

Glaeser, E. 2006 The economic impact of restricting housing supply. Rappaport Institute for Greater Boston Policy Briefs, PB-2006–3. Kennedy School of Government, Harvard University. Available at https://www.hks.harvard.edu/sites/default/files/centers/rappaport/files/glaeserhousing_final.pdf.

Glaeser E., Gyourko, J. and Saks, R. 2006 Urban growth and housing supply. *Journal of Economic Geography*, 6, pp 71–89.

Green Leigh, N. and Hoezel, N. 2012 Smart Growth's blind side, *Journal of the American Planning Association*, 78:1, pp 87–103.

Hopkins, L. 2001 *Urban Development: The Logic of Making Plans*, Island Press, Washington, DC.

Ihlanfeldt, K. 2004 Exclusionary land-use regulations within suburban community: a review of the evidence and policy prescriptions, *Urban Studies*, 41, pp 261–283.

Jacobs, J. 1969 *The Economies of Cites*, Random House, New York.

Karanja, F. and Rama, I. 2011 *Land Use Planning Challenges and Tools – Tradable Development Rights: Design Considerations*, 55th Conference, Australian Agricultural and Resource Economics Society, Melbourne, Australia. Available at https://ideas.repec.org/p/ags/aare11/100701.html.

Kim, J. 2011 Linking land use planning and regulation to economic development: a literature review. *Journal of Planning Literature*, 26:1, pp 35–47.

Kirkland, S. 2013 *Paris Reborn: Napoleon III, Baron Haussmann and the Quest to Build a Modern City*. St, Martin's Press, New York.

Krawchenko, T. and Schumann, A. 2017 *The Use of Land: Why Planners Cannot Go It Alone,* OECD Observer, March 3. Available at http://oecdobserver.org/news/fullstory.php/aid/5666/The_use_of_land:_Why_planners_cannot_go_it_alone.html.

Lafferty, R. and Frech, H. 1978 Community environment and the market value of single family homes: the effect of the dispersion of land uses, *Journal of Law and Economics*, 21, pp 381–394.

Lubell, J. 2016 Preserving and expanding affordability in neighborhoods experiencing rising rents and property values, *Cityscape*, 10:3, pp 131–150.

Malizia, E. and Motoyama, Y. 2016 The economic development-vibrant center connection: tracking high-growth firms in the DC region, *Professional Geographer*, 68:3, pp 349–355.

Marshall, A. 1920 *Principles of Economics: An Introductory Volume.* Macmillan and Company, London.

Ministry of Housing 2014 *Ministry of Housing, Communities & Local Government 2014 Guidance: Community Infrastructure Levy.* Available at: https://www.gov.uk/guidance/community-infrastructure-levy.

Porter, M. 1990 *The Competitive Advantage of Nations*, The Free Press, New York.

Porter, M. 1998 Clusters and the new economics of competitiveness, *Harvard Business Review*, December, pp 77–90.

Portney, K. 2013 Local sustainability policies and programs as economic development: is the new economic development sustainable development? *Cityscape*, 15:1, pp 45–62.

Poticha, S. 2000 *Smart Growth and New Urbanism: What's the Difference?* Public Square, Congress of New Urbanism. Available at https://www.cnu.org/publicsquare/smart-growth-and-new-urbanism-what's-difference.

Saks, R. 2008 Job creation and housing construction: constraints on metropolitan area employment growth, *Journal of Urban Economics*, 64, pp 178–193.

Sayce, S. and McIntosh, A. 2002 Planning for leisure: time for a radical rethink or just a slight adjustment? *Journal of Leisure Property*, 2:3, pp 254–281.

Silva, E. and Acheampong, R. 2015 *Developing an Inventory and Typology of Land-Use Planning Systems and Policy Instruments in OECD Countries,*

OECD Environment Working Papers, No. 94, OECD Publishing, Paris. Available at http://dx.doi.org/10.1787/5jrp6wgxp09s-en.

Stull, W. 1975 Community environment, zoning, and the market value of single family homes, *Journal of Law and Economics*, 18, pp 535–558.

Swords, J. 2013 Michael Porter's cluster theory as a local and regional development tool – the rise and fall of cluster policy in the UK. *Local Economy*, 28:4, pp 367–381. Available through Northumbria Research Link at http://nrl.northumbria.ac.uk/11207/3/local_econ_submission.pdf.

Tiebout, C. 1956 A pure theory of local expenditures, *Journal of Political Economy*, 64, pp 416–424.

United States Environmental Protection Agency (EPA) 2018 Overview of the Brownfields Program. Available at https://www.epa.gov/brownfields/overview-epas-brownfields-program.

Van Geenhuizen, M. and Nijkamp, P. 2007 Cities and footlooseness: in search of place-bound companies and effective location policies, *Environment and Planning C: Government and Policy*, 25, pp 692–708.

Vermeulen, W. and van Ommeren, J. 2008 *Does Land Use Planning Shape Regional Economies?* Tinbergen Institute Discussion Paper TI 2008–004/3. Available at http://papers.tinbergen.nl/08004.pdf.

Welsh, I. 2016 Review of *The Economy of Cities* by Jane Jacobs, November 24. Available at http://www.ianwelsh.net/review-of-the-economy-of-cities-by-jane-jacobs/.

Wilkins, J., Riall, B. and Nelson, A. 2006 Does rural land use planning and zoning enhance local economic development, *Economic Development Journal*, 5:4, pp 24–33.

Wlodarczak, D. 2012 Smart Growth and urban economic development: connecting economic development and land-use planning using the example of high-tech firms, *Environment and Planning A*, 44, pp 1255–1269.

World Bank 2018 *Transferable Development Rights*. Available at https://urban-regeneration.worldbank.org/node/22.

Wygonik, E., Bassok, A., Goodchild, A., McCormack, E. and Carlson, D. 2015 Smart Growth and goods movement: emerging research agendas, *Journal of Urbanism*, 8:2, pp 115–132.

# 11 The profession of economic development

This chapter:

- ▶ Considers the nature of economic development as a profession and the ways in which practices are shaped by global markets, as well as local regulations and programs;

- ▶ Examines the ways in which the practice of economic development exhibits both similarities and differences across nations and how places can learn from each other;

- ▶ Discusses where employment opportunities lie for economic development professionals;

- ▶ Discusses the resources and opportunities available to practitioners to develop their careers and stay abreast of progress in the field;

- ▶ Examines the professional associations available to economic developers and the role they play in advocating for change;

- ▶ Documents information sources on employment opportunities.

PEOPLE HAVE BEEN promoting the growth of the places in which they live for all of human history. In some instances, this has been a deliberate act of place branding – think of the rather optimistic naming of Greenland – or it has taken shape through conscious attempts to secure better transport or water infrastructure, generate new markets through favorable trade deals or secure the favor of key decision makers. In many ways, the emergence of formal economic development programs and the rise of economic development as a profession simply represents one more chapter in a long-running story. It is now a discipline that has become professionalized, has considerably more resources – conceptual, fiscal and practical – than previously, and is practiced on a far greater scale than previously as more cities, regions and communities take on the challenge of local development.

Practitioners need to consider how economic development as a profession has changed over the last 20 years in order to ensure their day-to-day activities are in line with currently held notions of good practice. There is also a need to reflect on how to prepare for the next two decades of change. In this chapter we consider the capacity to learn from the experience of other places – communities, cities, regions and even whole nations – as well as the potential to take advantage of professional associations to further economic development objectives.

# ■ 11.1 Economic development in global perspective

The economic development profession has been transformed since the emergence of the first formalized programs of economic development in the early decades of the 20th century. Much of the economic development that took place after 1945 in the industrialized world emerged under the guidance, and often the specific assistance, of governments at a variety of levels. Centralized processes determined where employment opportunities would be located, the mix of industries to be developed and the strategies for providing the infrastructure needed to support them and their workforce (Hall 1969). From the 1980s previously untried approaches were experimented with in response to global economic recession, and the rise of innovative ways of thinking about the role of governments in fostering economic development. Greater emphasis was placed on the role of 'entrepreneurial' cities and regions carving out a niche within the global economy. This new focus on local action to capture the potential of a global economy was encapsulated in the term 'glocalisation' (Swyngedouw 1997), which argued a range of economic and policy drivers had seen responsibility for both economic development and enhancing the well-being of individuals and communities shift 'down' to local governments and 'up' to national governments.

Changes in the broader environment reconfigured the expectations placed on the economic development profession, resulting in new investment and revived development efforts in locations with already established programs. In many instances initiatives were introduced in places where previously economic development was not a priority. In Chapter 5 we discussed the five waves in economic development programs, and these shifts reflected both the consequences of social transformation and the need to develop new 'tools' in order to bring forward growth. What we have witnessed in many places has been a succession of new policies and initiatives, sometimes creating new institutions, and on other occasions announcing additional investment or strategies.

Many of the changes in the ways economic development is practiced have been shaped by organizations with a global reach: since the early 1990s the OECD has sought to better understand the determinants of growth at the local or regional scale. It set out to disseminate best practice and has encouraged member states to implement reforms that will deliver productivity improvements and wage growth. Similarly, the European Union (EU) has implemented policies to encourage the growth of less developed regions in order to build a more cohesive and productive Europe. It too has reshaped policy thinking, with its championing of smart specialization just one example of its influence on contemporary practice.

In any locality the nature of local or regional development activities will be determined by a number of factors:

- First, the needs of businesses and the disciplines of the marketplace are truly global. This means that economic development practitioners need to address a set of growth imperatives and hurdles that are common regardless of location:

- o  This results in strategies and programs that are very similar between cities, regions and communities regardless of which nation they are located within. Individual cities or communities cannot afford to overlook a successful strategy or program just because their neighboring region developed the idea first;
- o  The work of the OECD – which has been reviewed earlier in this text – has been influential precisely because of its capacity to zero in on shared economic drivers and the ways communities can better support them;
- o  At the same time, we need to acknowledge that context is crucial in local economic development. The precise suite of measures implemented in a community or city will reflect the current industry mix, the aspirations of that locality, the powers and authorities (including taxation) available, and the history of development in that region.

- Second, decision makers – whether public or private, local or in a distant capital – need to endorse and provide resources to economic development programs, and their views and processes inevitably determine activities of the ground. In Chapter 8 we discussed public sector processes and how they affect economic development efforts. We also considered how communities can both understand and successfully navigate their way through the many pathways of government funding and support:

  - o  In some places, national governments – or even supranational bodies such as the European Union – choose to support local economic development efforts and this almost inevitably results in efforts to deliver a standard set of services to all parts of their territory;
  - o  Differences are evident as you move from city to city and nation to nation, as decision makers have emphasized their own priorities or sought to tailor their efforts to achieve local objectives;
  - o  There are a number of very good texts that describe how local or regional economic development activities are organized in different nations (see, for example, Danson et al. 2000);
  - o  There is variation between places in how economic development is implemented across the globe and within individual nations. This variability reflects differences in the values and philosophies of key decision makers. In some instances the variations are minor, in other instances they are very substantial.

- Third, budgets have a substantial impact on the types of activities economic developers engage in. Many initiatives – such as cluster policies or business incubators – are relatively expensive while other actions – such as subsidies to incoming firms – come at a lower cost and only if the bid is successful:

  - o  Larger communities have the capacity to afford more costly ways of stimulating growth, while small rural communities may be limited to relatively simple measures that also meet other policy objectives, such as amenity improvement or community building.

- Fourth, in a world made smaller by improvements in transport and communications, new ideas and approaches to economic development move rapidly from one part of the globe to the next:
  - o Communities seek to replicate the success of other regions, with the rollout of industry cluster policies around the globe fueled by the argument that they replicate the success of Silicon Valley;
  - o Economic development agencies copy the strategies they have seen in other parts of the world or had introduced to them through influential policy forums:
    - The work of the OECD, for example, has been the catalyst for a number of policies and programs, including those that emphasize focusing on the needs of minorities in inner-city neighborhoods, new firm formation and startups, the need to address entrepreneurial culture and the development of business incubators.

The US experience for local economic development has been highly influential both in understanding *which* strategies to apply and also *how* to organize and deliver programs (Blakely 1994; Green Leigh and Blakely 2016). In many ways the US experience is distinctive: local organizations are much more prominent in economic development than in many other nations, and in part this reflects the fact that the US passes more responsibility for taxation and the provision of services to local governments, which in turn provides them with the resources to fund local economic development efforts. In addition, economic development is contingent upon access to resources found in specific localities, as well as the right to change land use to enable investment.

The involvement of local governments in economic development in the US reflects the coming together for three factors: first, their control of zoning means that they exert a determinant influence on where businesses locate and how communities develop; second, many have a strong incentive to actively shape development trajectories as growth adds to their base and the resources they have available to meet the needs of their community; and, finally, local governments have increasingly stepped into economic development roles as taxation-shy politicians at the state and national level have reined in the expenditures of central governments. Local officials – elected and professional – have filled the vacuum created by the withdrawal of the other tiers of government.

When we look at the economic development activities at the global or national scale we see a pattern of both similarities and differences. Sometimes the only variation is in the language used to describe a program, but elsewhere these differences are profound and may reflect the national constitution, or the commitments made by one government to others. For example, local governments in the US frequently have greater responsibilities and stronger powers than those in the United Kingdom, Australia or other nations, including the right to raise revenue through the issue of bonds and the generation of specific local taxes, such as a sales tax. Local governments in the US, therefore, have the capacity – should they decide to exercise it – to be a major participant in the implementation of economic development. Local governments in many other parts of the world lack that opportunity.

In nations that are part of the EU, economic development funding and practices are strongly influenced by the programs of that cross-national entity. The EU has committed approximately one-third its total budget for the period 2014–2020 to territorial cohesion (city and regional development) programs, representing €71 billion per annum. While national governments operate their own programs, the capacity to source funding from Brussels has a substantial impact on which initiatives gain national or local support.

## 11.1.1 A global profession

Commonly individuals who have worked as economic development professionals in one nation are able to find equivalent work elsewhere, and this is made possible by the ways in which places learn from each other, and new ideas find a global audience. In broad terms, we know that variation in economic development practice is often greater within nations than between nations (Reese 1993). Previously we were involved in a major study comparing regional development practices across four nations: the United States, Australia, Northern Ireland and England (Beer et al. 2003). When we asked economic practitioners to nominate their four most successful activities, we found a remarkable degree of convergence. Respondents to our survey said their most productive activities were:

- In the US – **business development and advice**; land preparation and site development; provision of grants or loans for business; **networking and building partnerships**; inward investment/promoting the region;
- In England – **business development and advice**; infrastructure planning and development; training skills/labor market programs; land preparation and site development; **networking and building partnerships**; inward investment and promoting the region;
- In Australia – **business development and advice**; infrastructure development and service provision; **networking and partnerships**; sector planning/development; tourism promotion/special events;
- Northern Ireland – **business development and advice**; training skills and labor market programs; working with the community sector; **networking and building partnerships**; managed workspaces/business incubators.

Across the four nations, providing business development and advice to established and incoming firms, and engaging in partnership building and networking featured in the five most effective actions in all four nations. At the same time, land preparation and site development was listed as one of the most productive actions undertaken in the US and England, but was considered one of the least effective strategies in Australia. The provision of business incubators and/or managed workspaces was the only strategy listed as an effective action that reflects recent trends in economic development theory, and even then it was only listed for Northern Ireland.

There are practical implications for the profession of economic development, as it is clear that a sound understanding of business fundamentals – as well as the capacity to connect easily with others – is central to success in economic development.

The similarities in economic development practice across nations are clear, but we need to acknowledge the significant differences in the broader intent of economic development agencies, the budgets they control, their relationship with other public and private sector actors, and their dominant style of operation. If we refer back to that earlier study we found that:

- A 'business-first' ethos was evident among US economic development practitioners and this was evident in their day-to-day activities. Industrial recruitment was more important to the work of US practitioners than evident elsewhere. Other prominent programs were Main Street or urban business development projects which involved approximately half the respondents to our survey, as was the supply of information on government programs and coordinating public sector processes. Overall, the 'flavor' of local efforts towards economic development in the US was one centered on a combination of the provision of direct subsidies to firms, and low-cost market facilitation roles. Programs of work which were relatively expensive and yielded diffuse collective benefits which were difficult to measure – supply chain associations, business incubators and so on – did not feature prominently in their work programs or strategies;
- Facilitation was the term that best described the activities pursued by Australian economic development practitioners who responded to the survey. In Australia the dominant activities were those which could be undertaken with modest expertise and resources: Australian respondents marketed their region; streamlined development approval processes; provided information on government programs; helped in gaining access to government funds; assisted with major events; undertook urban business district development; and promoted tourism. Similar to the US, Australian respondents were centrally involved in offering reduced taxes to firms and subsidizing the relocation of firms;
- English economic development practitioners worked in agencies that had the largest budgets of any of the nations considered in that study, but the greater financial resources brought with them much greater expectations. Their approach could be characterized as comprehensive: economic development activities were not only expected to deliver growth, but were also seen as an instrument for the delivery of a more dynamic and inclusive economy. English economic development practitioners were more likely than their counterparts elsewhere to be involved in property-led developments and in the delivery of new types of assistance to firms, including those that related to fostering clusters, building networks between firms and creating supply chain associations. In addition, there was widespread use of SME support. English respondents were much more likely to be involved in labor market training and recruitment;
- In Northern Ireland, community organizations were central to local economic development efforts, and the work they did indicated relatively little engagement with those aspects of economic development that needed to be integrated with the formal processes of government. No respondents from Northern Ireland, for example, offered tax abatements or equivalent relocation inducements, nor did they have a role in streamlining development approval processes. Few practitioners were involved with a science park or industrial estate, or in the delivery of land or buildings.

There was greater commonality across the four case studies when the focus shifted to activities that build the capacity of a region, city or community to grow and attract new investment. Some forms of economic development activity – including the analysis of the local or regional economy – were universally important. In addition, economic developers in the US and Australia were more likely to engage in lobbying and planning for local or regional infrastructure or telecommunications than those from Northern Ireland or England. Those working in England and the US were most likely to plan and develop business sites and premises, reflecting the long engagement with property-led development in both nations, while skills development and labor market training was prominent in the UK, but not in the US or Australia.

The development of land was a shared priority across all four territories included in the study, with approximately 50 percent of agencies focused on simplifying land use regulations and streamlining planning decisions in order to enable business growth. The coordination of government programs was an additional common priority, and in all instances improving local or regional strategic planning was seen to be critical to success.

Further evidence of the common elements and drivers of economic development practice is to be found in a second study of how places respond to significant economic opportunities or challenges (Beer et al. 2019). This research took place in six nations – the United States, Italy, Australia, England, Germany and Finland – with practitioners active in economic development asked to consider how their community would respond to two scenarios. The first scenario was the announcement of a major plant closure in their locality, while the second asked them to consider how their region or city would react to the announcement of a significant employment opportunity. Study participants were asked to focus on what would be done, who would be responsible for responding, what role already established strategic plans would play, and whether central governments and their political leaders would play a major role. The study found that while there were some critical differences across these very diverse economies, there was a far higher degree of commonality of strategy and action. For both scenarios:

- Responses would largely be dealt with at the local or community level, and would draw upon already established strategies and plans;
- Professional officers would play a leading role in developing and initiating responses, with local political leaders involved at key moments and in the taking of critical decisions;
- Local business networks would play a muted role, and individual businesses would be more likely to participate in any response if the anticipated change was to occur within their industry;
- The process of 'boundary spanning' was seen to be one of the key responses in all nations. That is, economic development practitioners would seek to reach out beyond their administrative and professional boundaries to bring about a coordinated response that mustered the resources of multiple agencies and tiers of government.

Both of the studies discussed above were able to identify many and strong common elements across nations in the practice of economic development at the local, community or regional scale. The first study demonstrated that the range of strategies and actions used by economic development practitioners across a range of nations was remarkably similar, while the second took a more dynamic perspective and was able to show that major events within local or regional economies triggered very similar sets of responses across developed nations. The former was also able to illustrate how the most effective actions and strategies for promoting the growth of places are not necessarily those that receive the most attention in the business media or academic press.

It is the convergence in regional and local economic development practices across nations that makes this text possible. In large measure the contents presented throughout this book reflect what is known – the evidence base – on the practices and priorities of economic developers. This shared focus and experience of economic development practices also allows students, practitioners and government leaders to look at developments in other nations or regions with a view to implementing similar processes and programs in their own city or community. Such policy innovation is essential for ensuring dynamism in economic development and the success of individual localities.

## ■ 11.2 Professional associations

The discussion so far in this chapter has underscored the critical skills needed by successful economic development practitioners and the need to continually 'upskill.' Economic development is not a one-dimensional activity, and professionals need to be able to demonstrate a deep knowledge of businesses, their processes and the environments they operate within, as well as understand public sector program guidelines, write successful funding submissions, engage with elected officials and central government civil servants, and communicate both successes and ongoing challenges to their stakeholders and communities. Professional associations, and the networks and resources they place at the disposal of their members, assist practitioners in fulfilling these diverse tasks.

Professions are largely defined by their associations and organizations that sustain them. Economic development practitioners are fortunate that there are strongly developed professional associations for them to join and engage with, ensuring:

- The currency of their credentials;
- Their familiarity with current policy thinking and programs;
- The strength of their networks with others working in economic development;
- Their awareness of major achievements by others;
- Their capacity to build their credentials over time.

Associations offer economic development professionals a range of services and benefits including:

- The opportunity to attend conferences;
- Short courses for professional accreditation;

- Policy and practice bulletins;
- Access to research reports;
- The opportunity to work with others to advocate for, and enhance, the profession.

Associations play a distinctive and important role within economic development as they are critical in socializing new graduates into the profession. We know from a number of studies that there can be a substantial gap between the research and teaching of academics in economic development and the activities that take place on the ground (Osgood et al. 2012; Currid-Halkett and Stolarick 2011).

Industrial recruitment strategies, for example, are far more prominent in the work of economic development practitioners than would appear from published research. Similarly, the economic development profession may interpret new ideas on encouraging growth in ways that are very different from their presentation and discussion by academics. For example, one study noted that while local governments and economic developers across the US were highly engaged with Florida's (2002) ideas on the creative class, most did not seek to introduce a comprehensive suite of measures to attract this key group within the labor force. Instead they simply reshaped the marketing of their community to emphasize its 'creative' credentials (Currid-Halkett and Stolarick 2011). The same research also found an enduring disconnect between the more theoretical understanding of economic development held by researchers and teachers and the realities of contemporary practice. Professional associations help those entering the profession to bridge that gap.

There is a second key role played by professional bodies, and that is the creation and maintenance of networks within the profession. Research undertaken in Europe has shown that economic developers are more effective, and more highly regarded by their colleagues, if they establish and maintain a network, both within their profession and in related areas of their working life (Sotarauta 2009, 2010). Economic development professionals operate by influencing the decisions of others, and by bringing together resources from across the governmental and private sectors; across utilities and planning; and through relationships with key decision makers. Associations are a key starting point for building links. They also provide insight into current and emerging best practice, act as an information resource on future employment opportunities and help practitioners gain first-hand insights into the impacts of new policies or development approaches.

## 11.2.1 The International Economic Development Council

There are a number of professional associations of potential value to economic development practitioners. The International Economic Development Council (IEDC) is based in the US and is a membership organization that sets out to meet the needs of economic developers. It is prominent in the US, but less well known in other nations, although its website claims more than 5,000 members across the United States, as well as Canada, Europe, Australia, New Zealand and other nations. The IEDC sets out to help economic developers do their jobs more effectively and efficiently, and raise the standing of the economic development sector. It measures its success against the capacity of its members to support the creation of additional high-quality jobs, develop more vibrant communities and generally advance the quality of life in a region. The IEDC provides information on trends and best practices, networking opportunities, professional development courses and numerous other services.

The IEDC seeks to meet the needs of practitioners working in the public and private sectors, in rural or urban locations, and those working at a very local scale or internationally. Its members are employed in a wide variety of settings including local, state, provincial and federal governments, public–private partnerships, chambers of commerce, universities and a variety of other institutions. It claims a membership that includes individuals and organizations that: work to persuade new businesses to locate in communities, regions or states; aim to help the businesses already located in a community to continue thriving and growing there; look for ways to turn distressed areas into vibrant hubs of economic activity. A portion of IEDC members work in major cities, while others practice their profession in remote or rural areas. Some are employed by public agencies, while others work for chambers of commerce, private nonprofit organizations, public–private partnerships or in the university sector. Some work with private sector consulting firms, and a significant group are sole practitioners active in the field. The IEDC would claim that at least one IEDC member has worked on every type of economic development project. In short, it argues that its members represent the entire range of economic development experience.

The IEDC promotes the following values:

* Social responsibility and a dedication to building healthy, just and competitive communities;
* Creation of wealth for individuals, businesses and communities;
* Advancement of both the economic development profession and professionals;
* Cooperation and collaboration;
* Diversity, tolerance and equity (IEDC 2018).

Its membership includes:

* Regional, state, county and city economic development organizations;
* Chambers of commerce and other business support agencies;
* Community and neighborhood development organizations;
* Technology development agencies;
* Utility companies;
* Educational institutions;
* Consultants;
* Redevelopment authorities.

The IEDC offers a range of programs and services to support economic development professionals and their activities. This includes the provision of training opportunities, the analysis and dissemination of information – including new reports and other publications, and the sharing of experience on how to improve the responsiveness of decision makers to economic development needs. The programs include:

- Opportunities to network with and learn from community leaders, industry experts and federal policy makers at our technical and annual conferences;
- Professional development that strengthens economic developers' careers and communities, and a certification program that unifies and sets the standard of excellence for the discipline;
- Advisory services and research that creates custom solutions for all types of communities, as well as federal agencies;
- In-depth analysis in the premier practitioner publication of the discipline – *Economic Development Journal* – and a bimonthly survey of economic development news and federal updates in the *Economic Development Now* newsletter;
- Public policy which monitors federal activity impacting the field of economic development and engages its membership in policy advocacy activities;
- The Accredited Economic Development Organization program, which provides organizations with independent feedback on their operations and recognizes excellence in local economic development efforts.

Finally, the IEDC conducts a number of conferences, including a leadership summit, a forum on working with US federal programs, an economic future forum and an annual conference.

## 11.2.2 The American Planning Association

As discussed above, economic development activities are frequently based in planning departments of local government, and the American Planning Association (APA) is a second source of professional support and development. The APA has 37,000 members and includes an Economic Development Division that 'provides an opportunity to join others who share an interest in and responsibility for matters related to economic development.' (APA 2018) It sets out to advance the practice and state of the art of economic development by:

- Increasing the understanding of economic development as a key element of public policy formulation at all levels of government;
- Promoting economic development as a critical element of neighborhood, community, regional and national planning processes;
- Disseminating materials and information about current economic development practice and theory to members of the division;
- Assisting APA in positively influencing economic development policy;
- Promoting professional communication among members of the division through a variety of member services, including, but not limited to, newsletters, web pages, conference sessions, workshops and other publications (APA 2018).

## 11.2.3 Economic development associations outside the United States

There are many organizations based outside of the US that provide services and support for economic development professionals working in these nations. Some of these associations are relatively large, while others are smaller, and they may reflect the size of the country and/or the commitment to locally based economic development. In many places there are both specialist economic development networks and divisions within other professional bodies, such as planners, local government professionals or national government-organized bodies. Examples include:

- The Economic Development Association of New Zealand (EDANZ) – economicdevelopment.org.nz;
- Economic Development Australia (EDA) – www.edaustralia.com.au;
- The Association of Finnish Local and Regional Authorities – www.localfinland.fi;
- The Economic Development Association of Canada (EDAC) – edac.ca;
- The Institute of Economic Development (IED) – www.ied.co.uk;
- The European Association of Economic Development Agencies (EURADA) – http://www.eurada.org.

These groupings provide valuable support for economic development practitioners in their constituent territories, and in large measure provide a broadly comparable suite of services to their members. There are variations that reflect differences in the policies of governments, and in the case of EURADA, some of their distinctive features are a function of the critical role of the European Union in shaping the nature and direction of economic development efforts.

In some places specific types of regional development strategy have dedicated associations to promote that form of development, and share best practice among members. Globally there are a number of nationally based cluster associations in their territories, including the Romanian Cluster Association and the Serbian Cluster Association, and both associations are part of the European Cluster Collaboration Platform. These bodies operate in addition to the industry-focused cluster associations such as those focused on clean technologies, urban logistics, the aerospace industry or bio-marine resources.

## 11.2.4 Academic resources

There are two major academic organizations that focus on issues of local and regional economic development. The Regional Studies Association (RSA) is based in the United Kingdom and Belgium, while the Regional Science Association International (RSAI) is prominent in the US. Both organizations, however, are truly global, with each represented in multiple nations including China, Ireland, India, Brazil, et cetera. The two organizations are broadly similar, though their focus varies. Both provide academic conferences, networks, research grants and support for individuals entering the field. They conduct large-scale conferences annually and host a number of smaller, regional events throughout the year.

## BOX 11.1  ACADEMIC ORGANIZATIONS WORKING IN LOCAL AND REGIONAL DEVELOPMENT

### The Regional Studies Association

The Regional Studies Association (RSA) recognizes that regions are key to examining the nature and impacts of political, economic, social and environmental change and innovation. The RSA works with its international and interdisciplinary membership to promote research at the highest standards of theoretical development, empirical analysis and policy debate. It is committed to examining processes at the national and local scale, and it is centrally interested in urban and rural questions.

The RSA is committed to exploring new ways of thinking about how development takes place on the ground, and this includes the investigation of city-regions and interstitial spaces – the spaces between major centers of economic activity. The RSA is interested in issues of economic development and growth, conceptions of territory and its governance, and in thorny problems of equity and injustice. Its journals, magazines and books, along with its global-to-local series of conferences and events, position it as a key forum in shaping and disseminating advances in regional studies and science. Members come from economics, geography, political science, planning and sociology backgrounds. Most work in academia but many are working in policy and practice, and membership is truly global.

The RSA embraces multiple research methodologies including quantitative and qualitative techniques, thoughtful comparative research, and the practice of spanning the boundaries between researcher and practitioner.

### The Regional Science Association International

Founded in 1954, the Regional Science Association International (RSAI) is an international community of scholars interested in the regional impacts of national or global processes of economic and social change. The work of RSAI draws on the expertise of many different disciplines and this multidisciplinary approach helps to facilitate new theoretical insights for tackling regional problems. In turn this provides an increasing opportunity for academics within the Association to engage more fully with planners and policymakers. Building on a strong foundation of quantitative methods, regional science is at the cutting edge of research into new model design for regional analysis and impact assessment.

In 1990, the Association changed its organizational structure to better reflect the growth and development of the field; the Regional Science Association International now serves as an umbrella organization overseeing three major superregional organizations in North America, Europe and the Pacific.

The main objectives of the Association are the fostering of exchange of ideas and the promotion of studies focusing on the region, including the utilization of tools, methods and theoretical frameworks, specifically designed for regional analysis as well as concept, procedures and analytical techniques of the various social and other sciences.

These objectives are supported through the acquaintance and discussion among its members and with scholars in related fields, by the encouragement of publication of scholarly studies and by performing services to aid the advancement of its members and the field of regional science.

Sources: Adapted from Regional Studies Association (no date); Regional Science Association International (no date).

They are important publishers, producing books and journals that represent the leading edge of knowledge in the field, as well as newsletters, blogs and statements on current issues in regional and local economic development. How each describes themselves is summarized in Box 11.1 below.

## ■ 11.3 Employment opportunities

Economic development as a profession offers a broad range of employment opportunities, and across the globe governments at all levels promote job growth and wealth creation. In the US the Economic Development Administration within the Department of Commerce has been active at the federal level since 1965, but there are other institutions operating within individual states, at the regional scale, and within communities and municipalities. Other jobs are to be found in the private sector, with a range of employers – such as utilities, chambers of commerce and retailers – committed to promoting their locality. Many qualified in economic development are hired as consultants or for site relocation agencies, with some consultancy work undertaken across national boundaries. International agencies with an interest in economic development issues include the World Bank, the OECD, the Asian Development Bank, as well as a number of foundations and charities.

The precise configuration of employment opportunities varies across nations, states and policy frameworks. In some places there is a more comprehensive set of policy and program instruments supporting economic development, while elsewhere there is both less activity and fewer employment options. In most parts of the world, local governments are active in economic development and represent an important source of jobs for those in the field. In Europe, various EU programs support the positions of practitioners working at the local or reginal scale; this includes the LEED program and work associated with S3 – the Smart Specialization Platform.

Fortunately, data are available on trends in economic development activity and employment in the US, and this analysis sheds light on where professional opportunities are to be found, and the types of activities developers engage in. Analysis of a survey undertaken by the International City/County Management Association (ICMA) in 2014 found that:

- Municipalities continue to be the primary body responsible for economic development and therefore the primary source of employment;
- Chambers of commerce are often partners in economic development efforts, and represent a second source of employment for those entering the profession;
- The preparation of strategic plans is an important feature of the work of almost half the respondents to the survey, which in turn emphasizes the importance of this capability set among graduates (see Chapter 8);
- The ICMA survey shows that practitioners need to have the skills and strategies that would enable them to both compete and collaborate with neighboring communities as circumstances dictate;

- Economic development makes substantial use of tax increment financing, and development professionals need knowledge in that area, especially in communities with 100,000 residents or more;
- The use of business attraction and retention strategies has grown over the past decade (Osgood et al. 2012).

There are also specialty organizations that support training and skills development among economic developers. For example, in the US, the Council for Community and Economic Research provides training and skills certification in the sources and uses of regional socioeconomic data and data analysis techniques. Members of this organization are spread across a wide variety of entities, usually in a research operation that is connected with local or state economic development efforts.

In addition to the well-known sources of information on employment, there are a number of web pages focused on employment for economic developers. These include:

- www.iedconline.org/web-pages/professional-development/job-listings/;
- www.eda.gov/careers/;
- www.linkedin.com/jobs/economic-development-jobs;
- www.governmentjobs.com;
- www.indeed.com/q-Economic-Development-jobs.html;
- www.econdev.info;
- www.caled.org/jobs/;
- https://jobs.theguardian.com/jobs/economic-development/;
- www.indeed.co.uk/Economic-Regeneration-jobs-in-England;
- www.edaustralia.com.au/employment/;
- www.workopolis.com/jobsearch/economic-development-jobs/ontario-canada;
- https://newzealand.recruit.net/search-economic-development-jobs.

## ■ 11.4 Conclusion

This chapter has considered economic development as a profession and has found it is a mature sector with well-developed professional associations and employment spread across a number of different sectors – local government, state governments, chambers of commerce and consultancy practices.

Economic development is a global profession, with some practitioners choosing – over the course of their careers – to work as an economic developer in more than one nation. Others operate as consultants, helping to translate practical and policy learnings from one location to another. This mobility within and between nations is made possible by the similarities in economic development practice between places, especially with respect to goals and objectives applied. The chapter found that many of the most effective economic development strategies used in one nation are also ranked highly in other nations, and that when confronted by major changes, places deploy similar responses, regardless of national context.

Where once economic development was often practiced as a network of long-established professionals who largely engaged in place marketing, the 21st century economic development practitioner will succeed by being:

- A keen observer of economic and social trends;
- Skilled in the conduct or use of advanced data analytics;
- Able to judge the risk–reward opportunities of incentivizing private businesses;
- Able to understand corporate and startup financing;
- Successful in building and engaging networks of leaders from the public, private and nonprofit sectors;
- Adept at communicating a vision of economic opportunity across multiple cultures and industries.

As a profession of the 21st century, there is an ongoing need to acquire the skills and knowledge essential to success as individual planners and economic development practitioners continue to work across the public and private sectors.

## Key messages

- There are a number of professional associations for economic developers in the US and other nations;
- These associations are an invaluable resource for those working in this field, providing networking opportunities, continuing education, and information on employment and career development;
- The broad principles applied to economic development practice in one city, region or community can be transferred to others, and this has been reflected in the spread of critical concepts and thinking at the global scale;
- There are a number of relevant academic associations that offer access to the latest thinking on the topic and substantial research resources; and,
- The context within which the profession of economic development is practiced shapes the day-to-day activities of practitioners and the delivery of programs to communities and businesses.

## Discussion questions

As individuals and in groups, think about the types of jobs that might attract you to the economic development profession. Give thought to: a) the type of community you may wish to work in (rural, small metro area, a commuter city, or major urban area); and b) the type of employer/activity you are likely to find attractive (site selection firm, city planning department, chamber of commerce, local economic development authority, community development department).

As a class, discuss the strategies and activities you will use to facilitate the development of your careers (e.g. further education, relocation to opportunities, professional affiliations and memberships).

# References

American Planning Association (APA) 2018 Available at https://www.planning. org/.

Beer, A., Ayres, S., Clower, T., Faller, F., Sancino, A. and Sotarauta, M. 2019 Place leadership and regional economic development: a framework for cross-regional analysis, *Regional Studies*, 53:2, pp 171–182.

Beer, A., Haughton, G. and Maude, A. 2003 *Developing Locally: Lessons in Economic Development from Four Nations*, Policy Press, Bristol.

Blakely, E. 1994 *Planning Local Economic Development: Theory and Practice*, Sage Publications, Thousand Oaks, CA.

Currid-Halkett, E. and Stolarick, K. 2011 The great divide: economic development theory versus practice – a survey of the current landscape, *Economic Development Quarterly*, 25:2, pp 143–157.

Danson, M., Halkier, H. and Cameron, C. 2000 *Governance, Institutional Change and Regional Development*, Ashgate, Farnham.

Florida, R. 2002 *The Rise of the Creative Class*, Basic Books, New York.

Green Leigh, N. and Blakely, E. 2016 *Planning Local Economic Development: Theory and Practice*, Sage Publications, New York.

Hall, P. 1969 *Urban and Regional Planning*, Penguin, Basingstoke.

IEDC 2018 Available at https://www.iedconline.org/.

International City/County Management Association 2014 ICMA Survey Research: Economic Development 2014 Survey Results. Available at https://icma.org/sites/default/files/306723_Economic%20Development%20 2014%20Survey%20Results%20for%20website.pdf.

Osgood, J. Jr., Opp, S. and Bernotsky, R. 2012 Yesterday's gains versus today's realities: lessons from 10 years of economic development practice, *Economic Development Quarterly*, 26:4, pp 334–350.

Regional Science Association International (no date) Available at www. regionalscience.org.

Regional Studies Association (no date) Available at www.regionalstudies.org.

Reese, L. 1993 Local economic development practices across the northern border, *Urban Affairs Quarterly*, 28:4, pp 571–592.

Sotarauta, M. 2009 Power and influence tactics in the promotion of regional development: an empirical analysis of the work of Finnish regional development officers, *Geoforum*, 400, pp 895–905.

Sotarauta, M. 2010 Regional development and regional networks: the role of regional development officers in Finland, *European Urban and Regional Studies*, 17:4, pp 387–400.

Swyngedouw E. 1997 Neither global nor local: 'glocalization' and the politics of scale. In Cox, K. (ed.) *Spaces of Globalization: Reasserting the Power of the Local*, Guildford Press, New York, pp 115–136.

# 12 Future challenges and strategies in economic development

This chapter:

▶ Considers the future working environment for economic development practitioners as we look forward 10, 20 and 30 years;

▶ Argues that the need for economic planning and practice will become more acute in the future as communities appreciate the challenge of building a future within a globalized economy;

▶ Suggests that new forms of city, region and community development will bring forward unanticipated growth opportunities locally, and places will need to be flexible and responsive if they are to benefit;

▶ Notes that many already established industries will remain prominent in future economies;

▶ Argues that sustainable development will be mainstreamed. New technologies and business models will deliver economic activities with a much-reduced environmental footprint;

▶ Highlights the importance of ICT for success in economic development now and in the immediate future. A strong Web presence, Facebook, Instagram, Twitter, Weibo, WeChat and other social media will be essential;

▶ Identifies the delivery of economic development assistance to minority groups as an area for greater attention.

IN THE INTRODUCTION to *Globalization, Planning and Local Economic Development* we discussed how economic development at the local scale is both a question of assets and processes: the resources within a locality – natural resources, human capital or infrastructure – provide the starting point for effective development activities, which are then complemented by effective and targeted action toward an agreed set of goals. This perspective on economic development leads us to acknowledge that the task of development – in its true sense – is ongoing. As the economy of a town or community evolves, its stock of assets transforms.

At the same time national and global markets shift and new technologies result in previously unexpected threats and opportunities.

Importantly, communities and regions react much more speedily and flexibly than national governments, and more generally the era of national government-delivered prosperity has passed. The practice of economic development can, and should, change over time, through evolution in the concepts deployed, shifts in the skill sets of practitioners and engagement with a pool of emerging entrepreneurs. There are many perspectives on what the economy, society and environment will look like in 10, 20 or 30 years, and this chapter considers these changes and what they mean for economic development practitioners.

## ■ 12.1 A future economy, the future of economic development practice

There are competing visions of the world and its economy over the next 30 years. Some authors continue to present a picture of a dystopia marked by adverse climate change, degraded environments, social dislocation, increasing inequality between the rich and the poor – both between nations and within nations – a shortage of arable land and increasingly large, and dysfunctional, cities. Others point to a more positive future marked by increasing wealth, greater life expectancy, higher standards of living and nutrition, better environmental management, higher housing standards, increased mobility and better technologies, including medical assistance. The future, of course, lies somewhere between these two visions. In planning for the future we need to acknowledge both disruptive events and the evidence already available to us of change within our social, economic and business environment.

Disruptive events cannot be ignored, but they cannot be predicted with meaningful accuracy. The terrorist attacks on American soil on September 11, 2001 rewrote history and reshaped many aspects of contemporary life, including international travel and strategic relations. Such events are difficult, if not impossible, to foresee. On the other hand, we can look to long-term trends and use them as a lens on the future. We know that:

- $CO_2$ levels in the atmosphere passed 400 parts per million for the first time in recorded history in 2013 (NASA 2014), and at current rates of increase they will reach levels that will take tens of thousands of years to return to preindustrial levels. Anthropogenic climate change is an inescapable reality and economic development will increasingly need to take both climate change and measures to reduce its impacts into consideration. Critically, it is an opportunity for, not a threat to, business;
- The world's population will peak sometime around 2050 at approximately 10 billion persons (Dorling 2013). Importantly, in 2008 the world's population switched from being predominantly rural to being more than 50 percent urban, and this change has been accompanied by growth in megacities, especially in the developing world, including South America, China, India, and other parts of Asia;

- After 2050 – well within the planning horizons of many institutions, cities, regions and corporations – world population will fall. The global economy will be entering new territory and communities will need to plan for how they adjust to the decline of some markets but the expansion of others;
- The world's population is aging. In 2015, 9 percent of the global population was aged 65 or over. By 2030 that proportion will rise to 12 percent and increase further to 17 percent in 2050 with a total of 1.6 billion older individuals (Roberts et al. 2018). This shift will likely be more pronounced in developed economies. The implications for labor markets cannot be overstated;
- The rise of China is both important and welcome. Between 1981 and 2005 the number of people living on less than US$1 a day around the globe fell by almost 639 million, with China accounting for 623 million of that gain. China has seen substantial growth in its middle class and continues to plan for a rise in the living standards of its poorest citizens. In the foreseeable future, India may deliver a similar contribution to improvements in global living standards. The rise of these new giants of the global economy will create new opportunities for both developed and developing economies and for the cities and communities that mobilize resources to engage with them;
- While we cannot predict disruptive events, we do know that new technologies with considerable capacities will arrive and reshape economic activity. Over the past decade these changes have included the expansion of Web-based communication technologies, the rise of new business models that allow for a more direct link between the provider of a service and the customer, viable alternative energy sources and an exponential expansion in the level of connectivity between parts of the globe. The Internet has come of age and it has powered new forms of commerce, community formation and information gathering and exchange. It is likely that we will see new forms of energy supply that are much more diffuse than those evident over the past 30 years. The use of graphene as a building material might be part of this equation, but it is inevitable that other technologies will also arise;
- Motor vehicle traffic is almost certainly going to remain an important part of the future. The conventionally powered car will disappear, but alternatives such as those that use hybrid technology, electric vehicles, gas-powered vehicles and hydrogen fuel cells will take its place. The deployment of autonomous vehicles may also profoundly change our relationships with automobiles, shifting our engagement with vehicles and our ownership of such to the purchase of 'mobility services.' These innovations will have profound implications for freight, commuter traffic and the functioning of economies. Public transit systems will become more common but in many areas – including rural communities – automobiles will remain central to social and economic life;
- Air travel and transport will continue to grow in the short term, but its longer-term future is less certain and more dependent upon further technological innovation. It may become more expensive in real terms over

time, but air hubs and access to airports will remain critical for economic development for at least the next 20 years;

- Virtually all developed economies have witnessed a substantial fall in manufacturing employment and an associated rise in services-related jobs. Where once 20 or 25 percent of a developed nation's economy was employed in manufacturing, in the 21st century somewhere between 6 and 12 percent of the workforce works within this sector. But it would be wrong to assume that the 'old' economy is dead. In many cases the shift in manufacturing technology is driving new levels of labor productivity. For example, in the US between 1997 and 2017, real (inflation-adjusted) manufacturing output rose by 13.6 percent while the number of manufacturing jobs in the US declined by 15.9 percent.[1] In addition, the development of products, and services, is being reshaped by new forms of enterprise and new markets. Shortened product and investment cycles have also meant that places that lost factories and employment under one set of economic conditions may see new investment and employment as currencies decline and broader circumstances change (Tate 2014; Tate et al. 2014; Bailey and De Propris 2014);
- Perhaps the technology change receiving the most attention at the end of the second decade of the 21st century is how artificial intelligence and automation may reshape the nature of many jobs and displace the need for labor in 'technically automatable activities' that could affect over one billion full-time-equivalent jobs globally (Manyika et al. 2017). This sea change in automation will create new industries and occupations requiring the economic development profession to be able to adjust economic development strategies with technology foresight, new talent pipeline regimes and, importantly, incumbent worker retraining programs.

These are the likely mega-trends that will shape world, regional and local economies over the coming decades. This list is not exhaustive, as we could add acknowledgment of the critical importance of the knowledge economy – as reflected in part by the increasing uptake of higher education and other learning, but it does provide a broad context for understanding future economies and the opportunities available to them.

## 12.1.1 The city, region and community of the future

What do the mega-trends shaping developed economies tell us about the shape and functioning of cities, regions and communities into the future? Will we see unexpected, disruptive change, or will these places continue to restructure in a more evolutionary way?

As we move to the middle of the 21st century we will see a 'patchwork' economy comprised of the old, new and 'new new' industries. We will continue to see conventional retail, distribution centers, manufacturing plants, construction activities, infrastructure development, schools, health services – including hospitals but possibly to a lesser degree – and office activities. But they will be overlaid with more flexible forms of economic activity that are empowered by new technologies.

The experiential economy – tourism and recreation focused on actively 'doing' rather than passively 'seeing' – will be strong. Importantly, there will be employment – and the associated demand for staff and supporting infrastructure – in each of these sectors. Economic development planners and practitioners will need to find ways to encourage growth in some or all of these segments of the economy.

When we consider types of communities, we need to acknowledge that cities will continue to dominate economic activity, and especially high-value activities such as research and development, innovation, and the command and control activities within the economy. But these functions will be held less tightly, with tele-working, commuting and other forms of Internet-enabled economic activity loosening the grip of central business districts on their workforce. In many places conventional markers of economic success – such as presence of skyscrapers or cranes on the skylines – will be replaced by less obvious markers of achievement, including the median incomes of places and the range of economic opportunities available to residents. Individuals will be increasingly employed for their specific skills and abilities, rather than for their capacity to fill a predesigned job specification. Flexible forms of engagement with the labor market will see individuals employed full time, part time, 'as needed,' as contractor or as self-employed. Uber – the informal taxi service – typifies this last business model. Successful communities will need to accommodate this wide variety of economic opportunities, and attract and hold individuals with desired skills. Cities and their individual suburbs will have to offer high-end jobs in globally competitive industries, but also provide employment in support industries, tourism and service occupations.

Many rural communities will continue to thrive. For some, the future will lie in their central role as transportation hubs, or in servicing agribusinesses. As discussed earlier, others will continue as amenity destinations, potentially strengthening their role as a source of recreation – and residence – as information technologies allow increasingly flexible engagement with an individual's place of employment. Some rural communities will build on their role in agricultural production as global demand for high quality food increases, with niche markets offering opportunities to move up the value chain. Population growth to 2050 will not simply add to the total demand for food, it will also result in a focus on better nutrition, with some elements of this trend already evident in the move to organic foods in many developed nations, and an escalating market for dairy products, high-quality seafood and red meat in nations such as China.

The restructuring of employment and the world of work will have important implications for the practice of economic development and planning over the next 30 years. As is currently the case, economic development planning and practice for the foreseeable future will remain an issue of 'soft power' – as communities and economic development practitioners have no levers with which to compel business investment. Economic development will remain an issue of tendering appropriate information, ensuring the supply of needed infrastructure, assisting with labor supply, helping local businesses grow and providing an appropriate regulatory framework.

Land use planning will continue to be one of the key tools for encouraging growth, as land is fundamental to all aspects of economic activity – it's a site for production, it provides a forum for interaction among entrepreneurs, it conveys advantages and disadvantages with respect to access to markets and suppliers, it is a cost to business, it determines access to appropriately skilled and available labor, and it is a set of regulations that can encourage or rule out certain forms of economic activity.

One of the key changes we anticipate is the integration of questions of sustainability into all forms of economic activity. Put simply, sustainable development will not be a focus of economic development into the future as it will be embedded in all forms of public and private sector business. There is already a long-established debate around 'food miles' in Europe and other places, and some major corporations award preference to local suppliers because of their smaller carbon footprint. More broadly, an increasing number of big businesses focus on corporate social responsibility (CSR) and how to report it to stakeholders, including those who own stock in the company. This new brand of environmentally informed localism has the potential to generate opportunities for many communities.

Finally, in considering the future of places and economic development planning and practice, it is important to acknowledge the diversity of strategies and actions potentially available. As the earlier sections of this text have shown, economic development in the 21st century has the capacity to call upon proven, evidence-based strategies that address the supply side of the local economy, provide mechanisms that stimulate demand for local products, offer the tactics needed to capitalize on globalization and the techniques central to encourage the success of locally grown businesses. There is also more information available to economic development planners and practitioners than in the past, and new ways of transmitting that knowledge to target audiences. For the economic development professional and economic development planner, the best of times may be the immediate future.

The remainder of this chapter considers some of the emerging issues in economic development planning and practice, and considers ways in which the transformation of the business environment can be harnessed to increase the impact of economic development efforts.

## ■ 12.2 The e-economy and economic development

### 12.2.1 New technologies and new models in e-business

The changes ushered in by the rise of new technologies have been both profound and complex. On the one hand, some industries and regions have been adversely affected by the rise of new, disruptive technologies and ways of doing business, but on the other hand, the same technologies have provided new tools and strategies for economic development. Surprisingly little attention has been given to how best to use these new technologies in the practice of economic development. This section considers these issues and discusses some of the strategies localities can use in order to generate greater prosperity.

New technologies have changed the operating environment for many established industries. In some sectors the impact has been relatively minor, with Web-based tools and smartphone applications used to more effectively reach an audience, allow for the ordering of simple through to complex goods – coffee, pizzas, flowers, travel or cars – and more efficiently manage business processes. In other sectors, more profound change is either in progress or has taken place: Airbnb and the transport service Uber are examples of new, disruptive business models that are revolutionizing established industries. They are examples of a process known as 'disintermediation' where technological change allows a more direct connection between the providers of a service and the consumer. Staying in someone's home via Airbnb, for example, creates a direct relationship between the home owner and the visitor. It is a transaction that does not involve traditional forms of employment or business activity, and may serve as an adjunct to conventional income generation. Importantly, while home businesses are a well-established feature of most local economies, the process of disintermediation allows for their extension into services as well as the production of goods.

All forms of economic activity are increasingly reliant on access to high-speed Internet connections. One of the basic tasks of economic development planners and practitioners is to ensure their community is served by high-speed Internet to assist established businesses and help new business models grow. In many communities, there is a case to encourage residents to engage with the more innovative business models: rural communities with few preexisting tourism facilities but natural assets can use existing farm stays and bed and breakfast accommodation to build their tourism sector. Increasingly, Web-based platforms can complement those already used by established enterprises and allow new entrants into the market.

## 12.2.2 Economic development practice in the electronic era

Critically, new forms of e-commerce are emerging all the time, with new business models, platforms, software and reputations. Increasingly, economic development agencies – in all their forms – across the globe need to apply similar technologies to promote their community or region and to make others aware of the services they offer to potential investors in their region. In our contemporary economy, businesses look to Web-based sources as their first – and sometimes last – source of information on a community or region as they look to invest or engage in trade.

The World Bank (2006) provided guidance on the 'best practice' features of investment attraction websites (Box 12.1). While the features identified by the World Bank (2006) remain relevant, in many ways both technology and best practice have moved on. Current best practice would include a formal website but also feature social media, such as Twitter, Facebook, LinkedIn, Instagram, Weibo, WeChat, YouTube and other applications, as effective ways of disseminating information and establishing a presence in global information flows.

Many economic development practitioners, and their agencies, struggle with the demands of an Internet presence. The World Bank's (2006) guidance reflects a clearly identified need at that time, and a study of institutional factors affecting growth in Australia concluded most local governments in Australia had websites that were poor at providing information on economic development opportunities and processes. Across the nation the average score for that index was just three out of a possible ten (Beer and Lester 2015).

---

## BOX 12.1 CHARACTERISTICS OF BEST PRACTICE WEBSITES FOR INVESTMENT ATTRACTION

### Information architecture

*Quick downloads.* Download times are getting shorter as users have faster connections. Investors or their agents will not wait for slow downloads.

*Guaranteed uptime.* Agencies should demand 100 percent uptime from their service provider.

*Worldwide accessibility.* IPAs should test their sites on different Internet browsers and different platforms. They should invite users to contact them if they have trouble viewing pages.

*Hierarchical organization of information.* Information should be grouped by key location factors or business interests, such as economic overview, priority sectors, operating costs and infrastructure.

*Finding home.* Navigational bars should allow users to click back to familiar territory, for example, home, about us, contact us, or site map.

### Design

*Ease of reading.* Text should be in common international business languages and presented in a format that can be scanned. Investors have much information to assimilate, so texts should be short.

*Color.* Colors should be used to enhance the legibility of the text but should not be overpowering.

*Graphics.* Well-designed and carefully positioned graphic elements are inviting, but graphics should be small to speed up downloads.

*Navigational aids.* Buttons and links should be well designed and intuitive. Warn users of large file sizes and nonstandard formats.

### Content

*Investor focus.* Ensure information meets the needs of investors. The site should be client-focused and reflect the end user's needs – primarily business conditions and operating environment.

*Summaries.* Summarize the reasons why the location is suitable for investment.

*Comparisons.* Provide data to help companies evaluate locations.

*Statistics.* Marshal current statistics to support claims. Cite only reputable sources.

*News.* Sections devoted to news and events should be current and of specific interest to business investors. Avoid news geared to general users or tourists.

*Testimonials.* If a major global company has invested, this will interest other investors.

*Downloadable fact sheets.* Key information should be consolidated in convenient downloads, saving effort for the investor and reinforcing the IPA's role as information gatekeeper.

*Sector-specific information.* Sections on specific priority sectors, industries or business functions should accentuate market availability for potential investors. Information should be sufficient to inform the investor of the key capabilities and priority industries of the economy, with case studies or testimonials provided for individual sectors.

*Contact information.* List agency contacts prominently. Name individuals with specific expertise and provide contact details for teams who work in particular sectors.

### Promotional effectiveness

*Finding the site.* The site must be easy to locate on major search engines. It should be meta-tagged with these search engines and well linked to other sites.

*Anticipating investors' needs.* Information should be tailored to investors' needs.

*Government affiliation.* Identify the relationship with the government and its ministerial affiliation.

Source: Adapted from World Bank 2006 pp 15–16.

Economic development planners and practitioners currently and for the foreseeable future will need to give equal attention to the e-economy and bricks and mortar businesses. Both will be important for local economies, and neither should be overlooked. Economic development practitioners need to enhance their own skills and put in place strategies to increase the knowledge and skills of their business communities. Relevant strategies could include:

- Hiring staff from different academic backgrounds but with relevant skills;
- Recruiting consultants to train agency personnel and the broader business community;
- Sharing resources with other agencies to ensure continuity in e-services at a more manageable cost;
- The use of interns from local educational institutions.

### 12.2.3 New data, new insights

Economic development as a profession has conventionally used a limited number of data sources to identify market trends, understand the needs of their communities and monitor performance. These sources have included census data, periodic surveys of businesses or communities, data purchased from the private sector and individual studies commissioned by one or more government agency.

Increasingly attention is being paid to the use of 'big data' as a determinant of success in business, and this sense of a 'new horizon' has extended into the practice of economic development. Big data includes information collected from social media sites, from the devices that make up the Internet of Things (IoT) – for example, sensors in retail shopping precincts, traffic sensors, et cetera – and from government-collected data – such as information on the number of bus tickets sold to a destination. It can be challenging to both collect and analyze, as big data is created on a continuous basis and the volume of the data sets requires specialist skills in managing and interrogating the information. Gretzel et al. (2015) suggested big data is characterized by seven features:

1. *Volume* – which refers to the quantum of data generated through the fast development of technologies and applications like Internet of Things, artificial intelligence (AI) and user-generated content (UGC) from online social media platforms;
2. *Variety* – that represents the diversity of data sources and multimedia formats, for example text, videos, photos, likes, comments, website statistics, log data;
3. *Variability* – which is related to the data whose meaning can vary significantly in context;
4. *Velocity* – which refers to the high speed of data generation through the growth of interconnected devices generating enormous amounts of data in real time and big data change, and created with the speed of light;
5. *Veracity* – which represents the data reliability, as data is worthless if it's not accurate;
6. *Visualization* – the science of visual representation of data and information in a way that is easily readable, accessible and understandable. Big data is recognized as a key source for creating;
7. *Value* – big data is considered to offer a compelling value proposition since it contributes to more efficient and effective operations such as optimal price setting, optimizing supply chain, minimizing errors and improving customer satisfaction (Beer et al. 2018 p 7).

M-Brain (2016) identified another characteristic of big data that makes its management difficult – its *virility*, which means that big data is quickly spread through viral online practices and social networks. As big data is spread and shared, it is commonly augmented, enriched and changed – which makes monitoring, capturing and understanding these sources of information difficult and laborious.

Practitioners working in the US can benefit from the commitment of governments to open data, and increasingly information is made available by government agencies that can assist development efforts (IEDC 2014, 2016). The IEDC (2014) noted the growing importance of both big data and open data, and found that the four most important data sources for economic development practitioners in the US were federal government agencies, local government, state government bodies and paid software sources. The research also concluded that over 80 percent of economic development agencies contacted collected primary data in some form.

On the global scale, not all governments are committed to open data, and practitioners seeking new insights are forced to look to other sources, including social media. Beer et al. (2018) found multiple platforms that could potentially provide insights into the performance of local economies, and do so in very short time frames. Some of these included:

• Hootsuite;
• Twitonomy;
• Discover text;
• Sprout social;
• Inside Airbnb;

- AirDNA;
- Neighbourlytics;
- Seek;
- Spendmapp.

Inevitably, this list is not comprehensive, nor does it cover all parts of every economy. Some of these services are likely to disappear over time, while others will emerge.

Big data represents substantial challenges for the profession of economic development and its future because, while it represents a considerable opportunity, it also presents challenges. Many of the commercially available data sets are relatively expensive, and both open data and purchased data requires substantial expertise in analysis and interpretation. These requirements are likely to be beyond the resource envelope available to many agencies and local governments. That said, it is likely that enhanced analysis of these sources, and the presentation of visualizations based on these data, will be an important part of the future of the profession.

## 12.2.4 Minority communities, indigenous communities and development

The OECD (2009, 2010) has argued that economic development efforts need to address both lagging and fast-growing regions because there is greater *potential* for growth in slower-growing places and it is likely that such places will generate greater economic and social returns on investment when compared with fast-growing places. A parallel argument can be applied to assisting minority and indigenous communities within local economies:

- Assistance delivered to these communities will spill over into substantial benefits for the local or regional economy as a whole;
- It is an important mechanism for bettering their life chances, especially in places where there is little formal employment and measures designed to create new businesses offer the best prospect for moving off welfare or income support payments;
- It will assist in integrating marginalized groups into the formal economy, raise incomes and develop skills that are of value to a wider pool of employers;
- It can revitalize economies.

Across the globe there are many minority groups that should form the focus of economic development efforts, including indigenous peoples such as Native Americans, Aboriginal and Torres Strait Islanders, and the Maori of New Zealand. But targeted assistance should also consider a wider remit, including the provision of business formation and other assistance to persons with a disability, historically underrepresented racial/ethnic groups and recent migrants. Such groups often have both a very high level of need and considerable, untapped, latent resources. Their culturally, linguistically or personally distinctive characteristics give them unique insights into society and the economy: they may perceive market opportunities that others ignore, and they may carry with them perspectives on business that unlock new enterprises. To focus on immigrants as one example, those who move are often the most dynamic and resourceful in their place of origin and are likely to be more entrepreneurial than the residents of the community to which they move. Many migrant communities are highly entrepreneurial: the Korean community in North America is acknowledged for its innovation and business acumen (Choi 2010), and the Afghani community in Australia is similarly entrepreneurial. A study by the Centre for Entrepreneurs and DueDil (2010) concluded that 14 percent of all businesses in the UK had been started by migrant entrepreneurs, totaling some 456,000 entrepreneurs and 465,000 businesses. As the world population grows, major population movements and the associated communities of immigrants will expand, opening up new opportunities for trade with their place of origin and the infusion of new ideas into the recipient city or region.

Migrants and other minority groups represent a significant asset for the broader community but too often economic development efforts in these domains are considered separate and distinct from mainstream development efforts. This limits the spillover of benefits into the wider economy and restricts the range of expertise deployed. Research undertaken in 2001 (Beer et al. 2003) found that while economic development agencies in England had a mandate to engage with, and assist, minority communities, their equivalents in the US, Australia and Northern Ireland did not. In many respects, this is an indicator of missed opportunities. It may be a function of high transaction costs in engaging with these communities in the first instance, but it also reflects the problems of 'policy silos' and the failure of agencies to adopt a sufficiently broad mandate.

##  12.3 Conclusion

This chapter has looked at some of the major trends likely to shape economies and society at the local level over the coming three decades. It is clear that the challenges of the past are not necessarily the challenges of the future, but it is also the case that the need for economic development planning and action will remain acute. Climate change, global population growth, the anticipation of population decline after 2050, the aging of the population, the ongoing rollout of new disruptive technologies, the need to incorporate sustainability into all businesses and the rise of new markets in China and elsewhere will inevitably generate a new economic landscape. Communities, cities and regions operating within that new landscape will need to be more nimble than previously if they are to take advantage of the opportunities in front of them. They will also be called on to take a lead in shaping their future. There will be an ongoing requirement to pay attention to questions of economic development at the local or regional scale, as well as greater integration between economic development planners and practitioners. A greater stock of knowledge on likely trends and new possibilities will produce better economic development outcomes.

This chapter has highlighted some issues that we consider likely to be more important over time. First and foremost, the nature of 'success' in economic development is likely to be very different from conventional indicators: the growth of service-based industries means that economic success is no longer inevitably associated with 'smokestacks.' Indeed, the quality of the local environment and the caliber of resident households is likely to be the strongest indicator of community achievement. Second, we have argued that the blue-collar economy is not dead; it simply no longer occupies the preeminent position of the past. There is an enduring need for economic developers to plan for and facilitate transport depots, manufacturing plants and associated industries. Third, the e-economy is large and will continue to grow. Economic development efforts need to both use the full suite of tools available to promote their own activities, and empower their business communities. The use of electronic communication methods represents a significant challenge for many agencies because of the need to maintain the currency of their website, an active Facebook presence and a community of Twitter followers. Finally, we acknowledge that as cities and communities grow they become more complex. Economic development in the coming decades will need to focus on serving the wider community by meeting the needs of identifiable groups.

Overall, the challenges of economic development will be greater in the coming decades than at any time in the past. In compensation, the potential achievements and rewards – professionally, personally and in with respect to community engagement – will grow also.

## Key messages

This chapter found that:

Macro level trends will exert an enormous influence on the nature and work of economic development professionals and planners over the next three decades. Some of these key trends include:

- The growth of the global population;
- The aging of the population and the workforce in developed economies;
- The embedding of environmental sustainability in all parts of the economy;
- The growth of new economies, including India and China, and their increasing prosperity will generate new opportunities for communities that reach out to these new markets.

The chapter also discussed the ways in which the profession of economic development is likely to change over the coming decades. This includes:

- A focus on the demand for high-quality, Internet-based assets and the use of social media to promote their communities;
- The use of big data and open data to obtain fresh insights into local economies and their performance;
- The growing diversity of populations and the opportunities they present at the local level.

## Discussion questions

The future is unknown, and while this chapter has presented a widely accepted view of how the national and global economy will change over the coming 30 years, it is inevitable that there will be unexpected events and economic trends that cannot be foreseen. As a class, debate what you feel to be the likely future for the economy. Are we moving to a period of pronounced and sustained economic growth, or is recession likely to affect national and local economies alike? How will attitudes to work change? Will increasing numbers of working-age individuals seek to limit the demands placed on their time by work, or will the labor force remain committed to longer hours? Will coming generations of workers seek to leave paid labor at younger ages? Finally, what will new technologies bring and how will these new capacities reshape the geography of economic activity at the global, national and local scales, and the work of economic development professionals?

## Note

1  The drop in manufacturing jobs in the US may have passed its trough. Preliminary estimates from the US Department of Labor show that US manufacturers added over 670,000 new jobs in 2018.

## References

Bailey, D. and De Propris, L. 2014 Manufacturing reshoring and its limits: the UK automotive case, *Cambridge Journal of Regions, Economy and Society*, 8:2, pp 1–17.

Beer, A., Haughton, G. and Maude, A. 2003 *Developing Locally: Lessons in Economic Development from Four Nations*, Policy Press, Bristol.

Beer, A., Hodgson, L., O'Connor, A. and Sigala, M. 2018 *Development and Evaluation of Economic Development Measures,* Economic Development Australia. Available at https://www.edaustralia.com.au/resources/development-and-evaluation-of-economic-development-measures/.

Beer, A. and Lester, L. 2015 Institutional thickness and institutional effectiveness: developing regional indices for policy and practice in Australia, *Regional Studies, Regional Science*, 2:1, pp 205–228.

Centre for Entrepreneurs and DueDil 2010 Migrant entrepreneurs: building our businesses, creating our jobs, Centre for Entrepreneurs. Available at https://centreforentrepreneurs.org/cfe-research/creating-our-jobs/.

Choi, H. 2010 Religious institutions and ethnic entrepreneurship: the Korean ethnic church as a small business incubator, *Economic Development Quarterly,* 24:4, pp 372–383.

Dorling, D. 2013 *Population 10 Billion*, Constable and Robinson, London.

Gretzel, U., Sigala, M., Xiang, Z. and Koo, C. 2015 Smart tourism: foundations and Developments, *Electronic Markets*, 25:3, pp 179–188.

International Economic Development Council (IEDC) 2014 *Making it Count: Metrics for High Performing EDOs*, IEDC, Washington, DC.

International Economic Development Council (IEDC) 2016 *A New Standard: Achieving Data Excellence in Economic Development*, IEDC, Washington, DC.

M-Brain 2016 Big data technology with 8 V's. Available at https://www.m-brain.com/home/technology/big-data-with-8-vs/, accessed June 28, 2016.

Manyika, J., Chui, M., Miremadi, M., Bughin, J., George, K., Willmott, P. and Dewhurst, M. 2017 *A Future That Works: Automation, Employment, and Productivity*, McKinsey Global Institute. Available at https://www.mckinsey.com/~/media/mckinsey/featured%20insights/Digital%20Disruption/Harnessing%20automation%20for%20a%20future%20that%20works/MGI-A-future-that-works-Executive-summary.ashx.

NASA 2014 Climate change: the relentless rise of carbon dioxide. Available at http://climate.nasa.gov/climate_resources/24/, accessed September 29, 2015.

OECD 2009 *How Regions Grow: Trends and Analysis*, OECD, Paris.

OECD 2010 *Regions Matter*, OECD, Paris.

Roberts, A., Ogunwole, S., Blakesless, L. and Rabe, M. 2018 *The Population 65 Years and Older in the United States: 2016*, ACS-38. US Census Bureau, Washington, DC.

Tate, W. 2014 Offshoring and reshoring: U.S. insights and research challenges, *Journal of Purchasing and Supply Management*, 20:1, March, pp 66–68.

Tate, W., Ellram, L., Schoenherr, T. and Petersen, K. 2014 Global competitive conditions driving the manufacturing location decision, *Business Horizons*, 57:3, May–June, pp 381–390.

World Bank 2006 *Investment Promotion Agency Performance Review 2006, Providing Information to Investors: A Report of Global IPA Performance Results,* Multilateral Investment Guarantee Agency, World Bank, Washington, DC, pp 15–16.

# Author index

# Subject index

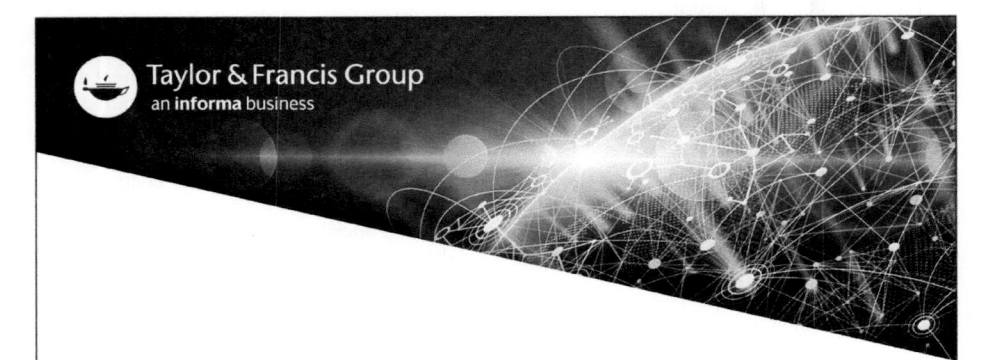

T - #0159 - 050919 - C264 - 246/174/12 [14] - CB - 9781138810303